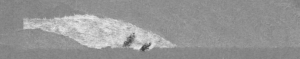

THE
DRAMATIC
VISION OF
AUGUST
WILSON

AUGUST WILSON
1945–

~THE~ DRAMATIC VISION OF AUGUST WILSON

Sandra G. Shannon

HOWARD UNIVERSITY PRESS
Washington, D.C.
1995

Howard University Press, Washington, D.C., 20017

Manufactured in the United States of America

This book is printed on acid-free paper.

10 9 8 7 6 5 4 3 2 1

Library of Congress Cataloging-in-Publication Data
Shannon, Sandra Garrett, 1952–
    The dramatic vision of August Wilson / Sandra G. Shannon.
      p.   cm.
    Includes bibliographical references and index.
    ISBN 0–88258–069–8 (alk. paper)
    1. Wilson, August—Criticism and interpretation.   2. Afro
  -Americans in literature.   I. Title.
  PS3573.I45677Z88   1995
  812′54—dc20   95–17758
                                                                       CIP

Cover Illustration: *Mill Hand's Lunch Bucket*, by Romare Bearden, inspired August Wilson's
play *Joe Turner's Come and Gone*. Illustration courtesy Estate of Romare Bearden.

CONTENTS

PREFACE

I read *Fences* in 1987 and was so moved by its portrait of the deeply
troubled Troy Maxson that, as soon as I had turned the last page, I vowed
to read everything I could get my hands on that was written by August
Wilson. I felt that this man had somehow peeped into my own past to
reinvigorate a part of my life that had for years lain dormant in my
memory. Troy Maxson was my father—crude, domineering, hardworking, hard-loving, and fiercely proud of his ability to provide for his
family. I was drawn closer to this character by memories of my father's
recent death, for he had just succumbed to lung cancer the previous year
after sixty-three years of constant responsibility. As one of the oldest, he
had essentially reared his brothers and sisters; he had learned to build a
fire from scratch, make biscuits, tree a possum, skin a rabbit or a catfish,
and plow a straight row before any of them. He bought his first piece of
land for $2,750, largely with money he had saved while a private in World
War II; his own father died while he was away fighting Hitler. Like Troy
Maxson's, his education was cut short at the insistence of a father who
felt his son could best be a man by getting a job and assisting him around
the farm. His professional career had also been severely restricted because
of the lingering influence of Jim Crow and racism, yet his strong work
ethic enabled him to manage a comfortable living for my mother, my
sister, my four brothers, and me.

I suspect that many others who have read or seen any of August
Wilson's plays have been similarly struck by the autobiographical reflections that they engender. His characters have an uncanny knack for
conveying universal thoughts and emotions, even as they speak in street
idioms or as they bemoan or celebrate particular moments in their lives.
His ability to stimulate his audience's consciousness to produce atavistic
images from their cultural past or memories of actual experiences is
fundamental to his skills as a dramatist. He is a prophet of his race,
resurrecting crucial moments in African American cultural history to
inspire healthy spiritual and attitudinal adjustments within his people.

He fashions these moments into constructive myths that point his characters toward the future.

I met August Wilson for the first time in November 1991. Prior to this I had already amassed an impressive collection of data on him—from a stack of reviews about productions of his work at the Yale Repertory Theatre and on Broadway to a supply of "August in November" buttons generated by the Washington, D.C.–based writers' group Millennium6 Exchange, whose members greatly admire Wilson's work. For four years I had been unwittingly preparing for the extensive interview that took place at Washington's Kennedy Center. *Two Trains Running* was in rehearsal then, with Rosco Lee Brown heading a list of veteran actors and Lloyd Richards grooming the play and the cast for what turned out to be yet another Broadway run. Wilson had already been grilled about various aspects of the play by *Washington Post* critic Megan Rosenfeld, *Where* feature writer Colleen Grewing, and America's Black Forum's host Julian Bond when I sat down with my tape recorder, list of questions, and camera. Surprisingly, he showed no signs of impatience. In fact, during the entire three-hour session, the playwright responded at length to my questions while frequently assuming the personas of certain of his robust characters and citing their exact lines from a number of scripts to embellish a story. He held my attention with humorous and touching recollections involving cast members for *Ma Rainey's Black Bottom* and *Fences* and recounted several near disastrous decisions about the course of his career. He seemed genuinely pleased to have me listen. During the consumption of some four or five cigarettes and an ample supply of coffee, Wilson outlined his dramatic vision and revealed a man quite capable of achieving it. *The Dramatic Vision of August Wilson* expands upon much of the information Wilson provided during this generous interview and draws upon seven years of my own research and writing on his works. Added to this is a genuine admiration and respect for the artist.

The structure of this book mirrors the chronology of plays as Wilson wrote them, even though his history cycle plays, in particular, have their own chronology and cover a fictive time span of some seventy years. Because it is the first published study of Wilson, I have attempted to integrate multiple aspects of Wilson as man and writer. Also, because Wilson's early education was in writing scripts for stage productions as well as in becoming a skilled writer of plays for publication, significant attention has been given to his initiation to both the stage and the larger arena of performance. The bulk of my study constitutes in-depth analyses of Wilson's six plays that are components of his self-proclaimed ten-play discourse on African American historical experience since the 1900s. Within the respective chapters dedicated to examining these plays, I explore their larger political, social, and thematic implications while situating each work within its historical and cultural contexts.

Each of Wilson's "moments-in-history"—*Jitney!* (written in 1979), *Fullerton Street* (written in 1980),[1] *Ma Rainey's Black Bottom* (1985), *Fences* (1987), *Joe Turner's Come and Gone* (1988), *The Piano Lesson* (1990), and *Two Trains Running* (1992)—also documents his own painstaking evolution from a collector of rejection notices to a collector of Pulitzer Prizes. Thus, in addition to discussing these works within the larger context of Wilson's declared agenda, this study will examine how the plays indicate his growth as an artist. While details of his life are helpful in comprehending his magnum opus, the six plays in his revised version of African American history are viewed outside the shadow of biographical references. Attention is directed instead toward the intrinsic dramatic qualities of these plays as self-sustaining texts.

The Dramatic Vision of August Wilson is a lesson in the making of an artist, for it traces the evolution of a major voice in American theatre from his boyhood interest in black literature to his phenomenal success as an adult at writing plays of the black experience. As the quality of his plays improved in their dialogue, in their structure, and in their characterization, Wilson's vision strengthened as well. His career moved laterally from writing plays to prove his competence as a dramatist to focusing his energies upon reexamining the broad, neglected expanse of African American history. This study demonstrates Wilson's gradual emergence as a master of effective stage as well as literary production.

ACKNOWLEDGMENTS

I wish to thank August Wilson for granting me an exhaustive interview in November 1991, during which he gave me what has turned out to be most helpful advice about writing: "You [don't] have to have the whole thing in your head when you [sit] down to write. You discover as you go along." These words were a welcome source of comfort to me as I mapped my way through approximately thirty years of the playwright's life as a writer and through some twelve of his plays.

Wilson's bit of wisdom, along with assistance and encouragement from several other sources, also kept me on a steady course from the book's inception in 1990 to its completion in 1994. The National Endowment for the Humanities Fellowship for University Teachers was a Godsend for me, for it supported an extremely productive sabbatical leave from Howard University during which I made significant progress toward revising and ultimately completing my manuscript.

I also wish to thank Pamela Jordan and Fran Oliver of the Yale School of Drama Library and Press Office for giving me prompt and easy access to materials on Wilson and for helping me find answers—often within a matter of hours—to important questions related to productions of his work. I also extend my gratitude to Wilson's former assistants, Emily Kretschmer and Jessica Morell, both of whom graciously provided me with crucial primary research material and allowed me unguarded access to Wilson for publication-related matters.

Many kisses and hugs go to my daughter Kristen, who was born in the midst of writing this book. I am grateful for the joyful balance that she provides in my life between being "Mama" and "Dr. Shannon, the author." I am especially indebted to my most supportive husband, Michael. Finally, I pay special homage to my mother, Eula Mae Garrett, and to my deceased father, John Luke Garrett, who set examples of hard work, ambition, and Christian faith.

ABBREVIATIONS

CDY	*The Coldest Day of the Year*
EMM	*An Evening with Margaret Mead*
ESD	*Eskimo Song Duel*
F	*Fences*
H	*The Homecoming*
HCSP	*How Coyote Got His Special Power*
JR	*The Janitor*
JY	*Jitney!*
JT	*Joe Turner's Come and Gone*
MR	*Ma Rainey's Black Bottom*
PL	*The Piano Lesson*
TT	*Two Trains Running*

CHRONOLOGY

1945	On April 27 born Frederick August Kittel in Pittsburgh, Pennsylvania. xv
1959	Student at Pittsburgh's Central Catholic High School.
1960	Drops out of school at 15.
	Discovers "Negro Section" in the Pittsburgh Public Library where he reads Ellison, Hughes, Baldwin, among others.
1962	Enlists for a three-year term in the Army.
1965	Begins career as writer with purchase of first typewriter for $20.
	Is introduced to the blues with discovery of Bessie Smith's "Nobody Can Bake a Sweet Jelly Roll Like Mine."
	Biological father dies.
	Moves out of his mother's house and into a rooming house on Bedford Avenue.
	From 1965 to 1973 preoccupied with "finding his voice as a poet."
1965–68	Encounters other black writers at Halfway Art Gallery and forms Pittsburgh's Center Avenue Poet's Theatre Workshop.
	Is introduced to the ideas of Malcolm X.
1967	Gets involved in cultural nationalist activities.
	Starts Pittsburgh's Black Horizons Theatre with Rob Penny and others.
1969	Stepfather David Bedford dies.
	Marries local Pittsburgh girl named Brenda Burton.
1970	Legally adopts his mother's name in early '70s.
	Daughter Sakina is born to Burton and Wilson.
1971	Temporarily gives up efforts to write plays and turns to writing poetry and short fiction.
1972	Breakup of first marriage.
1973	Writes *Recycle*.
1976	First produced play *The Homecoming* is staged for Kuntu Theater, a local amateur group in Pittsburgh.
	Makes another attempt at writing drama but abandons script

that he later develops into *Ma Rainey's Black Bottom*.

Writes *The Coldest Day of the Year*.

Gives a staged reading for a series of poems about Black Bart.

1977 Accepts invitation from friend and fellow Pittsburgh native Claude Purdy to fly to St. Paul, Minnesota, to develop the poems into a play.

Discovers the art of Romare Bearden.

1978 *Black Bart and the Sacred Hills* is given staged reading at the Inner City Theater in Los Angeles.

Makes St. Paul permanent residence.

From 1978 to 1980 works writing scripts for Science Museum of Minnesota.

1979 Begins to appreciate "voices of the people I'd grown up with all my life. And I started writing them down."

Writes *Jitney!* and *Eskimo Song Duel*.

Turns to revising *Ma Rainey's Black Bottom*.

1980 Receives from friend Rob Penny brochure from O'Neill Center and is encouraged to submit his work there.

Writes *Fullerton Street*.

Black Bart is produced in St. Paul's Penumbra Theater.

1981 Completes *Ma Rainey* and submits it to O'Neill Center.

Marries second wife, Judy Oliver.

1982 Begins to "write plays in earnest."

Ma Rainey is accepted at O'Neill Center for playwright's workshop.

First meeting with Lloyd Richards.

Undergoes intensive training in writing plays at O'Neill.

Meets Charles Dutton at O'Neill.

Jitney! is produced at Pittsburgh's Allegheny Repertory Theater.

1983 Writes *Fences*.

Fences is accepted at O'Neill for staged reading.

Mill Hand's Lunch Bucket (later *Joe Turner's Come and Gone*) workshopped at New Dramatists in New York.

Mother dies.

1984 *Ma Rainey* opens on 6 April 1984 at Yale Repertory in New Haven.

Ma Rainey opens on 11 October 1984 on Broadway.

Writes *Joe Turner's Come and Gone*.

1985 *Ma Rainey* wins New York Drama Critics' Circle Award for best new play of 1984–85.

Fences opens on 30 April 1985 at Yale Repertory.

Publishes *The Janitor* in *Short Pieces from the New Dramatists.*

1986   *Joe Turner* receives first production at Yale Repertory.

Writes *The Piano Lesson.*

The Piano Lesson is presented as a staged reading at O'Neill and opens at Yale Repertory.

1987   *Fences* opens on Broadway and wins Pulitzer Prize, Tony Award, New York Drama Critics' Circle Award, American Theater Critics' Association Award, Drama Desk Award, and the Outer Critics' Circle Award.

Joe Turner opens at Washington, D.C.'s Arena Stage.

1988   *Joe Turner* opens on Broadway and is voted best play of 1987–88 season by New York Drama Critics' Circle.

Piano Lesson is produced by Yale Repertory at Boston's Huntington Theater.

1989   *Piano Lesson* opens at Kennedy Center in Washington, D.C.

Writes *Two Trains Running.*

1990   *Piano Lesson* opens on Broadway.

Receives second Pulitzer Prize for *Piano Lesson.*

Two Trains is produced at Yale Repertory.

1991   *Two Trains* opens at Kennedy Center.

1992   *Two Trains* opens on Broadway.

1995   *Seven Guitars* opens at Chicago's Goodman Theater.

The Piano Lesson airs on CBS Hallmark Hall of Fame.

THE
DRAMATIC
VISION OF
AUGUST
WILSON

INTRODUCTION

The body of August Wilson's work as an acknowledged playwright—from *Jitney!* to *Seven Guitars*¹—represents his piecemeal effort to draw renewed attention to certain historical moments in the African American past since 1900. Although Wilson did not initially set out to construct what has so far become a museum of African American cultural artifacts, at some point he realized a fortuitous pattern emerging from the plays he had written: *Joe Turner's Come and Gone*, set in 1911; *Ma Rainey's Black Bottom*, 1927; and *Jitney!*, 1971. Once he discovered this unplanned chronology with each play set in a different decade, Wilson actively adopted an impressive ten-play mission and an equally impressive artistic agenda

> to focus upon what I felt were the most important issues confronting Black Americans for that decade, so ultimately they could stand as a record of Black experience over the past hundred years presented in the form of dramatic literature. What you end up with is a kind of review, or re-examination, of history. Collectively they can read certainly not as a total history, but as some historical moments. (Powers 52)

Wilson's mission goes beyond recording history merely to inform. By transforming select moments in black history into dramatic reenactments, he attempts to forge new attitudes among black Americans about their past and the role they played in its making. The resulting plays display a variety of tactics to forge a link between generations separated by a pronounced cultural breakdown. According to Wilson, in an age when far too many African Americans have been corrupted by materialism and have become disinterested in their past, their salvation lies in lessons resurrected from bountiful examples provided by the past. To drive home these lessons, he takes liberties with factual information, often expanding on it to include people and places of his own making. While he claims a sort of poetic license to avoid research, he consistently grounds his plays in very credible historical contexts complete with startlingly real dialogue, setting, and prevailing attitudes among both his black and his white characters.

Some have likened Wilson's ambitious undertaking to rewriting history, but the playwright stops short of such a monumental task. As theatre scholar Jay Plum asserts in his essay "Blues, History, and the Dramaturgy of August Wilson,"

> Wilson's dramaturgy challenges the secondary position of African Americans within American history by contextualizing black cultural experiences and, in turn, creating an opportunity for the black community to examine and define itself. Rather than writing history in the traditional sense, Wilson "rights" American history, altering our perception of reality to give status to what American history has denied the status of "real." (562)

Thus, Wilson's interests lie with the audience's response to his mythical interpretations of various historical moments. Unlike Bertolt Brecht, whose epic theatre consciously sought to alienate its audiences in order to provoke emotionally unencumbered thought, Wilson leads his audiences to recurring cultural epiphanies about their collective pasts and sweeps them toward the cathartic awareness that therein lie their greatest strengths.

Much has been made of the fusion between history as we know it and the fictional embellishments of the writer. In particular, critics charge that such works blur the lines between reality and fantasy and cast the writer as one who creates history while simultaneously conveying it. Thus, the fictionalizing of any real person or event poses special concerns for those interested in sorting fact from fantasy, no matter what genre. Wilson's historical approach to drama reintroduces the arguments that surround works such as Amiri Baraka's *The Death of Malcolm X* (1969), which re-creates events leading to Malcolm X's assassination, or Edward Albee's *The Death of Bessie Smith* (1960), which dramatizes events surrounding the wrongful death of the blues singer. These issues are hardly new; some of Shakespeare's plays also raise issues concerning the place of history in drama. For the historical dramatist, history becomes secondary to his or her imagination, which often becomes the dominant force at work.

This complex relationship between the fantasized and the real is most evident in personalities that Wilson dramatized while employed as a script writer at the Science Museum of Minnesota and, later, in his depictions of blues singers Blind Lemon Jefferson and Gertrude Rainey. For example, *Ma Rainey's Black Bottom* (1984) is based upon the real-life singer, yet both the play's setting and plot evolve from the playwright's imagination.

Each of Wilson's chronicles, to date, acquires much of its form and substance from the playwright's imagined reality of the historical milieu it represents. Often while listening to a blues album or studying an artwork, Wilson discovers the people of his plays for whom his scripts fashion credible circumstances. He avoids the "straitjacket" effect of researching the respective decades, taking cues instead from his own intuitive perceptions of what African Americans must have experienced and how they must have reacted and felt during each of the decades featured.

Wilson believes that artistic imagination overshadows any need for historical accuracy, especially as he tries to deconstruct entrenched misconceptions about African Americans among his wider audiences and, by so doing, alter customary patterns of behavior and thought. He believes his mission is not so much to challenge the past but to bring it once again into focus to exemplify for today's audiences how African Americans emerged triumphant. The importance of history, then, is as a way of knowing the present world and of predicting and shaping the future. Ultimately Wilson becomes a mythmaker, recasting the African American past in the crucible of his memory. The products of his mental alchemy are plays that, as their characters make decisions in the light of the hard-learned lessons of their ancestors, point to the future.

August Wilson's own life plays a major role in this study. In fact, he once told a baffled reporter, "I'm working on a four-hundred-year autobiography. I'm as old as the black experience in America" (Watlington 113). Although this figurative characterization of the playwright's mission to reexamine certain historical moments of the black experience since 1900 may have caught the journalist off guard, Wilson was, in fact, proclaiming the extent to which he has willfully merged his life into his art. Much like novelist John Wideman, a fellow Pittsburgh native, Wilson sometimes weaves details of his life through the tapestries of his fictitious settings. He has linked himself to the continuum of African American experience. He explains, "It's my autobiography of myself and my ancestors" (interviewed by the author).

Although several recognizable images of Wilson's life occasionally surface in his plays, he insists that his writing is not consciously about himself. Nevertheless, elements of the playwright's own experiences provide an ever-present backdrop for his works and surface in the tormented male protagonists he portrays, whether in the thinly veiled tribute to his stepfather in *Fences*'s Troy Maxson or in *Joe Turner's Come and Gone*'s profoundly vexed nomad, Loomis. Reestablishing linkages with the past—stretching across the black experience in America to Africa—involves tapping the resources of his memory, both conscious and subliminal. He willingly becomes a medium for synthesizing elements of his past and the imagined pasts of thousands of African Americans to produce inspirational new adaptations of recorded history. Aided by the melancholy strains of blues lyrics, a poet's sensitivity, and extraordinary intuition, he essentially wills a better world through his plays.

In varying degrees each of the plays that make up his chronicle of past moments in African American history is a product of the playwright's personal quest to "exorcise the demons of memory" (Henry 7) from his own troubled psyche. These memories come as a result of a past that combines his growing up poor and fatherless in a Pittsburgh ghetto, his quest to discover his own genealogical ties with Africa, and his sustained belief that African Americans of the present generation urgently need to ground themselves in Africa's cultural past.

Wilson the playwright is both subject and object in his ten-play process of exorcizing these demons from what he calls his "blood's memory." He admits, "When your back is pressed to the wall you go to the deepest part of yourself, and there's a response—it's your great ancestors talking. It's blood's memory" (C. Brown 122). He sees himself as a "conduit of antecedents," giving voice to millions of African ancestors and their descendants—from slaves tossed overboard during the Middle Passage to his grandmother, who reportedly walked from North Carolina to Pittsburgh during the post-Reconstruction mass exodus of blacks from the South.

Obviously influenced by revolutionary playwrights of the 1960s who sought to agitate their audiences by any means necessary, Wilson chooses a toned-down version of their more sensational attempts at didacticism. Plays such as *Fences*, *Ma Rainey's Black Bottom*, and *Two Trains Running* do not focus upon blaming white America for the conditions under which blacks live but instead look more closely at the underlying emotional scars blacks bear. That is not to say that Wilson is oblivious to the ubiquitous racism and oppression endured by past generations of black Americans; however, he feels that an entire landscape of experience has not been explored. While he reexamines select past moments in black history, he also targets the individual: "I concretize the values of that [black] tradition, placing them in action in order to demonstrate their existence, their ability to offer and provide sustenance for a man once he's left his father's house—so that you're not in the world alone, so that you have values that will guide you in your life" (Freedman, "Playwright Talks" C3). Wilson considers his drama to be that sustenance—that which blacks might substitute for the missing stories of their lives.

August Wilson is not the first dramatist to manipulate history for the edification of a contemporary audience. Historical plays are as old as the Greeks. Shakespeare figures prominently in the tradition, putting a dramatic spin upon the Tudor dynasty's view of their role in history. While relying a great deal upon historical details recorded in *Holinshed's Chronicles* as well as other sources, Shakespeare portrays English kings and barons in a manner that, according to Sabodh Gupta, presents their history "for its dramatic significance rather than for its doctrinal value" (18). Wilson's chronicles of the black experience, like Shakespeare's history plays, work within and around recorded history to reconfigure events according to a different worldview. While neither claims to be a historian or a scholar, each provides valuable insight about the political, social, economic, and racial milieus depicted in the various settings—information that is frequently excluded or glossed over in history books.

Had Eugene O'Neill completed his ambitious cycle of plays on American history tentatively titled *A Tale of Possessors, Self-Possessed*, his work undoubtedly would have become a yardstick for assessing Wilson's related venture. Instead, from the outset, O'Neill's work was doomed: first, because of his deteriorating health, and second, because his elaborate conceptualizations of the project made its writing impractical and its staging nearly impossible. Travis Bogard notes in *Contour in Time*, "In plan, the cycle was a staggeringly difficult work. Writing it was comparable to grasping along a web, tracing the strands of character, motif, and theme through the generations" (381–82). Unfortunately, O'Neill's frustration over the project got the better of him. In

1953 he and his wife burned the bulk of the works in progress, leaving only several scattered scripts.

Although O'Neill succumbed to his anxieties about *A Tale of Posessessors, Self-Possessed,* he had envisioned a plan not unlike that which Wilson is well on his way toward completing. He, too, sought to use American history as the backdrop for plays that were grounded in recognizable cultural and historical realities yet embellished for the stage. In earlier stages of the project, O'Neill outlined his ambitions for the cycle in a letter to an associate at the Theatre Guild: "It's a cycle of seven plays portraying the history of the interrelationship of a family over a period of approximately a century" (qtd. in Bogard 375).

Although O'Neill's proposed cycle never materialized, a contemporary Pulitzer Prize–winning playwright, Charles Fuller, is well on his way toward completing a venture comparable to Wilson's mission of recasting the history of black America via a series of dramatic reenactments. In a series of five plays he calls *We* (to date he has completed *Sally, Prince, Jonquil,* and *Burner's Frolic*), Fuller explores what life was like for blacks in the years just before and just after the emancipation of slaves in America (1863 to 1900). Like Wilson, Fuller is convinced that those who wrote the history books have misrepresented the role of black people in the country's making. He argues:

> We are all victims of dead men. The amazing thing about life is we predicate who we are on the basis of the history we have of ourselves. So the truth is, we really live out the dictums of dead men who died hundreds of years ago. If that's the case then by exhuming the body and re-examining it and essentially learning the truth about why it died, you get to understand more about why it died, you get to understand more about how the people who are living function. (Kucherawy 17)

In his campaign against "dead men," Fuller articulates concerns that mirror those of Wilson. Both men consider the culprits of widespread historical distortion to be "others" who took it upon themselves to record events of black history during a time when keeping such accounts was nearly impossible for a subjugated race of people barely able to write their names, much less record events of their lives.

Fully cognizant of the numerous pressing issues blacks face today—gun violence, teenage pregnancy, AIDS, drug and alcohol addiction, and so on—both Fuller and Wilson choose to bypass these concerns and focus instead upon experiences from years past. To them, the richness of history can now serve in a medicinal capacity. Contemporary black audiences, especially the youth among them, are given doses of their history through the respective series of plays and invited to take lessons from those who have gone before them. Whether as a series of five plays of the Reconstruction era or as a decade-by-decade journey from 1911 to 1971, history, in the hands of both playwrights, becomes instructive.

Despite differences in the scope of their work, Fuller and Wilson have a similar goal. In his series Fuller anatomizes several of the stereotypes about blacks that abounded, particularly after Emancipation, through the dilemmas and debates of his characters. For example, in *Burner's Frolic*, the fourth play in the projected series, the newly freed slave Tiche demonstrates for the contemporary audience the inherent dangers of passivity. When challenged by Burner (a disciple of what Wilson calls the warrior spirit), who spearheads political opposition among fellow freedmen in his community, Tiche replies, "Why is everything you do decided by a fight? Most colored people accept things the way they is—gon' take us awhile to git ova' being' slaves! You can't expect folks to be votin' and doin' everything at once! Freedom new to us!" (Martin, Teacher's Guide 9). Tiche's perspective will, no doubt, agitate the consciousness of audiences toward both empathizing with and resisting his position. With a similar mission in mind, Wilson explores the most pressing problems blacks faced from as early as 1911 to as recently as 1971, overlapping Fuller's time frame with only one play of his history cycle, *Joe Turner's Come and Gone*. Although Wilson's history cycles command a larger canvas, he and Fuller essentially want to set straight the record of black experience in America. Fuller bases his entire series on the premise that it was in this period in history that the record of black involvement was most distorted: "After emancipation, a flood of reporters and travel writers came south. It is essentially out of their histories that a great number of myths and lies about blacks began. It wasn't until the late 1880s that the experience of slavery began to be reported by black people for black people. I want to attack the problem right there" (13–14).

Unfortunately the critical acclaim of Fuller's history series, as performed by the Negro Ensemble Company and directed by Douglas Turner Ward, has not been comparable to the fanfare Wilson's work received. The series debut *Sally*, for example, was roundly criticized at the 1988 National Black Theater Festival in Atlanta when it was presented after only one week's rehearsal. Various other limitations in stage size and lighting problems caused *Washington Post* critic David Richards to label it a "lumbering sprawl—21 episodic scenes crying out for focus" ("Trouble with *Sally*" E4). In spite of such negative reviews, Fuller continues to move toward completing his series—his goal not being to please critics but to enlighten his people.

Although the effect of his drama's cultural affirmation on audiences is so far ungauged, Wilson is satisfied that, as a writer, he is contributing to the development of black culture. When he writes about a railroad song or has his characters perform the juba dance or integrates lines from a blues tune into his script, he perpetuates a way of life that he feels provides healthy images for a floundering generation of African Americans. As a playwright, then, he considers himself to be part of a larger community of black writers who bear the grave responsibility of finding ways to sustain their heritage. He greatly admires writers such as Toni Morrison, artists such as Romare Bearden, musicians such as Muddy Waters, and fellow playwrights, such as Charles Fuller, who achieve in their work what he aspires to create in his plays—a sober, instructive journey back to investigate and draw strength from that which many would sooner forget.

To expand the black cultural dimensions of his plays, August Wilson turns to the works of collagist Romare Bearden. At thirty-two Wilson was introduced to the work of the world-famous artist. After examining a copy of *The Prevalence of Ritual*,[2] he experienced an epiphany much like the mind-altering spell under which he had fallen some twelve years ago upon discovering Bessie Smith's version of "Sweet Jelly Roll." Since that moment in 1977, Wilson has seen Bearden's work as expressing visually what blues lyrics stir inside of him. In a foreword to a recently published study on Bearden, Wilson writes:

> What for me had been so difficult, Bearden made seem so simple, so easy. What I saw was black life presented on its own terms, on a grand and epic scale, with all its richness and fullness, in a language that was vibrant and which, made attendant to everyday life, ennobled it, affirmed its value, and exalted its presence. It was the art of a large and generous spirit

that defined not only the character of black American life, but also its conscience. (Foreword 8)

For Wilson, Bearden and the blues both are provocative means of communicating the otherwise uncommunicable triumphs and tragedies of African American life. Joan Fishman argues that Wilson and Bearden have in common "the incorporation into their art of the elements that define traditional African performance forms. In the selection of their themes and the portrayals of their characters, they incorporate the true-to-life and the familiar into ritualistic drama recognizable and influential to their audiences" (133).

Bearden's often grim patchwork pieces offer Wilson another mirror image of himself—"a doorway. . . . A road marked with signposts, with sharp and sure direction, charting a path through what D. H. Lawrence called the 'dark forest of the soul' " (Foreword 9). Each familiar cultural signpost directs the artist's attention inward and facilitates his ongoing personal quest to understand his cultural origins as an African American. In scraps of cloth, clipped pictures, and carefully positioned images, Bearden's collages, like Wilson's plays, convey the rich cultural heritage of his people. Though their mediums differ, the two are united in their attempts to convey aspects of the black experience in art form. Wilson notes, "In Bearden I found my artistic mentor and sought, and still aspire, to make my plays the equal of his canvas."

The steel mills of Pittsburgh were common ground for Wilson and Bearden. Both knew firsthand of the back-breaking labor of the real-life "John Henry's" who stripped to their waists to endure the hellish heat from fiery furnaces and who, after a day's work, coated their bodies with cocoa butter to soothe their scorched skin. In 1920 Bearden lived in Pittsburgh with his maternal grandmother Carrie Banks, who with her husband, George, ran a boardinghouse. From the security of his grandmother's boardinghouse on Penn Avenue, young Bearden watched itinerants up from the South in search of steady work. He also saw the billowing clouds of smoke and heard the screeching whistles from nearby mills. For a brief time, he tried his hand at working in a nearby mill but wilted beneath the sweltering heat; he requested several transfers from jobs that were either too hot or too dangerous. Years later his *Mill Hand's Lunch Bucket* (1978) would document a domestic scene based upon this working-class environment and inspire August Wilson's *Joe Turner's Come and Gone.*

The short fiction of Argentine writer Jorge Luis Borges also contributes to Wilson's strategy for writing plays. Hailed as "a magician of language" (Giovanni 9), Borges regularly explored various metaphysical complexities in his short stories. What Wilson finds most intriguing about his work is its unorthodox manner of narration. He explained in an interview:

> I've been trying to write a play the way he writes a story. One of his techniques is that he tells you exactly what is going to happen. At the outset the leader of an outlaw gang with a bullet in his head would seem improbable. When you meet the guy, he's washing dishes, and you go "This guy is going to be the leader of an outlaw gang?" You know that he's going to get killed, but how is this going to happen? (interview)

His unpredictable plots make Borges not just a magician but a trickster; and "like all the best tricksters and poets [,] he makes us feel, when the trick is revealed and the poem is said, that it was always there, somewhere unexpressed within us" (Giovanni 9). Borges's metaphysical journeys capture the artistic imagination of Wilson, a playwright in search of the most effective way of conveying his numerous stories.

August Wilson's plays are also motivated by his desire to renegotiate what he perceives as crucial mistakes blacks have made since their emancipation—mistakes that have historically limited their involvement in education, employment, and economic opportunities in America. For example, his plays consistently demonstrate his beliefs that (1) the original sin committed by African Americans may be traced back to their massive postwar exodus from the South and their decision not to cling to the land; (2) African Americans do not sufficiently acknowledge and celebrate their cultural differences; (3) the salvation of today's African Americans rests with renewing ties with Africa and acknowledging their African heritage; (4) mainstream histories have systematically and consciously excluded and misrepresented African Americans; and (5) the only avenues that traditionally have offered African Americans limited acceptance have been sports and music.

Whether directly or indirectly, each of the plays that make up Wilson's cycle demonstrates the aftermath of the cardinal sin committed by the descendants of slaves: they abandoned the South rather than become landowners and gradually build a strong economic base. Wilson reasons,

We were land-based agrarian people from Africa. We were uprooted from Africa, and we spent 200 years developing our culture as black Americans. And then we left the South. We uprooted ourselves and attempted to transplant this culture to the pavements of the industrialized North. And it was a transplant that did not take. I think if we had stayed in the South, we would have been a stronger people. And because the connection between the South of the 20's, 30's and 40's has been broken, it's very difficult to understand who we are. (Rothstein, "Round Five" 8)

Essentially, this agrarian philosophy operating at the epicenter of Wilson's artistic agenda gives new meaning to the Reconstructionist theories of Booker T. Washington, who also saw that remaining close to the land was African Americans' most practical means of securing their future. And, like Washington's advocacy of self-help, Wilson's vision has been questioned; indeed, both views are challenged as inherently impractical on several grounds. Most crucially, Wilson's critics question the realism of expecting ex-slaves, at long last emancipated after years of physical and mental oppression, *not* to seek a less depressing environment when given the opportunity. Although the Emancipation Proclamation, "Juneteenth," and the myth of "forty acres and a mule" elicited some celebration at slavery's end, various remnants of the system went unchecked for decades. In the face of the South's "changing same" status, many freedmen opted to start a new life in one of several northern cities and thus escape their history as slaves.

In addition to wanting to exorcise the demons of their slave pasts, freedmen made their way north because they had little or no funds with which to purchase land. Whites were reluctant to offer any of their acreage for sale. The availability of sharecropping and tenant farming was, of course, merely a red herring employed to deflect attention from more deep-seated fears among these landowners: "With the destruction of the institution of slavery, whites looked upon land as their only important capital investment; and they were reluctant to sell land to Negroes, whom they did not want to enjoy the power that came from the ownership of land in the South" (Franklin 398).

But Wilson avoids such attacks on the logic of his ideal vision by transcending the detailed circumstances of oppression. He diverts attention away from the mire of historical details and toward the emotional landscape of the African American experience. Thus, he does not dwell on the actual "mistake" of leaving the South. Instead he is concerned about revealing the devastating irony of the move to the North: "We came North and we're still victims of discrimination and oppression in the North. [T]he move to the cities has not been a good move. Today in 1988 we still don't have jobs. The last time blacks in America were working was during the Second World War, when there was a need for labor, and it did not matter what color you are" (Moyers 167).

What Wilson seeks to explore in plays such as *Joe Turner's Come and Gone* and *The Piano Lesson* are the unmined regions of slavery's emotional milieu, the depths of which still remain fairly fresh territory for contemporary dramatists. With the notable exception of Amiri Baraka's *Slaveship* (1967), few dramatists have probed the long-term psychological effects of slavery. Until the recent publication of works such as Octavia Butler's *Kindred* (1979), Toni Morrison's *Beloved* (1988), and Charles Johnson's *Middle Passage* (1990), the slave experience was infrequently treated; even today, rarely has anyone delved into its lingering psychological effects upon subsequent generations as intimately as Wilson does.

Wilson seems most determined in his chronicles to assure African Americans not only that it is allright to be different from mainstream white America but that these important differences must be celebrated rather than repressed. He is often troubled by the unspoken desire among modern African Americans to distance themselves from their slave ancestors as if that part of their history did not exist. Conversely, he envies those people who are not ashamed today to keep such traditions as dancing the polka or celebrating Passover, and he finds it painful to consider the campaign by Jews to keep memories of the Holocaust fresh in minds of their people while far too many African Americans seem embarrassed by any African linkage. This attitude is best demonstrated during the first act of his 1982 play *Ma Rainey's Black Bottom* as Ma's bandmembers converse among themselves before a rehearsal session:

> TOLEDO: That's African.
> SLOW DRAG: What? What you talking about? What's African?
> LEVEE: I know he ain't talking about me. You don't see me running around in no jungle with no bone between my nose.
> TOLEDO: Levee, you worse than ignorant. You ignorant without a premise. *(Pauses.)*

Now, what I was saying is what Slow Drag was doing is African. That's what you call an African conceptualization. That's when you name the gods or call on the ancestors to achieve whatever your desires are.

SLOW DRAG: Nigger, I ain't no African! I ain't do no African nothing!

TOLEDO: Naming all those things you and Cutler done together is like trying to solicit some reefer based on a bond of kinship. That's African. An ancestral retention. Only you forgot the name of the gods.

SLOW DRAG: I ain't forgot nothing. I was telling the nigger how cheap he is. Don't come talking that African nonsense to me. (*MR* 32)

Slow Drag and Levee's response is typical for African Americans brainwashed into believing that by acknowledging their ties with Africa, they jeopardize total access to the American Dream. To this group, any derivative of the word *Africa* unleashes fervent denials and immediate defensive postures. In 1927 (the year in which *Ma Rainey's Black Bottom* is set), images of jungles inhabited by wild animals and scantily clad natives carrying spears did, in fact, represent the uninformed beliefs about Africa shared among "Americanized" African Americans. What's more, they shuddered, as if insulted, at the thought that such images had any association with them. But August Wilson is aware that these are often innocent defensive reactions to ubiquitous messages conveyed in a country seemingly growing less tolerant of cultural differences: "The social contract that white America has given blacks is that if you want to participate in society you have to deny who you are. You cannot participate in this society as Africans" (Moyers 177).

Africa plays a vital role in Wilson's dramatic vision. In varying degrees each of Wilson's history chronicles directs attention back to Africa, either by incorporating some visually familiar reference or, in some instances, by invoking supernatural or mystic phenomena. To counter self-deprecating emotions so symptomatic of cultural denial, Wilson writes to urge African Americans to "find their song" or discover their identity; otherwise, they will never understand who they are. Wilson is aware of the realities of assimilation among blacks in the twenty-first century, but early in his career he joined the ranks of writers like Langston Hughes and numerous others who, during the Harlem

Renaissance, knew the importance of cultural affirmation and who decided "to express our individual dark-skinned selves without fear or shame" (Hughes, "Negro Artists" 694).

While Wilson's plays illustrate his insistence upon demonstrating a linkage to Africa, their dramatic conflicts, in several instances, convey his belief that tragedy results when racism permeates either of the two areas in which African Americans have traditionally achieved limited success: music and sports. He finds potent drama by exploring what happens when these last avenues for even very limited economic and social advancement are blocked. What often results is a "transfer of aggression to the wrong target" (Savran 300). That is, instead of singling out the enemy among members of an entrenched white power structure, victimized African Americans make others of their race the unfortunate objects of their misdirected violence and aggression.

Wilson's dramatic vision also reveals his resentment of the ways African Americans have been misrepresented and unrepresented in history recording the last nine decades. He is very bothered that, for the most part, their history has been written by insensitive scholars alien to their culture and, unfortunately, subject to racism. For the last decade, he has been about the business of redressing this problem of African American exclusion and alienation from their own history by providing a more intimate look at moments in time when African Americans themselves had the power to choose their own destinies, despite daunting odds. He wishes to openly engage African Americans in a new historical dialectic—one that encourages affective as well as cognitive responses. By so doing, he reopens their history books, giving them a sense that they are participating in determining their own destinies.

August Wilson traces the source of his artistic vision to 1965—the year he was introduced to the blues. Perhaps it was providence that led him to purchase a three-dollar record player and to discover among some old seventy-eights he had bought Bessie Smith's "Nobody Can Bake a Sweet Jelly Roll Like Mine." As he listened to the record, he was inexplicably mesmerized by the emotions that Smith's sassy delivery exuded. The effect that Bessie Smith had on the then twenty-year-old Wilson was profound, for he had discovered the universal language of the blues. He had tapped into a nonverbal means of understanding the gamut of emotions locked up inside him.

Not only could this new language assist him in coping with the emotional vacuum left by his estranged white father or in identifying with his mother's African American heritage but it also would later inspire him to move beyond the bounds of his own life to convey the stories of the poor, illiterate, oppressed, and unrepresented African American masses. Wilson had, up until this moment, actively sought a means to define himself in a world where there were few gods in his image. Like James Baldwin, alone in Paris "with two Bessie Smith records and a typewriter" ("Discovery" 5), he found in the blues an image of himself that would, in time, also become a stimulus for calling forth the collective images of his people's ancestors. In 1961 Baldwin— whom Wilson quotes often—wrote, "One can only face in others what one can face in oneself. On this confrontation depends the measure of our wisdom and compassion. This energy is all that one finds in the rubble of vanished civilizations, and the only hope for ours" (13). Wilson would, perhaps unwittingly, adhere to Baldwin's wisdom, for it directs the African American writer to seek his or her voice in the cultural medium of the blues.

The year 1965 held several other memorable initiations for August Wilson. At nineteen he had moved out from Daisy Wilson's absolute rule and had rented a basement apartment in Pittsburgh's Hill District, where he fraternized with a group of writers and painters. The immediate environment of his new home was also peopled by ex-convicts, ex-counterfeiters, and drug abusers who would later be resurrected in his writing. As he committed to memory the vernacular rhythms of their speech, the idiosyncrasies of their personalities, and numerous visual images of this environment, Wilson gradually gained the much-needed substance of life that he lacked as a young novice poet. The dynamics of the blues, moreover, would eventually steer Wilson away from the restricted medium of poetry to the larger landscape of drama. This conversion allowed him to continue to draw upon his poet's sensitivity, his ear for dialogue, and his eye for visual detail, yet on a much more expansive scale.

Prior to Wilson's blues epiphany, his imagination had been limited by his own youthful inexperience and by the restraints imposed by poverty and an abbreviated high school education. As far back as he can recall, he wanted to be a writer; only his fortitude and singular vision enabled him to overcome the circumstances of his life to reach this goal. Wilson was born to poverty. Financially and emotionally abandoned by an indifferent German father, he, his two brothers, and two sisters were supported by the domestic wages his mother earned. They were healthy, clean, well-fed, and studious under Daisy Wilson's watchful care. Despite their father's negligence, Wilson's mother kept the family together until her children eventually matured and moved out on their own.

Although exceptionally bright, Wilson was bored with school and entertained early thoughts of dropping out. These thoughts soon became reality when he was accused of plagiarizing a term paper on Napoleon Bonaparte. Mr. Biggs, his black history teacher, considered the paper to be too well researched and written to have been authored by Wilson, gave it an "F," and charged the young student with cheating. Wilson reportedly tore up the paper, dropped its pieces into the garbage can, and never again returned to this class or, for that matter, to Central Catholic High School.

Wilson's education merely moved in other directions when he dropped out of ninth grade. While deciding how and when to inform his mother of his decision, he spent his truant days in the "Negro section" of the public library devouring the works of Langston Hughes, James Baldwin, and Richard Wright. Once she did learn of her son's plans, Daisy Wilson used the opportunity to nudge him out on his own. Without much of a fuss, Wilson moved out of his mother's apartment, took a job as a short-order cook, and began frequenting the tobacco houses, bars, and restaurants of Pittsburgh's Hill District. For Wilson, then known as "Youngblood" among the older men around him, this education was just as valuable as that provided by the system he had recently abandoned. These usually male-dominated establishments took the place of the stuffy classrooms where he had been fed a steady diet of Eurocentric writers. Here he listened to racy tales of love affairs and down-home blues stories, bolstered by heavy doses of braggadocio, the dozens, or just plain lies. Here in these smoke-filled watering holes where rough-edged men drank liquor, swapped tales, and laughed out loud, the adolescent Wilson found knowledge of a different sort. Like the familiar front porch setting, where the African American narrative tradition flourished in all of its uncensored glory, or the sacred ground before the African griot or African elder, these locations were essential for communal bonding.

Somehow Wilson was not fully drawn into the questionable company he kept at the Pittsburgh boardinghouse where he lived. Absorbed in dreams of becoming an accomplished poet, he would write for hours on end when not working at one of several odd jobs as porter, sheet metal worker, or short-order cook. During this time—before his introduction to cultural nationalism, Amiri Baraka, or Malcolm X—Wilson chose as his role model the Welsh poet Dylan Thomas. Thomas was a symbol of unadulterated rebellion, a Bohemian who ignored standards, drank profusely, and thumbed his nose at stuffy academicians of his time. His poetry favors themes suggesting the continuing processes of life, death, and new life that links the generations to each other. He was, moreover, brilliantly noncommital, having no interest in politics or society. But Wilson would soon realize that his African American heritage, grounded in the blues tradition, was at odds with this Welshman he had chosen to idolize. Although Wilson would not adopt all of Thomas's characteristics, certain of them stuck. For example, Wilson admired Thomas's fiery nature as well as his flamboyant style of dress and theatrical delivery. More substantively, Wilson's ten-play chronicle may have been influenced by certain of Thomas's ontological themes, specifically those regarding the continuum of life.

Wilson's education again veered when he discovered Pittsburgh's Halfway Art Gallery, a local rendezvous for the city's so-called Beat Culture. Here, among mutual lovers of poetry, he found not only an audience for his verse but also a network of lasting contacts with members of Pittsburgh's black literati—poets Rob Penny, Charley Williams, and Nick Flournoy. Together, the group formed the Center Avenue Poets Theatre Workshop and began a literary magazine to publish their verse. This trio of black artists also aided the neophyte cultural nationalist in his search for substance and voice by educating him about important contemporary writers. During lively forums they dissected and debated the writings of Ed Bullins, Richard Wesley, Ron Milner, Ishmael Reed, Maulana Karenga, Amiri Baraka, and Malcolm X and started Wilson to think about the artist's role in conveying the sentiments of the oppressed masses.

One indication of prevailing restlessness among blacks during the 1960s, the Black Theatre movement, exploded on the scene bringing with it scores of revolutionary plays. Wilson became part of this when, together with Rob Penny, he cofounded Pittsburgh's Black Horizons Theater. Keeping in line with its mission to "raise consciousness and politicize the black community" (Pointsett 74), Wilson and Penny staged all of Baraka's agit prop works in *Four Black Revolutionary Plays* and the entire series of plays published in a special Summer 1968 issue of *The Drama Review*.[3] In addition, Wilson got an opportunity to see some of his fledgling work brought to life on Black Horizons' stage.

However, he still recalls the initial insecurity about writing these first plays and managing a theatre:

> I tried to write a play but it was disastrous. I couldn't write dialogue. Doing community theater was very difficult—rehearsing two hours a night after people got off work, not knowing if the actors were going to show up. In '71, because of having to rely so much on other people, I said "I don't need this," and I concentrated on writing poetry and short stories. (Savran 290)

By the late 1960s, August Wilson had become a staunch cultural nationalist. By then, he had also completely purged his white father from his life and had chosen to affirm his mother's African heritage. To formalize the rejection of his European heritage, he legally changed his name from Frederick August Kittel (his father's name) to August Wilson. Heeding the chants of "Black Power," "Power to the People," and "Black is Beautiful," Wilson went further by adopting the African name "Mbulu," which means strength. In addition, to acquaint himself with the thrust of the movement, he studied the works of Malcolm X and the Muslim religion. For a while he also donned the black Muslim trademark black suit and bow tie and sold copies of *Muhammad Speaks*.

Totally absorbed in the ideology of the Black Power movement, Wilson found new avenues for his poetry. In a tribute to Malcolm X called "For Malcolm X and Others,"[4] he wrote:

> The hour rocks a clog,
> The midnight term,
> In bones no shape before
> Has warmed in such
> That loves these cold as dead,
> As stone; a flock of saints
> Run ground as thieves. (58)

He also shed the tweed jacket so characteristic of his former model Dylan Thomas and adopted his own trademark canvas jacket and cap.

During this nationalist period, Wilson also came to know the beliefs of the controversial poet, playwright, and activist Amiri Baraka, formerly known as LeRoi Jones—fascinated by his politically charged

poetry and inspired by his collection of fiery one-act plays. Baraka
awakened Wilson's sense of social awareness and provided another
means of affirming his own racial identity.

But Wilson was soon to discover that Baraka's style of poetic agit
prop was better admired than imitated: "I liked the language, I like
everything about [the plays]. In my early one acts I tried to imitate that
and then I discovered I wasn't him and that wasn't going to work"
(Savran 292). Although Wilson understood and agreed with his literary
colleagues of the Black Arts movement, who pushed for Afrocentric
artistic expression and "a radical reordering of the western cultural
aesthetic" (Neal, "Black Arts" 29), his inclinations as a poet led him to
assume a less political, less rhetorical posture. While Baraka wrote
"Poems are bullshit unless they are / teeth or lemons piled / on a step"
("Black Art" 223), Wilson wrote:

> We feel to begin
> The eye of the house opens
> Three angles.
> Think angels.
> There is something about living.
> The sheep runs from the wolves.
> The breaking of tradition.
> The horse fall from the sky.
> Life is (kawaida)
> Eternal Life (us)
> We are building a house. ("Morning Song" 68)

Apparently the lingering appeal of Dylan Thomas prevented Wilson from achieving total solidarity with black revolutionary artists.
Decades later he would write,

> as I bedded down each night with my immortal self the guns of
> social history and responsibility that went boom in the night
> and called the warriors to their stations were largely ignored. If
> I heard them at all they had no relation to my bearing as a poet
> determined to answer the question of how many angels could
> fit on the head of a pin, despite the fact that I was having
> trouble identifying the angels and the size of the pin. (*August
> Wilson: Three Plays* viii)

Although Wilson still considers himself an ideologue of cultural nationalism and is quick to acknowledge Amiri Baraka as a major influence,
he found the movement too extreme for his sensibilities and could not
capture its essence in his poetry.

August Wilson is the first one to concede that he was not a very
good poet. Still, he was fascinated by what he could do with words, and
he was fond of producing what was music to his ears but confusion to
those who would read or hear his poetry. The "anxiety of influence" did
not dissuade Wilson from mimicking the styles of accomplished poets
whom he admired in the late '60s and '70s. He freely admits to
"imitating everybody, all at the same time" (Patrick 42). As a result, his
verse emphasized eloquent abstractions at the expense of meaning and
content. He confessed,

> If you've got a way with language, you can really fool
> yourself. I was writing stuff that had no meaning, stuff
> like this—
> Though lovelier mo-
>   tion
> She dropped from her
>   immortal baggage
> A splintered pump
> And hell's mansions
>   rocked in torn winds
> For whom must we pray? (Patrick 42)

When questioned about the meaning of particular lines from his poem
"For Malcolm X and Others" (1969), he admitted the obscurity of his
poetry and explained, "it took me from '65 to '73 before I could actually
write a poem that I felt was written in my own voice" (interview).

Much has been written and said in the popular media about Wilson's conscious avoidance of major literary influences upon his work.
The unspoken and misleading assumptions are that the dramatist
chooses to deny what appear to be borrowings from his literary predecessors—especially Europeans—and that he creates in a vacuum, focusing only on his own experiences. While by his account Wilson has not
read Hansberry, Shakespeare, Miller, or O'Neill, he acknowledges that
he is well-grounded in the continuum of African American writers and
claims universal ties to all in his profession: "As you sit down to write

you are everyone. You are confronted with the same problems" (Berry B3). From his early discovery of Ellison, Wright, and Hughes in Pittsburgh's public library to his introduction to the works of Amiri Baraka and Toni Morrison, Wilson aligns his art with the well-wrought tradition of his black literary forerunners. He is well aware of numerous cultural practices familiar to African Americans and deliberately strives to include them in his work. For example, the storytelling and blues traditions as well as the railroad song and the juba dance signal that his work is grounded in a rich cultural legacy.

Although Wilson deserves his current acclaim for bringing black theatre once again into the American mainstream, he is working within an already established tradition. His success is owed partly to that tradition, for he has found a way to recast the valuable cultural inheritance of black experiences into the substance of his plays. Thus, the two-time Pulitzer Prize–winner and Broadway-seasoned playwright is but part of a larger whole. His predecessors, many of whom are no longer writing plays, include the firebrands of the 1960s, such as Ed Bullins, Ben Caldwell, Jimmy Garrett, Ron Milner, and Amiri Baraka, who presented harsh agitation propaganda aimed at indicting whites for their oppressive politics toward African Americans.

More broadly, Wilson draws on the nondramatic works of such important writers as W. E. B. Du Bois, Langston Hughes, Alain Locke, and Amiri Baraka. In his introduction to *Plays of Negro Life* (1927), Alain Locke encouraged black actors and black playwrights to "interpret the soul of their people in a way to win the attention and admiration of the world" (xv). Langston Hughes, in his landmark statement in "The Negro and the Racial Mountain" (1926), called for unabridged portrayals of "our individual dark-skinned selves without fear or shame" (694). In "The Drama among Black Folk," Du Bois revealed his dream "to get people interested in [the] development of Negro drama to teach on the one hand the colored people themselves the meaning of their history and their rich, emotional life through a new theatre, and on the other, to reveal the Negro to the white world as a human, feeling thing" (171). Amiri Baraka's essay "The Revolutionary Theatre" (1966) implores black people to "[storm] America with furious cries and unstoppable weapons," (214) an attack that should culminate in "actual explosions and actual brutality." Wilson's plays of the black experience combine aspects of Alain Locke's desire for universal appeal, Hughes's preference for uncensored material of Negro life, Du Bois's designs for the Negro as subject and object, and Baraka's brutally frank revolutionary theatre.

Wilson's literary influences go beyond writings of the African American experience. The first dramatic production he saw was Ed Bullins's *The Taking of Miss Janie,* but it was Athol Fugard's *Sizwe Bansi Is Dead* that instigated his interest in writing plays. Wilson has seen approximately fourteen of Fugard's works and admits that "he's probably had an influence on me without my knowing it" (Freedman, "Leaving His Imprint" 38). Argentine fiction writer Jorge Luis Borges, as already discussed, also affected the playwright's handling of relationships between structure and suspense.

August Wilson's dramatic vision is the result of years of maturing—as a black man in America and as an artist. As he discovers and comes to terms with the forces of history that controlled his fate and the fate of his ancestors, he also discovers and overcomes the weakness of his writing. To some extent, each of the plays that follow chronicles Wilson's personal journey out of an indistinct cultural past into a much more focused present. While sharpening his dramatic vision, he sees himself more clearly.

ONE

In Search of
a Voice

August Wilson
outside Eddie's restaurant
in the Hill neighborhood of Pittsburgh.
This establishment could serve as a model for
the setting of *Two Trains Running*.
Photograph © by Terry Clark.
Reprinted by permission.

August Wilson's inspiration to become a playwright had its genesis in the Black Power movement of the early 1960s. With Pittsburgh's Black Horizons Theater as backdrop and the revolutionary plays of Amiri Baraka as his textbook, he took his first awkward steps away from writing poetry toward composing one-act plays. But the conversion was a slow and painstaking one for Wilson. Although he had adopted the ideology of the Black Arts movement and had begun to observe and imitate the varying styles of playwrights such as Philip Hayes Dean, Ed Bullins, and Amiri Baraka, he still had not yet acquired a style and voice of his own. At that time, he saw little grandeur in the black experience and was not inspired by the conversations and lifestyles of fellow Pittsburgh natives.

Along with cofounder Rob Penny, Wilson's immediate concerns while affiliated with Black Horizons Theater from 1968 to 1971 were to raise his people's consciousness and to inspire them to take political charge of their lives. It was during this time that the reluctant playwright discovered the basis for an artistic ideology of his own. Despite remaining insecurities about the quality of his plays, Wilson was able to work out in his mind an artistic premise grounded in the Black Power movement's politics of empowerment and the Black Arts movement's emphasis upon cultural affirmation. His was not to be the belligerent, vindictive voice of Baraka or Bullins but the subtly provocative, yet equally effective, voice of a playwright with some thoughts of his own.

August Wilson's dramatic output while affiliated with Black Horizons Theater was minimal. Although he gained some directing experience, learned certain technical aspects of the theatre, and dabbled at writing a play or two, he still floundered. He had not yet been able to write dialogue that was convincing enough to capture the essence of his native Pittsburgh subjects; their conversations were stilted with figurative, unrealistic lines. Although Wilson's friend Rob Penny counseled him to "listen" to his characters rather than "make them talk," he had to move away from Pittsburgh before he could learn the key to Penny's wisdom. Before his departure, he believed that the speech patterns of fellow Pittsburgh natives, whom he had long known and with whom he had often spoken, had no qualities worth imitating in his work. Subconsciously he had regarded their talk as common, unpoetic street jargon. With distance, however, he began to pay attention to their voices in his memory, and his skill at writing dialogue greatly improved.

The lessons of Pittsburgh's Black Horizons Theater and Pittsburgh itself were interrupted when Wilson moved to St. Paul in 1978. *Black Bart and the Sacred Hills* (written in 1977), an ambitious script about the notorious rustler Black Bart,[1] turned out to be Wilson's debut as a serious dramatist; it also spurred this first major geographical relocation. In 1976, his friend Claude Purdy had heard him read a tribute in verse to the character Black Bart. Purdy saw dramatic potential in Wilson's series of poems about this adventurous western character and encouraged him to convert the poems into a play.

Wilson did just that; four months later he produced a 120-page script called *Black Bart and the Sacred Hills*, a musical satire with twenty-seven characters. This sprawling attempt was to be the pivotal point in Wilson's conversion from poet to playwright. Although Purdy acknowledged that the work still needed much revision before it could be staged, Wilson was moved by his words of encouragement. At Purdy's invitation Wilson flew out, intending simply to further revise *Black Bart*; eventually, he took up residence in this city in the northern Midwest. After some fine-tuning, *Black Bart* was staged in January 1978 at Los Angeles's Inner City Theater.

Wilson's business trip to St. Paul would also have an impact on the direction of his personal life. Purdy's wife introduced Wilson to her friend Judy Oliver, who became Wilson's second wife in 1981: "Wilson showed her one of his scripts; she made him dinner. She was struck by the honesty and the sense that he spoke with a 'true heart' "(Brown 124). Their meeting influenced his decision to relocate to St. Paul in the spring of 1978.

The move had consequences for his career more significant than the staging of one play. Prior to *Black Bart* he had already quietly experimented with *Recycle* (written in 1973),[2] *The Coldest Day of the Year* (written in 1976), *The Homecoming* (written in 1976), the script that eventually became *Ma Rainey's Black Bottom* (written in 1976, revised in 1981); and *Jitney!* (written in 1979); most of which were created for Black Horizons Theater. While under the tutelage of Purdy, Wilson gained confidence as a playwright, steadily improving as he revised several of these plays and completed new ones such as *Fullerton Street* (written in 1980). He found a strong network of support, a network formed by Purdy and aspiring playwrights like himself whom he met at the Playwright's Center in Minneapolis, from which he received a minigrant as a result of submitting *Jitney!*. Moreover, the change was just what Wilson needed to improve his skills at writing dialogue. Once removed from daily reminders of an environment he had known all of his life, he came to appreciate both the people of Pittsburgh and what they had to say: "In 1979, when I wasn't living in Pittsburgh anymore, I started hearing the voices of the people I'd grown up with all my life. And I started writing them down" (Patrick 43). Above all, Wilson learned to "listen." That is, rather than force manufactured dialogue into his characters' mouths, he allowed them to assume a life of their own. The more he listened, the more his characters revealed their painful pasts to him. Once Wilson overcame the tendency to manipulate his characters in obvious ways, their speech became infinitely more credible. This remedied what had been his greatest weakness as a playwright.

In learning to listen to his characters, Wilson stopped trying to cram a political agenda down their throats. Nevertheless, his theatre is not inattentive to the same concerns that dominated black theatre in the era of the Civil Rights and Black Arts movements. But out of the fire and rhetoric of this period, he emerged as a different brand of revolutionary playwright: not quite comfortable with direct racial affronts, he writes tributes to his people's culture and exposes the unheralded nobility in their endurance. For example, while Walker Vessels of Amiri Baraka's *The Slave* spends time accosting his white middle-class captives in their suburban home, Wilson's Troy Maxson—while aware of white oppression on his job and in the sports arena—turns his attention to grabbing as much gusto during his middle-aged years as he can. Wilson found that listening, not manipulating, was the key to writing realistic dialogue.

Prior to moving to St. Paul in 1978, Wilson had experimented with ritual and absurdist drama, which had been inspired by a troubled relationship with a girlfriend. The blues stemming from the failed romance and his continued search for a suitable form yielded the one-act play *The Coldest Day of the Year*, a rhetoric-laden script of twenty-three pages whose minimal action is confined to a bus stop during the bleakest part of the winter. Its rakish candor, latent surrealism, verbal calisthenics, and overall honesty are reminiscent of Edward Albee's *Zoo Story* and *Who's Afraid of Virginia Woolf?* as well as Amiri Baraka's *Madheart* and *Dutchman* and Samuel Beckett's *Waiting for Godot*. But, on a more interpersonal level, the play is an allegorical love story between Man and Woman, who finally are able to communicate and resolve their differences after years of separation and miscommunication.

While Woman continues what has come to be a daily ritual of
waiting on a bench located near a bus stop, she is spied by the homeless Man. After a guarded introduction, Man and Woman warm to each other's company. Man is concerned about the futility of Woman's daily waiting and slips into a role that allows him to uncover the source of her vigilant watch. A forthright conversation ensues, revealing that the man for whom Woman waits is her estranged husband. During the minidrama instigated by role-playing, Man becomes her former husband and lover while Woman reenacts both good and bad memories of their years together. After some verbal foreplay, they take turns disclosing episodes from their previous life together—a life fraught with mutual misunderstanding. Man, in a self-conscious dramatic moment, pretends to have stabbed himself to prove his gallantry; Woman fusses over him and reveals limitless compassion for him. Man's strategy works, for in reminiscing about certain episodes from her previous married life, Woman is able to move her thoughts and eventually her body beyond the bench setting; she invites Man to her small room to get out of the wind, for it *is* "the coldest day of the year." After a lengthy conversation, the two agree to meet again at this same rendezvous on a future date to continue their intimate (albeit staged) stroll through the mutual past they have created. They both keep their pledges and show up later to resume what promises to be a sequel to their earlier verbal ramblings. The lines blur between make-believe and reality at the end of the play, for once Woman and Man step out of their fictive roles, they discover that they have loved each other all along.

The Coldest Day of the Year displays the stilted, figurative dialogue that Wilson labored to improve from his earliest one-act plays to his very first attempts at writing scripts for Minnesota's Science Museum. During this time Wilson's characters merely approximated speech, frequently missing the mark. As soon as they speak, Man and Woman immediately become distant and symbolic characters, for their conversation is riddled with figurative allusions and self-conscious dramatic poses. Their talk is just as obscure and convoluted as lines from Wilson's early verse:

> MAN: You never knew me in barbershops, or scouting the funeral homes for bereaved widows . . . a ghost willing to be exorcised. Under your touch, lady, I moved toward an explosion, a becoming in my life, spirited and pointed toward the finish line. (*CDY* 6)

The Coldest Day of the Year also represents Wilson's early penchant for imitating the masters. Although he minimizes and, in some cases, denies influence by other artists, this early play bears a number of more than coincidental structural and thematic similarities to works by Amiri Baraka, Edward Albee, and Samuel Beckett. From Baraka comes the apparent influence of the witty sensuality of *Dutchman*'s Lula and Clay. Wilson's play, like Baraka's, develops out of a chance meeting between two larger-than-life characters—a man and a woman who eventually anger each other with wicked accusations and innuendoes. Perhaps the degree to which *The Coldest Day* does reflect European influence is due to Baraka's own acknowledged influence by such dramatists as Samuel Beckett. For example, the plays included in his *Four Black Revolutionary Plays—Experimental Death Unit #1, Madheart, Jello,* and *Black Mass—* which helped form Wilson's background as a playwright, by and large deliberately imitated European dramatists in parodying them. These dramatists could have indirectly affected Wilson's early work.

The influence of other modern dramatists also seems to be at work in Wilson's *Coldest Day*. The image of Albee's familiar bench setting from *Zoo Story* surfaces in the play, as does the pivotal chance meeting of two strangers and the emotion-charged dual between them. Moreover, like Beckett's *Waiting for Godot*, Wilson's play revolves around a remarkably static setting and a pervasive mood of futile expectation. Woman comes daily to sit and wait on a bench at "Fifth and Market," yet the man she expects has yet to arrive:

> MAN: I stood over there and watched you. I thought you were
> waiting on the bus . . . but it passed and you did not get on.
> WOMAN: I was waiting for someone.
> MAN: And they didn't come?
> WOMAN: No. He did not come.
> MAN: And you came back today?
> WOMAN: Yes. And tomorrow as well. (*CDY* 2)

As in Beckett's *Godot*, the time spent waiting is eventually consumed by highly charged conversation in which the two characters harangue about an abstract issue.

That Wilson may have been influenced by these and perhaps other dramatists at this point in his career as a playwright suggests his ongoing struggle for his own style. As of 1976 when *The Coldest Day* was written, he had not yet experienced the kind of concentrated writing and staging of plays that would later be afforded by various conferences and playwrights' institutes. Although he had been profoundly influenced by the blues, Amiri Baraka, and Romare Bearden, he was not yet able to convert this influence into a unique voice of his own. Still, he repeatedly denies being influenced by other than a select few dramatists who include Amiri Baraka, Athol Fugard, and Philip Hayes Dean: "I haven't read Ibsen, Shaw, Shakespeare—except *The Merchant of Venice* in ninth grade. The only Shakespeare I've ever seen was *Othello* last year at Yale Rep. I'm not familiar with *Death of a Salesman*" (Savran 292).

Although Wilson acknowledges his general affiliation with European playwrights, it is Baraka's style that he more closely emulates as he draws upon autobiographical details for his plays. *The Coldest Day of the Year*, like an earlier play written in 1973 called *Recycle*, mirrors an intimate side of August Wilson that involves love, marriage, the birth of his daughter Sakina, and divorce. The play not only shows a generic failed romance but it also draws specifically on his troubled marriage to a Muslim woman, which lasted from 1969 to 1972. In 1969, while still in Pittsburgh, August Wilson married his first wife, Brenda Burton. He was moved by the discipline and beauty of his wife's Muslim background and he strove to please her by increasing his knowledge of her religion. As his friend the poet Rob Penny recalls, "August tried hard to be a Muslim man. He sold *Muhammad Speaks*—the Muslim newspaper—and he wore a black suit and bowtie." Wilson's sister, Freda Ellis, also noticed a change in her brother, speculating that his immersion in the Muslim religion "might have put him in touch with the way blacks think, the way the black and white world treated each other" (C. Brown 124).

Although the salvation of Wilson's marriage seems to have prompted in him a mere passing interest in Elijah Muhammad and the Muslim religion, when he married Burton, he was already well aware of the legacy of Malcolm X. While standing on a street corner in Pittsburgh in the fall of 1965, a twenty-year-old August Wilson was presented an album of Malcolm X's speeches by a friend, Clarence Jones. At this point in his life, Wilson had moved out on his own, was supporting himself with odd jobs, and had adopted a set of politically active artists as friends. Nick Flournoy and Rob Penny were among those schooling Wilson in the politics of the Black Arts movement and encouraging his artistic pursuits.

Already sensitive to the plight of blacks in America—especially black men—Wilson was deeply moved by Malcolm X's words. Like the lyrics to Bessie Smith's blues song "Nobody Can Bake a Sweet Jelly Roll Like Mine," the words on the Malcolm X recording struck a resounding chord in Wilson. As one of thousands of young black men growing up in an oppressive, poverty-ridden urban environment, he knew that he needed a strong sense of direction to keep him from falling prey to the streets. While crime, drugs, and dereliction beckoned, Malcolm X offered the young fatherless Wilson a vision of black manhood: "When we saw or heard Malcolm we saw or heard ourselves. Whatever the self was: Malcolm the Bad Nigger. Malcolm the Boisterous. Malcolm the Defiant. Malcolm the Brave. He was all these and more" (Wilson, "Legacy of Malcolm" 89).

The spirit of Malcolm X remains with August Wilson and, to some extent, informs the behavior of each of his black male protagonists. Since a dominant theme in each of the six plays that make up his history cycle is how to survive as a black man in America, Malcolm X's defense of black manhood offers a fitting guideline: "His public stance was that of a man who did not hold his tongue, a man who was unafraid, a man who was not seeking approval from whites" (89). His outspoken nature, his persistence, his indomitable warrior spirit, and ultimately his martyrdom are traits Wilson often appropriated to create strong male characters.

Wilson's ideas on the importance of culture may be traced back some thirty years to his days as an avowed nationalist and disciple of Elijah Muhammad, Malcolm X, and Ron Karenga. Though he has since toned down some of his extremist views on cultural isolationism, he retains a strong belief in the importance of preserving elements of one's cultural heritage. For example, he still applauds Ron Karenga's criteria of culture[3] and Elijah Muhammad's contribution to origin myths as seen in the popular Muslim myth of Yacub.[4] He explains, "[If] you look at the criteria of culture using Maulana Ron Karenga's criteria of mythology, history, religion—we had all those things. But the one thing which we did not have as black Americans—we didn't have a mythology. We had no origin myths. Certainly Muhammad supplied that" (interviewed by the author).

But neither his marriage nor his fascination with the Muslim religion lasted—only the ideals of Malcolm X and Elijah Muhammad's emphasis upon discipline. Wilson and his wife Brenda drifted apart, reportedly not speaking for more than fifteen years. And so to exorcise himself of what he called "man and woman stuff," Wilson wrote several

plays whose conflicts are based upon a man and a woman communicating to resolve their differences. *The Coldest Day of the Year* is such a
play premised on a dialectical exercise in analyzing causes of incom-
patibility and demonstrating means of reconciliation. In the sense that
the play thinly veils Wilson's strained relationship with his first wife, it
becomes a therapeutic "rap session" in which Woman helps Man
identify the source of his despair:

> WOMAN: Something's bothering you. I can tell. The story you
> wear on your face like a mask. Why don't you tell me? I'm
> not good at talking much with fancy words and all, but I
> listen. Tell me.
> MAN: . . . We met at school. A curious detachment had already
> begun to settle in my bones and my life was a sweltering
> furnace of nonchalance, tempered with a certain vigor.
> When wanting my fullness and not a field of war . . . [,] she
> came into my life carrying in each hand the seed of both.
> What could I do with such fairness?
> WOMAN: . . . What happened?
> MAN: Stars crashed into each other. The universe stuttered. I
> missed my prayers. I awoke at dawn . . . sunlight crashing
> through the windows . . . and I ran to collect it, alive and full
> of motion and fuel, and . . . the bed beside me empty. Empty
> space. A black hole in the slit of time.
> WOMAN: You probably scared her. You're not an easy man to
> take. Your intensity inhabits like a wound. (*CDY* 18–20)

When it was written in 1976, *The Coldest Day of the Year* was not
unique among plays written by other contemporary African American
playwrights in treating man-woman themes. In fact, themes concerning
either the eradication or conversion of femme's fatales who were considered archenemies of the revolution were commonplace in the prolific
playwright Amiri Baraka's repertoire of revolutionary plays of the
1960s. At that time it was popular to focus upon the compatibility of
African American men and women, as black nationalists pushed, initially within the family unit, for solidarity, which— according to their
expectations—should ultimately spread to society at large. This message was too often brutally conveyed in works such as Amiri Baraka's
Madheart (1968), in which women are cursed, slapped, or humiliated

into submission. The blatant sexism of African American men like *Madheart*'s Black Man crushes their women's independence while they lord over them sexually and politically. This matter-of-fact dominance over women was the ordained scheme of things. To many staunch nationalists, the woman's role in the revolution was to worship their men. As both Baraka and Wilson knew well the teachings of Muhammad, one may surmise that Muslim beliefs about the role of women in the family and in society in some way shaped both men's perceptions. Baraka's *Madheart* typifies the extremely sexist roles relegated to women by those who followed the nationalist impulse during this time:

> BLACK MAN: I want you, woman, as a woman. Go down. *(He slaps again.)* Go down, submit, submit . . . to love . . . and to man, now, forever.
> BLACK WOMAN: *(Weeping, turning her head from side to side)* Please don't hit me . . . please . . . *(She bends.)* The years are so long, without you, man, I've waited . . . waited for you. (81–82)

Although Wilson's play does not address concerns immediately identified as nationalist, its tone is very similar to a number of plays written by African American playwrights during the '60s and early '70s specifically geared toward a nationalist agenda. During this time ritual drama was a popular subgenre of black theatre, primarily seeking an expeditious and uncomplicated means of communicating various nationalist concerns via the symbolic and the familiar. The trend that evolved, therefore, was to create allegorical characters who were recognizable on both literal and figurative levels. These characters would, in turn, speak, act, and dress to invite immediate recognition. Shelby Steele observes, "As a means of presenting the Black Experience through the nationalist perspective, ritual has emerged as a predominant force, both in the thinking of several Black playwrights and in the nationalistic theater they have created" (30–34).

But despite the play's nationalist tone and Wilson's allegiance to the nationalist cause, he apparently did not endorse the prevailing crude depictions of women. *The Coldest Day of the Year* accords Woman an abiding respect: "Here . . . allow me, Madam . . . my coat"; and "Loveliness is not just a patron of youth, Madam. Take it from one who knows about such things: . . . You are as lovely as a jaybird on a spring day" (*CDY* 2). This respect is reciprocal; Woman nurses Man back to psychological health by listening to his past and eventually falling in love with him. She neither fears him, snubs him, nor makes light of his suffering. Instead she listens to his story while gently counseling him and rebuilding his confidence. In what seems to be a staged exorcism, they both revisit the past to examine Man's part in destroying the relationship:

> MAN: Why didn't you help me?
> WOMAN: I did. I was healthy for you. But I wasn't ready to be responsible for nobody's happiness. Even my own. I couldn't carry that weight. You poured all of your will into me and when hot ambition cooled . . . you fell to stumbling blocks. It's not my fault.
> MAN: You were the fuel and I moved smoothly, an engine racing toward the future worlds. I needed you to complete my journey. (10–11)

What results is a ritual purging of Man's past and a renewed faith in love.

The Homecoming, another one of Wilson's one-act plays written in 1976, remains unpublished; it was first produced by Kuntu Theater, a local amateur group in Pittsburgh. He dedicates the seventeen-page script "to the memory of Blind Lemon Jefferson and to the countless 'unknown' blues singers, whose story remains largely untold" (1). The play's deceased protagonist, Blind Willie Johnson, is a fictionalized rendering of the itinerant blues singer-guitarist Blind Lemon Jefferson, who was born in July of 1897 in Couchman, Texas, and died on the streets of Chicago in December of 1930. He achieved fame by freelancing his guitar-picking and singing skills at various public events around small Texas towns, such as Waco, Galveston, East Dallas, and Silver City.

Blind Lemon Jefferson (a.k.a. Deacon L. J. Bates and Elder J. C. Brown) was born blind on a small farm. One of seven children born to Alec Jefferson and Classie Banks, Blind Lemon eked out a modest living in Texas, Louisiana, Mississippi, Alabama, and Virginia as a singing beggar at picnics, parties, and on street corners. Black pianist Sammy Price, who was impressed by Lemon's music, recommended him to Paramount Records. He recalls, "Blind Lemon was using the term 'booger rooger' and playing in that boogie-woogie rhythm as far back as, oh, 1917, when I heard him in Waco. . . . A little later, in Dallas, he used to spend every day walking from one end of town to the other, playing and singing on the street and in various taverns for tips" (Palmer 107).

By the mid-twenties Blind Lemon Jefferson had made a name for himself among southern folk as a top-rate singer and guitarist. In the process of panhandling his blues, he had amassed an impressive list of songs, such as "Pneumonia Blues" (recorded by Paramount Records in 1929), "Broke and Hungry Blues," "Lemon's Worried Blues," and "Stocking Feet Blues," which often conveyed his private dispair. Several of his blues songs, such as "Hangman's Blues" (recorded by Paramount Records in 1928), "Blind Lemon's Penitentiary Blues," and "Prison Cell Blues," reveal his compassion for prison inmates. Others, such as "Eagle Eyed Mama," "Gone Dead on You," "Piney Woods Mama," "Peach Orchard Mama," "Southern Woman Blues," and "Deceitful Brownskin," speak to the heavy hearts of the lovesick, betrayed, and downright depressed southern lovers.

Paramount Records realized that Blind Lemon Jefferson "had developed a fluent and apparently idiosyncratic blues guitar style" and that "his lyrics were among the most inventive in the blues genre" (Titon 114). They invited him to Chicago, where, at the time of his death, he had recorded ninety-seven titles. At the height of Jefferson's career with them, *The Paramount Book of Blues* proudly advertised the blues virtuoso in a brief narrative recounting his legendary rise to fame. Jefferson's blindness became a commercial gimmick, and the more Paramount drew attention to his tragic status, the more he piqued the curiosity of northern audiences fascinated by anything even remotely exotic or primitive. Also, through Paramount's popular mail-order service to southern rural areas, Lemon's fame spread even more extensively.[5]

But there was to come a dark end to a life already deprived of light. Blind Lemon Jefferson reportedly died of a heart attack brought on by exposure to Chicago's wintry weather. In 1930 he was buried in an unmarked grave at Wortham Negro Cemetery in Wortham, Texas.

The Homecoming explores the mystery surrounding Blind Lemon Jefferson's death through creating a blues singer, Blind Willie Johnson, whose life and death parallel the real singer's. Although historical records do not actually implicate anyone in Jefferson's demise, August Wilson concretizes the villains in the form of two white talent scouts from some northern record company. As the story went, before going up North, Blind Willie was regarded as such a crowd-pleasing guitarist and blues singer in those parts that men idolized him and women flocked to be near him. Unfortunately, Blind Willie's fame had caught the attention of a rival record company on a talent-scouting expedition to various southern backwoods. According to Blind Willie's friends, the crafty northern agents enticed the blind man to come up North to record a collection of his best blues songs. Once they had committed all of Blind Willie's tunes to records, they turned him out into the winter weather where he eventually died of exposure.

The play takes place in a small abandoned train station in rural Alabama where three black men await the corpse of the legendary blues singer. This solemn occasion is interrupted by two white talent scouts looking to bag and take back up North some of the raw talent springing up around southern towns in 1927. By coincidence, these men intrude upon Blind Willie's last rites, scheduled to begin when his frost-bitten body arrives at the depot from Chicago. The dead man's welcoming party, aware of the circumstances of his death, immediately recognize the two scouts as the same kind of white men who had unmercifully exploited their friend. After masterfully deceiving their visitors by pretending complete ignorance to all of their questions, the two men, aided by Blind Willie's son, rough up the scouts and leave them to die in a boarded-up, airtight room at the abandoned station.

Out of pitiable circumstances August Wilson creates a heroic drama in which disarming, backwoods vigilantes avenge the death of one of their own. In the process, Obadiah and Leroy join a long line of tricksters extending as far back as Charles Chesnutt's Uncle Julius of *The Conjure Woman* (1899) and forward to Rutherford Calhoun of Charles Johnson's *Middle Passage* (1990). Wilson has created an example of what he refers to as "the warrior spirit" by inverting the stereotype of the docile and dimwitted black southerner of 1920s Alabama. Their flip sides may be described in terms of a "willingness to do battle, even to death. . . . Not all of them are in the penitentiary, but some, because of that spirit, find themselves on the opposite side of society that is constantly trying to crush their spirit" (Moyers 179). Wilson admits, "For a long time, I thought the most valuable blacks were those in the penitentiary. . . . They were the people with the warrior spirit. How they chose to battle may have been wrong, but you need people who will battle. . . . Just like there were people who didn't accept slavery. There were Nat Turners" (Freedman, "Voice" 49). Although this warrior spirit has its genesis in *The Homecoming*, it recurs in a number of Wilson's subsequent plays—in *Ma Rainey's Black Bottom, Fences*, and *Joe Turner's Come and Gone*. Levee, Troy Maxson, and Herald Loomis are all formed in the same militant mold as Obadiah and Leroy; they all are wrong in the eyes of society, but according to Wilson, committing various crimes and moral indiscretions is better by far than acquiescing to the dead-end lives society has prescribed for them.

The Homecoming is an obvious precursor to *Ma Rainey's Black Bottom*, completed five years later in 1981. In fact, Wilson gives a brief tribute to Blind Lemon Jefferson by including several lines of one of his blues songs in the opening pages of *Ma Rainey*:

> They tore the railroad down
> so the Sunshine Special can't run
> I'm going away baby
> build me a railroad of my own. (*MR* x)

Both works are preoccupied with the exploitation of the blues performer by record companies vying to control the rights to their music during the 1920s. Yet *The Homecoming* leads to a more satisfying catharsis, as the potential victims become the victors. In Wilson's later two-act play, the latent aggression within *Ma Rainey* and her band takes the form of compensatory actions that avoid indicting the white man as the source of their troubles (e.g., playing the dozens, singing the blues, stalling the rehearsal session, and stabbing the piano player for accidentally stepping on a new pair of shoes). In contrast, as soon as Obadiah and Leroy encounter the white talent scouts, they begin to unfold a deliberate plan of retaliation. This plan begins with a display of naïveté and downright ignorance to deflect any suspicion and moves toward the swift and aggressive immobilization of the two white scouts:

> *(Will Jr. comes out. They begin to take the plywood and nail up the windows and door).*
> LEROY: You nail up around on that side Will.
> GEORGE: Hey! Hey! What are you doing! You can't do that! You can't do that! Please Fellas! You can't leave us without food and water . . . we'll . . . we'll . . .
> IRVING: We'll die! George, we'll die!
> LEROY: Yessir. A man can't get no food or water'll die sure enough. *(He continues nailing.)* Say Obadiah . . . you say Blind Willie starved to death?
> OBADIAH: Froze. (*H* 16)

By granting African American characters of the 1920s the power and the will to avenge a wrongful death, Wilson becomes a contemporary mythmaker, who—in the tradition of Richard Wright, Arna Bontemps, Amiri Baraka, and others who use literature to empower—demonstrates that "black people have power" (Gibson 82). Obadiah and Leroy, like Richard Wright's Bigger Thomas (*Native Son*), Arna Bontemps's Gabriel Prosser (*Black Thunder*), and Amiri Baraka's Walker Vessels (*The Slave*), violently break down barriers of stereotyping that society has imposed on them. Although each of the above reluctant heroes does, in fact, carry out or contemplate a murder, the emphasis is not so much upon inflicting death but upon their exemplary valor in overthrowing or outsmarting their oppressors; that they are "warriors" gains them automatic respect. Like Baraka, Bontemps, and Wright, August Wilson caters to the part of the human spirit that empathizes with the downtrodden under-classes, relishing any advantage they may gain over their oppressors.

The Homecoming, though comparatively brief, is surprisingly well crafted, displaying dramatic skills that, even as early as 1976, revealed a promising future for the aspiring playwright. When Wilson wrote *The Homecoming*, he had not yet relocated to St. Paul. Thus, his ear for dialogue was still in its undeveloped state. Yet despite his frequently admitted difficulty in writing credible lines for his characters, the con-versations of Blind Willie's Alabama neighbors Obadiah and Leroy and the aggressive white northerners George and Irving are convincing. For example, as Obadiah and Leroy engage in some tongue-in-cheek fun with the agents, they mock, in particular, the men's unshaken confi-dence in knowing their prey:

> IRVING: Come on now, you're pulling our leg.
> LEROY: Huh? Who me? Nossir, I ain't pulling nothing. Nossir, I ain't touched your leg. You can see I ain't moved from here. (*H* 4)

Again, later:

> OBADIAH: What's the name of this singer you looking for?
> IRVING: He ain't got no name . . . he's just somebody.
> LEROY: Nossir, everybody around here got a name. (5)

Wilson seems well versed in the racial politics of Alabama in 1927, and the dialogue suggests the realities of surviving in such an environment. However, he does not tamper much with the written word to denote southern, backwoods dialect. For example, he does not use "hya" for "here" or "Yassuh" for "Yessir." In fact, with the exception of an occasional "naw" or "nossir" or "usta," the conversations of both Leroy and Obadiah could have taken place virtually anywhere in the United States.

The Homecoming is as structurally sound as any of Wilson's later plays. In fact, this seventeen-page play seems anachronistic; the sprawl and artificial dialogue that plagued the novice playwright later in *Black Bart and the Sacred Hills*, *Jitney!*, and *Fullerton Street* are conspicuously absent. *The Homecoming* employs a story line that requires very few characters, and Wilson's stage notes—when they do occur—rarely exceed a sentence or a phrase. Characters come and go with very little fanfare, and all of the action takes place in one central location: an abandoned train depot. Obadiah, Leroy, and Will Jr. are stationary throughout the play, and the set is only twice broken into: first, by talent scouts and, second, by the train delivering Blind Willie's body.

The Homecoming is a crucial play in Wilson's career. It marks a decided departure from what he calls "disastrous" experimental works written while he was under the influence of the Black Theatre movement, Pittsburgh's Black Horizons Theater, Amiri Baraka's *Four Revolutionary Plays*, and the 1968 special issue of *Drama Review*. Still, Wilson was far from realizing his full potential as a dramatist. There would be several other flawed attempts to follow. After Wilson left Pittsburgh in 1978 he would confront and overcome, with each subsequent play, the problems that frustrated his efforts to master the genre.

Inspired by the aesthetic distance and relative serenity that St. Paul offered, Wilson polished not only his playwrighting skills but also increased his productivity. One of his first jobs in Minnesota was at the Science Museum, where he wrote scripts for its affiliated theatre troupe. This experience gave him the special satisfaction of being a *paid* writer; he was commissioned to create one-man skits on men and women of science, such as Margaret Mead, and educational minidramas highlighting cultural practices among various peoples. But perhaps more important, the discipline Wilson acquired while producing acceptable scripts on a regular basis significantly diminished many of the novice playwright's early anxieties. The museum brought Wilson's work to life on stage as part of its offerings to the public. This experience at writing plays brought him a large degree of satisfaction, for he was compensated triply for his work: he received a regular paycheck, public exposure, and practice in writing on a regular basis.

The relative ease and effectiveness that characterize Wilson's brief dramatic episodes about science and anthropology reveal a steadily improving ear and eye for drama as well as a growing confidence that would serve him well when he would later venture to write full-blown plays. For example, *The Eskimo Song Duel: The Case of the Borrowed Wife* (1979), though basic in plot and structure, demonstrates his gift for fashioning drama out of otherwise ordinary life circumstances. The play is a dramatic lesson on Eskimo moral codes regarding husband-wife relationships. The eight-page script, which was adapted from a taped anthropological series,[6] focuses upon the custom, perfectly acceptable to Eskimo natives, or Inuit, of wife sharing or wife stealing. In fact, according to background information on Eskimo culture that frames the play, such practices were sanctioned by the Eskimo community to encourage the men to be good husbands, hunters, and providers. Wilson writes in the play's epilogue: "It is the response of the community that decides who is right and who is wrong. For the community has a vested interest in peace" (*ESD* 8).

The Eskimo Song Duel highlights a verbal contest between an ineffectual, undeserving husband and a skilled huntsman and provider. Since Eskimo women were few in number, it was not uncommon for men to compete for them—even for another man's wife. Thus, according to their custom, a man who acquired and maintained a wife enjoyed a special status within the community, for it was a testament to his valor. Conversely, a man without a wife or a man who could not keep his wife was persecuted and shamed. So when an obviously more industrious and skilled huntsman coveted and won the wife of a lesser rival, he did so with his society's blessings. As matters of morals and ethics were settled by the Eskimo community, men were encouraged to settle their disputes by resorting to various types of duels wherein members of the community would serve as jury and judge.

Such is the case between the play's Eskimo rivals Kakachick and Kowicki, who put the Eskimo code of ethics to the test. Kakachick is a poor hunter. On a particularly bad day, his spear bounces off the hide of his prey, and he comes home without food for himself and his wife. His disappointed mate, in turn, does a poor job mending a tear in his kayak, and he nearly drowns during the next day's hunt. His ineptitude leads to a "breakdown in the survival system" (1). Noticing the dismal circumstances of Kakachick's marriage, Kowicki announces his intentions to duel for Kakachick's scorned and poorly kept wife. On a predetermined day, the men faceoff in a battle of songs. With the Eskimo community looking on, Kowicki and Kakachick compete for the woman by exchanging witty lyrics that detail for the community the substance of their dispute. After several displays of lyrical dexterity, Kowicki emerges the victor, and Kakachick "walk[s] off . . . his head hung in shame" (7). The conclusive result of the Eskimo song duel in settling this dispute is regarded with as much honor as a verdict rendered in any court of law: KOWICKI gains a wife and partner in survival while KAKACHICK is destined to a grueling existence as an Eskimo man without a woman.

Another one of Wilson's Minnesota Science Museum projects, *How Coyote Got His Special Power and Used It to Help the People*, is what anthropologists call an "etiological myth"—that is, its purpose is to explain an origin, often our own. This familiar narrative pattern, shared by many cultures, addresses certain mysteries of the universe, including questions about what lies behind a name or about the rationale for various chains of being. As in the case of *How Coyote Got His Special Power*, this is often done through anthropomorphized animals performing preternatural feats, which are told in an oral history. The brief myth that Wilson fashions about the relationships between wildlife nomenclature and certain animals' roles in nature draws on Native American lore and features Coyote as its heroic figure. His comrades, Fox, Eagle, Bear, and Deer (the "Animal People") are all assigned by a Spirit Chief separate domains to lord over.

The tale is passed on by a narrator who relates at the outset to his listeners, "I have no son to hear the tale. I grow old and lest this wisdom die with me, I tell the tale to you" (*HCSP* 1). The myth is then recalled by this wise old griot, who beseeches his audience to "profit" from its moral. Having absorbed generations of oral history, he is compelled to pass it on verbally for posterity.

Narrator introduces the folk legend in fairy-tale fashion: "It was in the beginning, in the time before there was a time, when the people were animal people, and moved about and talked together just like human beings, that the Spirit Chief called a meeting of all the animal people" (1). At this gathering he announces his plans to award new names, change ill-suited names, and issue arrows on a first-come, first-serve basis. Coyote, who detests his present name, vows to be the first to come before Spirit Chief for another, yet because he oversleeps the next day, he discovers when he finally arrives that each of his preferred names has been already granted to another one of the animal people. But Spirit Chief is actually pleased that Coyote is late. He explains:

> Don't be sad, for I have a special power for you. I wanted you to be the last one to come. I have work for you to do and you will need this special power. With it you can change yourself into any form. When you need help call on your power. Fox will be your brother. He will help you when you need help. Now, go among the people and help them change what it is they need changed. (2)

Equipped with a "special power," Coyote becomes a hero several times over as he travels the countryside coming to the aid of his fellow Animal People. Fox, who has been ordained as Coyote's assistant, frequently counsels him on the best means of reversing the various misfortunes of their fellow creatures. The minidrama ends with a homily from Coyote, savior of the Animal People, on ways to exist harmoniously with nature: "Cut only wood you can burn. Help the old people who are blind from the smoke of a thousand night's fires. Shoot elk. Eat them. Dance. Behave properly. Do not point at rainbows, your fingers will fall off" (8).

Wilson's charming beast fable, though written for the Science Museum of Minnesota, is more fantasy than science. Yet for its prospective audiences, it also proved instructive on the role myths play in cultural development. Wilson not only adheres to a pre-existing structure for his narrative but he also targets a lay audience not yet ready for—or perhaps not very enthusiastic about—a documentary on wildlife. As his playwriting skills continued to improve and as his dramatic vision came into focus, Wilson realized even more that myths were vital to the communal psyche of black people. As discussed earlier, he has credited Elijah Muhammad with creating a much needed mythic base for black Americans.

Yet another sample of Wilson's early inclinations as a dramatist while affiliated with the Science Museum of Minnesota is *An Evening with Margaret Mead: An Anthropological Look at America*, a one-woman skit sampling insights from the noted educator, scientist, journalist, humanitarian, wife, and mother. One of the best-known American anthropologists, her years as a field investigator among lesser-known civilizations yielded three of her most important anthropological publications: *Coming of Age in Samoa* (1928), *Sex and Temperament in Three Primitive Societies* (1935), and *Growing Up in New Guinea* (1939). On the one hand, Margaret Mead (1901–78) confounded her professional peers, who frequently took exception to her scientifically unorthodox yet widely popular theories on a wide range of subjects, from parenthood and children to abortion and the "generation gap." On the other, Mead's ability to bring science to the average American earned her celebrity status among the lay public. She was also "a prolific writer on civil rights and race, always placing her thoughts within the context of cultural analysis, as in her 'talking book' with writer James Baldwin *A Rap on Race*" (Cassidy 13). Thus, she was in constant demand on the lecture circuits and often inundated by requests to speak to a variety of eager audiences.

In *An Evening with Margaret Mead*, August Wilson adopts a form quite suitable for conveying familiar aspects of Mead's character while at the same time demonstrating her style of lecturing and providing a sample of her candid observations on human subjects. The thirty-two-page script begins as the audience looks in on Mead writing an acceptance letter to a former colleague from Johns Hopkins University. Among her numerous invitations outstanding, she chooses to accept Professor John Badrig's overture to address the Pacific Arts Council. She attributes this decision to what she calls "a curiously odd American trait" (*EMM* 1)—the tendency to feel a sense of community in the least likely circumstances. Because Mead and Badrig were once both affiliated with the same faculty club when she taught at Johns Hopkins, she accepts his invitation out of a sense of communal obligation.

Wilson invites the audience of this play to share some private moments with Mead, who uses her response as an occasion for musing about what it feels like to be an American, about the importance of "hometown," about America's love for the past, and about the American habit of joining organizations—all of this while sitting alone in a room of her home. While Mead contemplates the wording in her letter of acceptance, the audience is invited into her consciousness to experience her customary inductive, practical, and clear thought processes as she decides upon a lecture's topic and its contents. For example, nostal-

gia for former acquaintances at the Johns Hopkins Faculty Club leads
her to draw some conclusions about the meaning of "hometown":

> Americans establish these ties by finding common points on
> the road that all are expected to have traveled, from one place to
> another in America, resting for long enough to establish for
> each generation a "hometown" in which they grow up, and
> which they leave to move on to a new town which will become
> the hometown of their children. Whether they meet on the
> deck of an American steamer, in a hotel in San Francisco,
> Singapore, or Minneapolis, the same expectation underlies
> their first contact—that both of them have moved on and are
> moving on, and that potential intimacy lie in paths that have
> crossed. Europeans, who pride themselves in the fact that their
> ancestors have not moved at all, are puzzled by this "hometown
> business." They fail to realize, nine out of ten times the "home-
> town" is not where the person lives, but where he has lived. (4)

But Mead's soliloquy, which takes the form of a kind of stream of
consciousness as she talks to herself as well as indirectly addresses an
intrusive audience, is interrupted by a return telephone call from Professor Badrig, whom she had called earlier to personally thank for extending the invitation. During their conversation, Mead learns that Badrig's
wife is expecting a child. This particular point of reference helps Mead
fashion her forthcoming lecture:

> Listen, that's rather appropriate I think. I was thinking about
> giving . . . as the subject for my talk . . . giving a talk about
> the making of the American character . . . or something of that
> sort . . . a kind of turning of the interpretations we anthropolo-
> gists often give another culture . . . a turning of that sort of
> dissecting eye onto American society . . . or perhaps, more
> specifically, the child in American society. So I think that's
> rather appropriate that your wife is expecting a child. (8)

Thus, the anthropologist's thoughts on hometown and childbirth—
grounded in the particulars of a long-standing faculty club relationship,
an invitation to lecture, and news of an impending birth—are transformed into material for her lecture.

While August Wilson does devise an effective dramatic format to credibly portray Margaret Mead's character and intellect, *An Evening with Margaret Mead* allows him little room to flex his creative muscles. In Mead's conversations throughout the skit, Wilson adheres to her own characteristic style. For example, her familiar way of "answering each query thoughtfully and concisely—sometimes with a single word, sometimes sharply and most often with humor" (Metraux 9) is apparent in her writing as well as her speaking. One of Mead's habits on the lecture circuit was to ask members of her audience to write down questions that they wanted her to address. Although she fielded numerous questions during each lecture, she just as heroically responded to a large number in monthly contributions to *Redbook Magazine* from 1963 to 1979. These probing responses, posthumously collected in *Margaret Mead: Some Personal Views* (1979), reflect her style of mixing social commentary with a good deal of prudence and common sense. Mead became familiar to the American public, and Wilson's main task in writing this skit seems to have been to capture the essence of her personality and style, not to create intriguing new characters or searing dialogue.

Though Wilson routinely downplays the importance of research for the stuff of his plays, *An Evening with Margaret Mead*, like his other Science Museum projects, bears the obvious influence of biographical study. In fact, his fleshing out of Mead's character anticipates treatment of other personalities whom he chooses as subjects in later plays. What is no less evident in *Mead* than in plays such as *The Homecoming* and *Ma Rainey's Black Bottom* is Wilson's skill at fashioning drama out of real-life circumstances and real-life people. His portrayals of blues singers Blind Lemon Jefferson and Gertrude Rainey smoothly combine fact with a generous addition of the playwright's own creative imagination.

In general, however, the body of Wilson's writing for the Science Museum of Minnesota shows little sign of the genius of his subsequent work. Although each assignment is singularly effective in satisfying its immediate audiences and conforming to the prescriptions of his employer, Wilson's dramatic output during this phase of his career would yield an unfair and premature assessment of his potential as a playwright. Yet behind the self-consciousness of these early works is a notable ease with words and a poetic melding of the colloquial and the profound.

Wilson's first few attempts at playwriting did draw some attention in St. Paul; however, that he had not yet undergone the rigors of professional training in playwriting was evident. Not until he sent the musical satire *Black Bart and the Sacred Hills* and a play about a group of Pittsburgh cab drivers, *Jitney!*, to the Eugene O'Neill Theatre Center's National Playwright's Conference in Waterford, Connecticut, was he forced to focus more upon details of his craft. The O'Neill Center rejected both plays, but by this time Wilson was convinced that his writing was as good as any. Sure of this, he dusted off *Jitney!* and rerouted it to the Playwright's Center in Minneapolis. This time *Jitney!* was not only accepted for staging but Wilson was also awarded a $2,500 stipend to participate in its workshop activities for new playwrights.

Increasingly Wilson realized that writing realistic dialogue, creating more complex central characters, and improving focus were only a portion of what he needed to master to become successful at writing plays. He also needed to learn technical aspects of the craft, specifically those that required a working knowledge of what actors can and cannot do on stage during a performance, and to become familiar with what stage crews could perform within a limited time frame. Most important, he needed to know his responsibility, as a playwright, to the audience. Of course, Wilson's schooling on some of these concerns did not occur until much later, when he was challenged to write for the stage under the guidance of Lloyd Richards. However, his tenure at the Playwright's Center in Minneapolis and his work with the local Penumbra Theater provided significant lessons in these matters.

While mingling among fellow aspiring playwrights and enjoying the benefits of expert professional coaching, Wilson was more comfortable with identifying and addressing weaknesses in his unrefined style. The unwieldy story lines, unrealistic dialogue, and lack of proportion that detracted from early plays were confronted in an environment of constructive criticism. Under the auspices of the Playwright's Center, he witnessed staged readings of *Jitney!* and wrote a promising new play he called *Fullerton Street*. Inspired by the encouragement his work was receiving there, Wilson decided to try the O'Neill Center once again; this time he sent his latest work, *Fullerton Street*. However, much to his disappointment, the O'Neill Center remained unimpressed; they rejected *Fullerton Street* just as they had rejected *Jitney!* earlier. Wilson was still undaunted. Reasoning that perhaps those at the O'Neill Center had not actually read *Jitney!* at all before rejecting it, he again sent them the play; again it was rejected. Finally, Wilson conceded to repeated concerns that "*Jitney!* was too slight, and *Fullerton Street* was unworkably big" (C. Brown 125).

The string of rejection notices from the O'Neill Center forced Wilson to grapple with several conventions of composing that as a poet he had not been willing to consider. He learned that the written products of his inspired moments were not enough to sustain the expansive weight of the play, or, for that matter, keep an audience seated and interested for long periods of time. In short, Wilson's plays needed discipline. Thus, barely chastened, he challenged himself to write another play to demonstrate his mastery of recurring problems that were undermining his dramas. The result of Wilson's resilience and perseverance was a problematic fifty-nine page, two-act play he called *Ma Rainey's Black Bottom*. Troubles with length and coherence notwithstanding, the O'Neill Center immediately accepted the play. Once it had undergone major revisions there, it moved on to open at the Yale Repertory Theater in April 1984. In October 1984, *Ma Rainey's Black Bottom* opened on Broadway to impressive reviews.

Ma Rainey, which obviously was an enormously important breakthrough for Wilson, will be discussed in Chapter 3; but the play also had indirect significance in initiating the invaluable relationship between Wilson and Lloyd Richards, then dean of the Yale School of Drama and artistic director for the Eugene O'Neill Center and the Yale Repertory Theatre. When Richards discovered *Ma Rainey's Black Bottom* among the hundreds of plays submitted to the Eugene O'Neill Center for his review, he was immediately impressed by the playwright's raw talent. Even though Richards saw that the play needed major revisions, its dramatic potential convinced him to accept it for the center. He recalls,

> The talent was unmistakable. The characters were alive. They were people I had met in the barbershop on Saturday morning, talking about baseball, philosophy, politics. You'd hear humor, imagery, poetry—the poetry of oppressed people who have to create a sense of freedom in their words, people living more in their vision than in their actuality. (C. Brown 125)

The 1982 summer internship program at the O'Neill Center gave Wilson an opportunity to reap the benefits of Richards's many years of experience in nurturing unheralded talent such as his. From directing Lorraine Hansberry's *Raisin in the Sun* to coaching Sidney Poitier, Ruby Dee, and Harry Belafonte to stardom and promoting the works of South African playwright Athol Fugard, Richards has generously lent his talents to grooming these theatrically gifted artists. In Richards, Wilson found a powerful professional mentor and ultimately a friend. The internationally known director took Wilson under his wing, introduced him to producers and agents, and advised him of grant opportunities to support his work.

In addition to enabling Wilson to build a network of theatre associates, the Eugene O'Neill Center proved enormously helpful in the development of the maturing playwright. While working with some of the country's most noted dramaturges, he squarely confronted and overcame his aversion to rewriting. He also learned how to revise under extreme pressure and how to write a play with logistical concerns in mind, such as the need to allot time in the script for changing costumes or for rearranging the set. Under pressure to perform in the O'Neill Center's frantic yet perfectionist environment, he learned to work expeditiously, especially in solving any problems that surfaced in the script. In an atmosphere of concentrated study, he learned to work out any kinks that might weaken particular scenes.

Prior to his intensive training at the O'Neill, Wilson had not quite comprehended the relationship between writing scripts and writing texts. His early fascination with writing poetry and short stories had well equipped him with skills needed to produce powerful language and eloquent stage notes; however, his concept of writing plays had not moved enough beyond the page. Moreover, he had not yet come to understand the demanding and sometimes vicious world of the theatre—a world where the success of a play is too often based upon the name gracing the marquee rather than the artistic merit of the script, where concerns over ticket sales and good reviews frequently supersede the talent of the playwright, and where a playwright's fame may depend upon whom he or she knows and the circles in which the dramatist travels. Just as nerve-racking are the difficulties Wilson faced as a black playwright seeking acclaim in a traditionally white-controlled arena.

His monthlong training at the O'Neill Center helped ready Wilson to join the ranks of America's premiere dramatists. The entire experience is summed up by one participant as "a trial by paradise in a four-week Eden, a working idyll where they [playwright trainees] are privileged and condemned to create in a state of grace-under-pressure" (Kowinski 79). Wilson's development into a world-class playwright got its biggest boost at the O'Neill Center, where his work was unveiled and dissected before various audiences of critics; yet he has successfully sustained basic elements of the same unmistakable style that had first opened the O'Neill Center's doors to him.

During the early 1980s, Wilson got a chance to demonstrate what he had learned in the intense O'Neill Center setting. He and other playwrights accepted a fundraising challenge to write a four-minute play. *The Janitor* (1985) was Wilson's response to the task set: "I came up with the idea of the janitor, who is someone whom this society ignores and someone who may have some very valuable information, someone who has a vital contribution to make, and yet you have relegated him to a position where they sweep the floor" (interview). Wilson's compact drama focuses upon a black cleaning man who becomes a celebrity-for-an-instant when he exchanges his broom handle for a microphone that has been set up in preparation for a scheduled National Youth Conference. Although his job is to sweep the floor for the imminent "big important meeting," for a brief time he forgets his station, imagines himself as the guest speaker for the evening, and proceeds to expound into an open microphone. He fully intends to give a speech to flatter and inspire the group of well-educated, economically comfortable members of his race who will crowd the room later.

During his impromptu moments before the microphone, he struggles with discussing the word *youth*, which he had seen earlier on a sign hanging across the ballroom. Instead of a polished speech, what comes from his mouth is a series of cliches mixed with words and phrases mercilessly out of context. But as he works up a sweat trying to find a style befitting the sophisticated audience to appear later, a disarmingly honest, perceptive, and unpretentious black man emerges—one whose unrehearsed wisdom deserves as much of an audience as the pat speeches of the event's scheduled lineup. Ironically the clearest and the most genuine advice the janitor can muster comes when he drops the mask of sophistication and speaks from the heart:

> So . . . to the youth of the United States I says . . . don't spend that sweetness too fast! 'Cause you gonna need it. See. I's fifty-six years old and I done found that out. But it's all the same. It all comes back on you . . . just like reaping and sowing.

Down and out ain't nothing but being caught up in the balance of what you put down. If you down and out and things ain't going right for you . . . you can bet you done put a down payment on your troubles. Now you got to pay up on the balance. (*JR* 82)

Reality interrupts the imaginary scene when Sam the janitor is reminded by his white supervisor, Mr. Collins, to "quit wasting time and get this floor swept" (82). In another instant, Sam is transformed from a distinguished speaker to his role in the eyes of Mr. Collins: just an old cleaning man. "Yessuh, Mr. Collins. Yessuh," the janitor replies as he picks up his broom.

Wilson's focus upon the marginal man also resonates with autobiographical influences. His sensitive portrayal of the working-class individual, as represented by Sam, could easily be a tribute to his mother, Daisy Wilson, who found work as a janitor when Frederick Kittel, her husband and Wilson's father, left her with five children to support. Wilson not only acknowledges her as the model for his female characters, strong and independent yet warm and maternal, but also, thanks to her legacy, he came to understand the exclusionary tactics of class distinction and stereotype. His defense of underprivileged, underrepresented, and frequently overlooked members of society shows up regularly in later plays in characters such as Ma Rainey and her bandmembers, and Gabriel, Hambone, and Sterling. When asked during a 1991 interview what inspired *The Janitor*, Wilson revealed his compassion for working-class individuals living on the fringes of society: They do it [work in menial jobs] for some years, and never once do we think to say, "Hey, do you have anything to say about anything? Do you have any contribution to make other than being a janitor or running an elevator or whatever?" (interview).

Despite its brevity, *The Janitor* contains several themes that become part of Wilson's dramatic arsenal. For example, his obvious compassion for the marginal man or the social pariah that emerges in characters such as Herald Loomis and Troy Maxson includes the cleaning man. Just as he does in *Joe Turner's Come and Gone* and in *Fences*, Wilson spotlights a character who would otherwise remain silent—overshadowed by the lives of the more visible, the more vocal, the more economically advantaged. He affords such characters both an audience and the time to express their concerns. *The Janitor* also demonstrates Wilson's skill at creating works with figurative resonance. On one level, the impersonal title is indicative of the distant regard for such employees; on another, it represents the cool dismissal of blacks in America. Since in the United States the profession of janitor is typically held by blacks, Hispanics, or other minorities on society's lower economic rung, it is a fitting title for emphasizing the struggles of both class and race. While Mr. Collins may represent the barking voice of white America that stretches as far back as slavery, Sam mirrors an untapped source of knowledge and inspiration pent up in those from whom America does not want to hear.

Whether Wilson was aware of it or not, he had been preparing for his cycle of plays of the black experience all his life. During his first forty years, he accumulated an impressive dramatic store, fortified by his persistent drive to learn to write poetry and plays and to explore his mother's cultural heritage. His fledgling attempts to write drama in Pittsburgh and in Minnesota, though flawed, show evidence of artistic skills that later would lead to his Pulitzer Prize–winning status. Wilson's exploratory phase as a playwright, although marked by rejection letters and unkind reviews, produced works that gave an early indication of his genius and established a style of writing that would later mature, becoming the basis for some of his most critically and commercially successful work.

TWO

Pittsburgh on His Mind: *Jitney!*

Ariel view of Pittsburgh. Jitney cabs
ply their trade in and around this area.
*Reprinted by permission of GRM Associates, Inc.,
agents for the* New Pittsburgh Courier.
From the issue of June 23, 1979.
Copyright © 1979 by the
New Pittsburgh Courier.

Jitney! marks the beginning of both a private and professional journey for Wilson. It demonstrates what would prove to be a continued dependence upon his native Pittsburgh as the backdrop for his dramatic agenda. Growing up in and eventually escaping from Pittsburgh still rest heavily upon the playwright's mind. He returns to the city in his writing out of bittersweetness, for he knows that he could have easily been any one of the down-and-out characters about whom he writes. With the exception of *Ma Rainey's Black Bottom* (set in Chicago), in each of the subsequent plays in his proposed cycle, Pittsburgh figures prominently. At times he may resurrect a street name, feature a former Pittsburgh locale, or borrow the name of a boyhood acquaintance from the Hill District for one of his characters. In retrospect he sees that his ability to transcend the potential doom of life on the streets is due largely to the attitude of self-preservation he developed as a young boy—one that led him to listen to the wisdom of elders, work hard, and hold steadfast to his dreams.

Jitney! also marks Wilson's first experience with standing-room-only success as a professional playwright when Pittsburgh's Public Theater performed the play in the late '70s. Created specifically for this stage, *Jitney!* was so well received by Pittsburgh's audiences that "a large portion of the black audiences going to the theater for the first time refused to leave when told the show was already sold out" (Powers 52). Written in 1979, this sprawling, two-act play set in a gypsy cab station also opened the first of a succession of doors for its author. Sometime during 1980 the then relatively unknown Wilson submitted the play to the Playwright's Center in Minneapolis, and it was accepted. Time spent in Minnesota and at the center proved to be an important incubation period for Wilson's emerging talents. The experience—the first of its kind for Wilson—expanded his scope, both in terms of improving his skills as a dramatist and establishing a lasting network of support from other beginning artists: "I remember walking into a room with sixteen playwrights and thinking 'Wow, I must be a playwright'" (Savran 291).

Aside from giving Wilson his first small-scale taste of public success, *Jitney!* is important as his first mature work and as the first installment in his ten-play chronicle of African American history since 1900. Of course, Wilson had no idea that the play would later gain this distinction; at the time it was written, he had his doubts about writing a single successful play, much less a history series. But as he came to realize a decade-by-decade pattern emerging in his collective work, *Jitney!* logi-cally became his dramatic commentary upon the 1970s.

Jitney!'s plot is relatively straightforward, anticipating several of Wilson's subsequent works featuring a common gathering place where troubled characters are able to vent their emotions. Here, the place is an already dilapidated building within the city limits of Pittsburgh, sched-uled for imminent demolition. For years it has been the site of employ-ment for a group of irritable hackies, who range from a perpetual drunk to a Vietnam veteran. Each sings his share of the blues, but the circum-stances of the station owner, Becker, overshadow their troubles.

The play opens with news that Becker's only son, Booster, is about to be released from a twenty-year jail sentence. Instead of jubilation, Becker astounds his employees with indifference about the pending release; in fact, he loathes his son for committing a crime that indirectly led to the death of his first wife, Booster's mother. The source of their long-standing father-son feud may be traced to Booster's youthful fling with a young, wealthy white girl who accused him of rape when her irate father discovered the two having sex in a parked car. After being arrested and released on bond for the crime, Booster paid her a visit and wound up killing her and wounding her father. For the double crime, Booster is sentenced to die in the electric chair, which so affects his mother that she wastes away and dies shortly thereafter. She dies before learning that Booster's sentence is eventually commuted to a twenty-year prison term.

When the two finally meet in the station, Booster and his father engage in a father-son showdown that rivals the exchanges between Troy and Cory Maxson in *Fences* (1986). Becker, whom his son accuses of "selling out," is forced to admit why he had been so passive in gaining political advantage on his job:

> "Why didn't you knock the foreman on his ass?" You wanna know why? I'll tell you why. Cause I had your black ass at home crying to be fed! Crying to have a roof over your head! To have clothes to wear to school and lunch money in your pocket. That's why! Because I had a family and I had responsibility. If I had knocked him on his ass you would have went hungry! You wouldn't have had clothes to wear or a roof over your head! I done what I had to do. (*JY* 39)

Like Troy Maxson, Becker has great ambitions for his son's future—

so much so that he willingly puts his own career on hold so that he can nurture that warrior spirit in his maturing son. For much of his life, he has been secure in the knowledge that this rebellious spirit would serve to vindicate him and justify his own submissiveness. But Becker is doubly disappointed in his son. Not only is Booster a murderer and convict but he also refuses to find steady work; once out of jail, he immediately falls into the numbers racket and latches onto a financially secure woman to support him. Becker, a broken man whose business will soon fold, dies in a freak accident at a local steel plant. The hardships of several other characters intersect in *Jitney!*; however, the central conflict of the play is the irreparable gulf between this father and son.

Longtime natives of Pittsburgh, such as August Wilson, understand that the proliferation of gypsy cab services in the city around the 1970s was an outgrowth of the city's racial polarization. Simply put, white-owned and operated cab services shunned the predominantly black areas of Pittsburgh. Out of necessity, therefore, unauthorized transportation enterprises became quite commonplace.

The idea for *Jitney!* was conceived while Wilson and his wife Judy Oliver drove home from a trip back to his boyhood home in Pittsburgh's Hill District. Jitney stations were part of this area's local color then, and many still remained. Their images stuck with Wilson as he made his way back to the relative serenity of St. Paul, Minnesota, and nostalgia set in. He recalled that "the men who drove the private shuttles would kill time between calls playing checkers and swapping stories. A perfect setting for a play" (C. Brown 125). But Wilson was most concerned with how resourceful these men were: "I simply wanted to show how the station worked, how these guys created jobs for themselves and how it was organized. . . . I just wanted to show how these guys could be responsible. They make jobs out of nothing. The important thing was for me to show these five guys working and creating something out of nothing" (interviewed by the author). Back in his new surroundings in St. Paul, he turned his nostalgia into the fifty-nine-page *Jitney!*: " . . . he took his pad to a "fish-and-chips place. In ten days he had a draft. He was dizzy. He had turned an enormous corner" (Brown 125).

As a period piece, *Jitney!*, like subsequent plays in Wilson's history series, embodies the spirit of the decade in which it takes place with particular emphasis upon the often untold stories of African Americans. Set in 1971, the play has as its backdrop a politically and socially restless era during which Americans reeled from the effects of both domestic and international mayhem. The decade began in controversy with 425,000 American troops in Vietnam and an administration deadlocked in its war policy. In the summer of 1972, the Watergate scandal drew the media spotlight with events that began with five Republican agents being caught and arrested for breaking into Democratic National Committee headquarters in Washington, D.C., and ended in August 1974 with the resignation of President Richard Nixon. The presidency of Jimmy Carter was weakened at home by "malaise" and abroad by the so-called Iran hostage crisis. Still, in 1976, the country was able to pull itself up out of the mire of domestic and foreign turmoil to celebrate its two hundredth birthday.

But the 1970s did not inspire all Americans to celebrate. African Americans, in particular, as Frederick Douglass had done some one hundred twenty years earlier, found any Fourth of July celebration to be a sham for those who remained oppressed. Discrimination still existed on all fronts, from the classroom to the workplace to the housing market. The Supreme Court regularly pressured reluctant school districts to propose desegregation plans for their public schools; unemployment rates—especially among African American veterans—pushed up the national average; and blatant housing discrimination went unchecked.

For much of the decade, the Vietnam conflict was foremost in the country's psyche; from the 1960s through the early 1970s, thousands of young American soldiers fought an undeclared war that lacked significant public support. For many of the survivors who were fortunate enough to return, extreme psychological agony and remorse set in as they reacted to their country's rejection and, indeed, hatred of them for their efforts. African American veterans of the Vietnam War found even less recompense for their military tour of duty. Once back in the States, they realized that they indeed were "first in war, last in peace, and last in the hearts of their countrymen" (Tyler xi). Instead of parades and commendations, they found a double dose of rejection. Still in place were remnants of Jim Crow and other forms of systemic racism in housing, employment, and education. African American Vietnam veterans became even more marginal citizens as they shared the brunt of America's scorn for all U.S. servicemen and women who participated in the conflict. Some of the lines from Marvin Gaye's 1970s song and political query, "What's Going On?" (1971), epitomize the African American veteran's difficulties readjusting to postwar America:

What else is new, my friend, besides what I read?
Can't find no work. Can't find no job, my friend.
Money is tighter than it's ever been.
Say, man, I just don't understand
What's going on across this land. (Jobete Music 1971)

Wilson praises this song for being among the few popular rhythm and blues recordings that responded to social issues.

Although only one of Becker's crew (Youngblood) is actually a veteran of the Vietnam War, they all are soldiers of another cold war taking place in their own country—the fight to survive. They fight to keep dead-end jobs that require only a driver's license and knowledge of the city streets to succeed. The majority of them see playing the right lottery number as their only way of escaping this monotony. For those who dare hope to improve their lot—by saving to buy a home, for example—fate intervenes in the form of a wrecking ball to level their refuge and place of employment. Becker has been served a notice that, along with the entire city block, his cab station must be destroyed to make room for the city's proposed renovations.

Pittsburgh is a city historically polarized by residential segregation. Black migrants from the South after World War I crowded into the city to fill the labor demand created by Pittsburgh's steel industry: "Migration and natural increase combined raised the total black population from 54,983 in 1930 to 100,692 in 1960, the largest three-decade increase in the history of Pittsburgh" (Darden 7). Unfortunately, this burgeoning black population led to the same exploitation in housing that post-Reconstruction migrants faced in large cities, such as Chicago and New York; after the "white flight" out of urban dwellings, landlords converted spacious homes into multiple-unit housing and charged exorbitant prices to families and individuals desperate for any type of accommodations. Even run-down houses in deplorable neighborhoods commanded extraordinarily high prices.

The early '70s represented a time of renovation and change in Pittsburgh. Organizations such as the Regional Industrial Development Corporation and ACTION-Housing implemented ambitious and innovative programs as part of their plans for Pittsburgh's urban renewal. But despite massive revitalization efforts directed toward housing and business establishments, the programs failed to include the human factor in their revival of the city. According to a documentary history of

Pittsburgh, published in 1976, "the black population was concentrated in those areas most affected by urban redevelopment plans, thus suffering the main burden of disruption and relocation. In Pittsburgh and other cities, postwar urban renewal was characterized by large-scale clearance, emphasis upon the central business district, and indifference to the impact of renewal upon family and neighborhood life" (Harevan and Thernstrom (179). With this renaissance came the destruction of several of the city's landmarks and the displacement of a population who sought refuge among them.

Interestingly, the impending demolition that looms in the background of *Jitney!* surfaces again in a much later play—*Two Trains Running* (1992)—also set within the time frame of the late '60s to early '70s. In both, Wilson utilizes potential destruction as a paradoxical dramatic force that mobilizes characters who have, for years, existed as virtually half-alive. At the same time, however, drastic changes in their immediate environment rob them of much-needed communal and cultural havens. The threat of losing familiar surroundings moves Wilson's otherwise static characters to at least consider alternative jobs, but it also jeopardizes what has been, for some of them, their only source of certain and steady income.

Jitney!'s taxi drivers act out the disillusionment and frustration experienced by many African American men during the post-Vietnam years of the '70s. Their nerves are frayed from pressures of trying to be men in a society that regards them as "leftovers from history" (*MR* 57). That is, according to Ma Rainey's philosopher/pianist Toledo in Wilson's 1981 play *Ma Rainey's Black Bottom*, "we don't know that we been took and made history out of. Done went and filled the white man's belly and now he's full and tired and wants you to get out the way and let him be by himself" (58). As "leftovers" from the proverbial "melting pot," the black men featured in *Jitney!* are forced to pursue less than glorious ways of making a living: they are numbers runners, taxi drivers, hustlers, and steel mill workers. Out of this diversity, three significant categories of men emerge: the hopefuls (Youngblood); the defeated (Fielding, Turnbo, and Becker); and the warriors (Booster).

Youngblood is clearly a breed apart from his mostly middle-aged colleagues. At twenty-four, he is the youngest of the cab drivers, as his name suggests. What also distinguishes this recent Vietnam veteran from his seniors is his faith in the American Dream. He actually believes that he can take advantage of the GI Bill to afford a comfortable home for his girlfriend and their child in the Penn Hills section of the city.[1] Unlike several of his get-rich-quick friends, Youngblood believes in working within the system and saving for a home. He rehearses how he will meet his monthly payments:

> Let's see . . . if I make two hundred dollars a week . . . that'll be eight hundred dollars a month. . . . Then with what Rena gets . . . then you got three hundred dollars a month mortgage . . . hell that ain't nothing. I can make that with no sweat. What scares me is that thirty years! Damn! That's your whole life . . . to be paying for a little old house. Don't make sense. I don't know how these white folks figure. (*JY* 24)

Although Youngblood is just as alarmed as others are about the imminent demolition of Becker's cab station, he is not devastated. He has cautiously and wisely saved enough of his fifty-dollars-a-week, untaxed wages to proceed toward settlement. As his friends mourn Becker's accidental death and reluctantly prepare to disperse when the demolition crew arrives, Youngblood prepares to move his family into their new home. That Youngblood is able to negotiate a housing loan through the GI Bill is indicative of positive trends in Pittsburgh's real estate market in the early '70s. The emergence of black real estate brokers and black-owned financial institutions greatly improved the chances of minorities being able to purchase homes in a wider cross-section of the city.[2]

Becker's jitney station is more than just headquarters for dispatching taxis. It also doubles as home for several men who have lost their way in the world. Fielding, a hopeless alcoholic, and Turnbo, a meddlesome busybody, frequent this dilapidated building. When they are not out on call, they routinely may be found hanging around the station sneaking a sip from a hidden bottle or gossiping about someone else's personal affairs. They both are defeated, though each has a gimmick to deflect attention from what is otherwise obvious. Wilson does not reveal much about the forty-nine-year-old Fielding or the fifty-three-year-old Turnbo beyond the alcoholism of one and the meddling of the other. Unlike Youngblood or Becker, neither alludes to a life outside of the station, and the jitney station employees appear to be their only family.

The sixty-year-old station owner, Becker, is defeated because he cannot recover from the grave disappointment of having reared a failure

of a son. Thus, his depression keeps him barely above Fielding and
Turnbo. He has a home and a second wife, and he is making a fairly
comfortable living, yet he is heartbroken over Booster's lackadaisical
attitude about life and loathes his son for having indirectly caused his
first wife's death. Becker tells his son, "You ain't nothing! After twenty
years I'm looking at you and I can see that you ain't nothing. You less
than the day you was born" (*JY* 38). Becker's misery makes him lax in
the management of his jitney station, and he seems but a shell of a man.
He responds very little when he learns that his business will be demolished, for he has already been crushed by the prospect of no heir to take
his place. His accidental death at the steel mill is a tragic end for this
already defeated man.

The remaining characters, Doub and "the numbers man" Shealy,
have developed tough-skinned attitudes toward their situation. Neither
seems particularly bitter about the limitations placed upon him. In fact,
Shealy routinely supplements his income by combining his job as a
jitney driver with his one-man numbers operations. Becker's business
becomes a convenient front for incoming bets.

While Shealy is a hustler, Doub is perhaps the most temperate
member of the jitney station's crew. Slow to anger, he is quick to defend
anyone who becomes the helpless target of his colleagues' ridicule. For
example, he intercedes on behalf of Youngblood as Turnbo verbally
chastises him for the way he treats his girlfriend, the mother of his child.
Doub volunteers that Youngblood is "alright. Just young. Got a lot to
learn. That gal keep after him, he'll be alright" (11). Yet Doub is just as
adamant with Youngblood as he tries to convince the angry young
veteran that blaming "the white man" for the poorly timed demolition
of Becker's station is just a red herring. He rejects Youngblood's hasty
conclusion:

> Boy, that white man ain't paying you no mind. You ought to
> stop thinking like that. They been planning to tear these shacks
> down before you was born. You keep thinking everybody against
> you and you ain't never gonna get nothing. I seen a hundred
> niggers too lazy to get up out the bed in the morning, talking
> about the white man is against them. That's just an excuse. (40)

Like Fielding's and Turnbo's, Doub's life does not extend beyond
the confines of the station. With his pension intact and only himself to

support, he is not worried that the station's closing will lead to his financial ruin. But he still cannot envision a future that does not include working with Becker and driving jitneys. When asked about his plans after the station has been leveled, he responds, "I don't know. Becker talking about quitting. I wanted to get together and see if we can find a place to move the station. If that don't work, I guess I'll just run the bus line until something else happens" (42).

At the core of *Jitney!* are two characters whose opposing images repeatedly surface in Wilson's later plays. The ambitious Vietnam veteran Youngblood and Becker's rebellious son Booster represent alternating images of the warrior spirit. He applauds this disposition in "people who look around to see what society has cut out for them. Who see the limits of their participation, and are willing to say, 'No, I refuse to accept this limitation that you're imposing on me'" (Moyers 179). Paradoxically, these warriors become criminals more often than not, for in saying "No," they find themselves choosing crime over conformity. They are battling a society that would break their spirit of opposition.

Booster is the first of Wilson's warriors. Like his successors, he refuses to work a nine-to-five job, considering such conformity tantamount to "working for the white man." Although he has no better option for making a living, he prefers being unemployed and in so-called complete control of his life to collecting a weekly paycheck. To his father, who is eager to get him into the work force now that he is out of jail, he says:

> No thanks, Pop. That's not for me. That's why I didn't accept that parole five years ago. I figure after all that time, five more years wouldn't make much difference, and when I got out I would be free. Wouldn't have no parole officer telling me to get a job and watching over me to see what I do. Naw, I didn't want that. Now I'm my own man. I don't owe nobody nothing. (*JY* 37)

For the warrior, such as Booster, going against the system is the same as scoring a victory, and being in control of his own fate is being a man. Neither homicide nor the death of a loved one draws much response from this stoic individual, for displays of grief threaten to expose weaknesses in his armor.

While Booster epitomizes the heroic though impractical warrior spirit, Youngblood is the essence of hard work and conformity. Although they both are fairly young African American men of the 1970s, they have distinctly different priorities: one tries to beat the system, and the other tries to exist within it. Youngblood was, above all, a willing draftee in the Vietnam War. He understands the blatant contradiction of serving his country overseas and facing a hell at home as a veteran trying to afford a decent home for his family and himself. Yet instead of dodging his civic responsibility—as Booster certainly would have done—Youngblood acquiesces. He does so, however, with full knowledge that he is a victim. When Doub tries to direct his anger away from the white establishment, claiming that "they don't even know you is alive," Youngblood grumbles, "They knew I was alive when they drafted me and sent my ass over to Vietnam to be shot at. They knew I was alive then!" (40).

The distinctly drawn personalities in *Jitney!* confirm that, as early as 1979, Wilson was consciously working at making his characters more multidimensional and credible. At the risk of the play's substance being seen as too slight, Wilson focused his attention not on achieving unity but on developing a set of characters with whom his audiences could identify. He explains that his purpose in writing the play was to "show these guys could be responsible" (interview). This emphasis upon character worked in Wilson's favor; the standing-room-only success that *Jitney!* enjoyed when it premiered in the small Pittsburgh theatre earned it a repeat performance the following year. This time Wilson revised the script "to expand the dramatic world from the rather narrow 'slice' of the first play" (Powers 52).

August Wilson himself is the first to admit that he was far from being a successful playwright when he wrote *Jitney!* He told colleagues at the Martin Luther King Center in St. Paul, where the play was performed in January 1985, "You could fit in a thimble what I knew of theater" (Livingston 184). Despite its popular acclaim, the play suffers from a vague story line and simply too many characters. *Jitney!*'s busy station is typical of Wilson's well-populated, bustling settings where characters come and go freely. However, with so many personalities vying for center stage, it becomes difficult to identify one protagonist and follow a single story line. The play does not provide an organic whole or present a focused, cathartic end. In fact, Wilson describes Becker's death as a "dramatic convenience arrived at when the playwright couldn't imagine the character's next scene" (Livingston 184). As a result of this dramatic non sequitur, the play ultimately lacks resolution. Becker's death precipitates neither action nor any appreciable change in his son or the remaining drivers; instead they sit around in their "funeral clothes" uttering cliches. The only encomium that any one of them can muster in Becker's honor is that he was "alright with me." Even his son can come up with no more than the bitterly ironic, "He deserved better than what life gave him" (*JY* 59).

With *Jitney!* Wilson gained a measure of respect from Pittsburgh audiences as well as a very favorable reputation among audiences at the Playwright's Center in Minneapolis. However, his confidence was shaken when the play was twice rejected by the Eugene O'Neill Center for being "too unwieldy." "Maybe it's not as good as I think it is," Wilson thought to himself. "I have to write a better play but how the hell do you do that?" (Savran 291). He worked out a solution to *Jitney!*'s problems in writing *Ma Rainey's Black Bottom*.

THREE

The Blues on Broadway:
Ma Rainey's Black Bottom

Theresa Merritt as Ma Rainey
in the spring 1984 Yale Repertory
Theatre production of *Ma Rainey's Black
Bottom*. In this scene, Ma joins her band
in performing one of her trade-
mark sassy blues tunes.
*Photograph by
William B. Carter.
Reprinted by permission.*

Fortunately the success of a play is determined by more than what satisfies the tastes of reviewers. To the delight of many a playwright, the audience's reactions frequently override the cool, clinical assessments of the seasoned critic. Such was the case with the sold-out performance of Wilson's *Jitney!* in his native Pittsburgh. The play's unqualified acceptance by its audiences did wonders for Wilson's ego as a playwright—so much so that he turned his attention toward completing a script about a 1920s blues singer that he had started and then abandoned in 1976. With *Jitney!*'s weaknesses in mind, Wilson resurrected and completed the script about a cantankerous blues queen and her backup band. When Wilson was introduced to the blues, he was mesmerized by a blues singer wailing notes that penetrated his soul. In the '70s Gertrude Pridgett "Ma" Rainey sang to him just as Bessie Smith had done in 1965, and this time the product of his musical revelation was "a fifty-nine-page, ill-organized script" (Savran 293) that he named after a dance popular among blacks during the decade following the Great Migration and just before the Great Depression.

Ma Rainey's Black Bottom at one stroke marked Wilson's transition from novice to celebrity. Although the play depicting the plight of blues musicians in the 1920s was far from polished when it caught the attention of Lloyd Richards, director of Eugene O'Neill Center in Waterford, Connecticut, it bore the unmistakable signs of a potentially first-rate dramatist. Flawed as the play was, Lloyd Richards saw past the playwright's awkward attempts to merge two separate plays into one to discover what he called "a new voice" ("Wilson" *CLC* 275). This important work by the then unknown August Wilson would initiate a history-making collaboration with Richards, win Wilson a coveted place in the playwright's workshop at the Eugene O'Neill Center and later at the Yale Repertory Theatre, garner him the New York Drama Critics' Circle Award, give him his first experience on Broadway, and pave his way toward receiving two Pulitzer Prizes.

But before all of these rewards were to be realized, Wilson had to come to grips with some realities about his skills as a playwright. Despite being plagued—but not defeated—by difficulties writing realistic dialogue, producing meatier plots, and allowing for such practicalities as time for costume changes, Wilson put into *Ma Rainey's Black Bottom* all of the best he had learned over his years of writing poetry and plays. As he later realized, "I felt that I was growing as a playwright and moving toward learning more about the craft and how to articulate my

ideas dramatically. I had submitted a couple of other plays to the
O'Neill, but I'm glad they weren't selected. I'm glad my exposure was
with *Ma Rainey* because I think it is a stronger play than the others I had
submitted" (Powers 52).

The idea for the play sprang from Wilson's curiosity about the
economic exploitation of black performers during the 1920s. This curiosity was fueled by his belief that sports and music historically have
been the only avenues open to blacks for gaining a secure economic
base. When either of these avenues is blocked, according to Wilson,
tragedy on a grand scale results. Therefore, the blues that permeates *Ma
Rainey's Black Bottom* is the black performers' means of responding to
not having sole authority over their music. Their strained emotions—
despair mixed with moments of comic relief—surface in their songs,
their conversations, and their unwillingness to surrender their talents to
the white power structure.

Although Wilson had undoubtedly polished his playwriting skills at
the Playwright's Center in Minneapolis and had benefited from the
excellent counsel of friends affiliated with the theatre, the Eugene
O'Neill Center forced him to address and overcome more rigorously his
lingering problems with sprawling, poorly organized scripts and awkward logistical maneuvers:

> The important thing I learned was to rewrite. Not just patch-
> working here and fixing there, but exactly what the word
> means—rewriting. When you write, you know where you want
> to go—you know what a scene, a particular speech is supposed
> to accomplish. Then I discovered that it's possible to go back
> and rewrite this speech, to find another way to say it. In a poem
> you rewrite six or seven times before you end up with what you
> want. But I didn't think of theatre as being like that. And I
> learned to respect the stage and trust that it will carry your
> ideas. The intensity of the O'Neill process—working in four
> days, working fast—was also good experience. It comes down
> to problem solving. But there's no one correct solution. The
> O'Neill made me more conscious of what theatre is about.
> There's nothing like encountering the problems of costume,
> lighting, set design—What do you mean by this? Where is this?
> Where is the window?—which make you more aware of the
> totality of what you're doing. I discovered with *Fences*, for

example, that I had a character exiting upstage and coming back immediately with a different costume. That's really sloppy but I was totally unaware. I never thought, "This guy's got to change his costume." I've become conscious of things like that and it's made me a better playwright. But I don't want to lose the impulse, the sense, as with *Ma Rainey*, that anything goes, that you may do whatever you desire to do. Maybe I wouldn't have written *Ma Rainey* as I did, had I been aware of the problems with casting and with the music. (Savran 293)

For Wilson, the O'Neill Center experience offered just the kind of discipline and intense honing his work needed. For approximately one month, he and other select novice playwrights were subjected to grueling days of writing and rewriting their scripts in preparation for the stage. The motto "Every day is a week" (Kowinski 80)—adopted by those who survived the summer workshop—describes both the frantic four-day rehearsal schedule so familiar to all participants and the entire tightly controlled program. While the labor is intense for new recruits, the guidance they receive is second to none. Under the watchful eye of experienced actors, directors, and other theatre professionals, they come to grips with and overcome flaws that fledgling playwrights often do not notice. They improve their dramatic skills, surrounded by the beautiful and serene setting of Eugene O'Neill's boyhood home.

Without doubt, gaining the attention and respect of Lloyd Richards and having access to the facilities of the O'Neill Center and ultimately the Yale Repertory Theatre bolstered Wilson's confidence. Other fringe benefits of this association included important contacts with a network of producers and agents and Richards's assistance and prestige in securing several generous grants, fellowships, and other awards to support his writing.

Once Wilson agreed to allow Richards to produce *Ma Rainey's Black Bottom* at the Yale Repertory Theatre, he gained both a mentor and a convenient homebase for his work. In the academic setting that the Yale School of Drama afforded Wilson, the director was understood to be Lloyd Richards, whom Wilson trusted implicitly; stage managers and technicians were drama school students and interns who were expected to carry out the tasks as meticulously as professionals. Yale Rep audiences served as ready-made critics whose assessments of each play's production were taken seriously as it was honed toward a definitive

script. Exhaustive notes on what worked and what needed improvement became the basis for classroom discussion as well as for future
revisions to the work in progress. Wilson was left free to observe *Ma
Rainey's Black Bottom* and subsequent productions of his work at the
Rep from an aesthetic distance and to determine the feasibility or the
extent of any suggested changes.

Perhaps the most important aspect of Richards's influence upon
Wilson was not only that he became a mentor and friend but that he
was also an African American man, as intimately familiar as Wilson
with the lives that Wilson translates to the stage. Richards, like Wilson,
had been forced to become a "street smart kid" when he was only a
teenager. At thirteen he was forced to find work during the Depression
to support his family after his father died of diptheria and after his
mother's improperly treated glaucoma led to blindness. Just as Wilson
had pounded the mean streets of Pittsburgh's Hill District in search of
odd jobs to help Daisy Wilson make ends meet for her five children,
Richards and his brother Allan found work to support four siblings and
their physically disabled mother. When asked if being black was a factor
in their collaboration, Richards replied, "I think he has said that the first
time that we went to the rehearsal and I talked to the cast about his play,
he learned things, and he learned that I understood his work and all of
the ramifications of it and that it wasn't necessary for him to sit in the
room and check me because we were both coming from the same place"
(Shannon, "From Hansberry to Wilson" 126).

In addition to his insight into the world of Wilson's characters,
Richards shared with Wilson his shrewd business savvy gained from
years of working on both the artistic and commercial ends of play
production. Richards's advice, for example, steered Wilson clear of a
dubious, yet potentially lucrative, offer to convert *Ma Rainey's Black
Bottom* into a musical.[1] This sealed the working relationship between
Lloyd Richards and August Wilson. Richards essentially took Wilson
under his wing and began tutoring him—not just in his playwriting
skills but also in the sometimes crude realities of commercial theatre. At
this point in Wilson's writing career, he yielded to Richards's wisdom
and experience, and the two set out on a collaborative venture to
chronicle ten decades of the black experience in America.

Once *Ma Rainey's Black Bottom* was turned over to Lloyd Richards
and the Yale Rep, he set about identifying its flaws and coaching Wilson
on ways to correct them. Two major difficulties—neither seen by Wil-

son when he wrote the play—emerged as Richards began to adapt the original script for the stage. Structurally, *Ma Rainey's Black Bottom* at first consisted of two distinct plays: "a play that took place in the recording studio and a play which took place in the bandroom. . . . So if you took the little play about the recording studio, she [Ma Rainey] was the central character in that; if you took the little play in the bandroom, somebody else was the central character in that" (Shannon, "From Hansberry to Wilson" 128). There were choices for revision: (1) to retain the two plots as equally important and blend them more coherently, (2) to eliminate one of the plots, or (3) to determine which plot should be emphasized and which de-emphasized. Settling on the third option, Wilson and Richards decided to give Ma Rainey a role as a peripheral character, whose story is secondary to what goes on in the bandroom among the black men.

This decision to shift the focus of the play from Ma Rainey was informed by more than the desire to achieve a smooth stage adaptation. Wilson recalled his return to the script in 1981:

> In my head I suddenly saw the four musicians sitting in the bandroom. . . . When I discovered the musicians, I opened the door to the play. . . . At stage right is the recording studio and at stage left is the bandroom. I decided to examine the meaning of the lives of the musicians, to show where the music came from. So I blended the two ideas—Ma Rainey's life and the lives of the musicians. (Mitgang C15).

Therefore, the apparent disorder in the script was not the result of muddled writing. Rather, it is typical of what occurs when Wilson yields to images and voices from his subconscious that crowd his head: he allows them to determine how they are to be represented on the page and ultimately onstage.

Another problem surfaced as Richards tried to prepare Ma Rainey for the stage. Since the play called for four musicians, he had to decide whether it would be more prudent to hire four musicians and have them study their respective roles in the script, hire four actors and require them to learn to play assigned instruments, or hire four actors and play taped music. That he had unknowingly written another staging problem into the script was another revelation to Wilson, as he was concentrating his efforts on writing credible dialogue and meatier plots.

He had much to learn about what was possible during a live perform-ance, and grappling with the special problems associated with staging *Ma Rainey* opened his eyes to many concerns.

Much to the chagrin of some critics and blues fans (who viewed the play as a potential blues concert), Richards convinced Wilson to hire actors and blend live and recorded music. The solution drew disap-proval from reviewers such as *The Nation's* Paul Berman, who argued that preliminary sounds from the makeshift musicians seemed notice-ably artificial when compared to the smoother, more professional taped musical numbers that followed. However, as the play demonstrates, Richards's emphasis was not upon providing coherence in the music but upon highlighting the band's limitations. As I have argued elsewhere ("The Long Wait" 137), "Forever practicing to become but never actu-ally 'arriving' describes each of the musicians' predicament." Further-more their practicing is often interrupted by minor errors and disagreements, and it seems futile to practice what they know so well. Practicing and playing are worlds apart for Cutler, Toledo, Slow Drag, and Levee. They all know that forces conspire to keep them rehearsing their roles as backup musicians, never allowing them the economic and emotional independence to strike out on their own.

Unfortunately Wilson's early creative strategy caused this work and subsequent plays to be labeled "sprawling," "unwieldy," and "ram-bling." His naïveté about staging at this point in his writing career made Richards's work challenging at best. Here, the director's delicate task was to find a way to make audiences focus their immediate and lasting attention on the bandmembers while, to a lesser extent, allowing them an intimate look at the personal plight of a black female blues singer in a decade fraught with both racism and sexism.

The plot of the substantially overhauled *Ma Rainey's Black Bottom* develops around Ma's freak automobile accident and subsequent brush with the law. When the abrasive Ma Rainey and her entourage of hangers-on sweep into a dingy recording studio where she is scheduled to sing some of her popular works for an album, the white organizers of this recording session are already irritable because of her lateness, and they cringe at her demands for a Coca-Cola, more heat in the studio, and the microphone for her stuttering nephew, who she insists will announce her on the album before she sings.

While Ma Rainey tries the patience of her two promoters, her crew of black male musicians waiting in the basement bandroom argue and amuse each other with bouts of the dozens and pseudo-philosophical wisdom. Their conversations, which slip from an argument over the correct spelling of the word *music* to an existentialist discussion of black history, gradually intensify and unexpectedly erupt when a common-place incident leads to murder. The self-made philosopher and pianist Toledo inadvertently steps on the new Florsheim shoes of the sulking trumpet player Levee. Apparently still angered by the recent refusal of one of Ma Rainey's promoters to launch his musical career, Levee becomes enraged and stabs Toledo in the back.

The final version of the play opened at Broadway's Cort Theater on October 11, 1984, and subsequently was published in 1985; it signaled Wilson's success. The two blended miniplays worked fine on Broadway although several critics who missed the intentional focus on the band-members expressed dismay that the work did not feature more of Ma Rainey's story. Others lamented the dearth of actual musical numbers in the play—conditioned as they were to expect such in a Broadway play about black life. Despite these few sour notes, the play received rave reviews from New York theatre critics, one of the most notable coming from the *New York Times*'s Frank Rich, who wrote, "In *Ma Rainey's Black Bottom*, the writer August Wilson sends the entire history of black America crashing down upon our heads. The play is a searing inside account of what white racism does to its victims—and it floats on the same authentic artistry as the blues music it celebrates" ("Wilson's *Ma Rainey's*" C1).

Taking Ma Rainey to Broadway introduced a number of new concerns for Richards, Wilson, and the play's producers. One of the most disconcerting involved Richards's dual role as dean of Yale School of Drama and as director of Wilson's Broadway-bound drama. Though Richards was exemplary in executing his duties at Yale, expanding his theatre work beyond campus did not sit well with some Yale adminis-trators. They claimed that any ambitions for Broadway posed conflicts of interest in the overall mission of the school, yet Richards held fast to his belief that the Broadway experience was an appropriate extension of the Yale classroom. The mission of this school as he sees it, and accord-ing to founder George Pierce Baker, is "to find, to discover the most talented persons in every area of the theater and to provide them with the best training toward their participation in the profession of theater that was possible and to give them some kind of a bridge into profes-sional work" (Shannon, "From Hansberry to Wilson" 125). Richards also responded to growing complaints about his inaccessibility to drama school students as well as to conflict of interest charges by discounting Broadway as an ultimate goal. He explained, "Broadway is never the goal; it never has been. The first audience that sits in the theater right here at Yale—that's who I create for" (126). Still, the movement of this first collaboration between Wilson and Richards from the Yale Rep to Broadway sparked a controversy that mounted with each subsequent play following the same performance route.

Ma Rainey's Black Bottom also initially caused a great deal of worry among Broadway producers Robert Cole, Ivan Bloch, and Frederick Zolla, who feared a financial fiasco. In 1984 Broadway was in a slump: any play that deviated from previous formulas for success was considered an extreme risk. As a play featuring blues performers, *Ma Rainey* made its backers nervous. They wanted the relative financial security of a musical rather than a conventional drama. The play's chances of success on Broadway were also doubted because some felt that a play featuring "the voice of the playwright wrestling with the Afro-American experience" (Tighe 95) would essentially bore Broadway audiences and devastate ticket sales. However, *Ma Rainey's* excellent reputation, from the time it premiered at the Eugene O'Neill Theater Center to its run at the Yale Rep, was enough to stimulate high attendance at New York performances. As a novice to Broadway, Wilson defied the odds and piqued the curiosity of theatregoers who had heard "ecstatic word-of-mouth and critical raves" (95).

In addition to a solid script and good financial backing, the Broadway success of *Ma Rainey's Black Bottom* was due to careful casting. For the $700,000 venture, producer Robert Cole secured former classical singer and television sitcom star Theresa Merritt to play the title role of Ma Rainey and Yale School of Drama graduate Charles Dutton to play the part of Levee. No doubt Merritt's physical appearance (she has an abundant frame) and her ability to sing without taped assistance figured heavily in the decision to cast her. In addition to getting used to "those nasty, suggestive blues," Merritt's only reservation about playing the legendary Mother of the Blues was doing justice to her music. She recalled, "I knew I could say the lines. But I'd never sung blues before. I got her records and listened. I put something of me in the songs but I tried to get her phrasing, her style and the style of the period as much as I possibly could" (Campbell B3).

The relationship between Charles Dutton and August Wilson goes back to the Eugene O'Neill Theater Center, where they met in 1982.

After impressing Wilson and Richards with his acting ability, Dutton was offered a leading role in *Ma Rainey*. In 1985 he received a Tony nomination for his riveting performance as the paranoiac trumpet player Levee. Because of his abundant energy and emotional range, Wilson later tapped Dutton to play leading roles in *Joe Turner's Come and Gone* and in *The Piano Lesson*.

August Wilson keeps his dramatic vision sharply in focus by concentrating more upon writing effective scripts and less upon casting media darlings to attract audiences. In fact, he was interested in Dutton mainly because he did *not* carry the baggage of superstardom. Later, he wrote scripts specifically for the actor so that Dutton might demonstrate his wide range of acting capabilities; however, Wilson and Richards agree that a play's success should not rely on the appeal of any one cast member, no matter how stellar. Of course, their philosophies did not stop producers of *Fences* and *Two Trains Running* from casting James Earl Jones and Mary Alice as Troy and Rose and Roscoe Lee Browne and Laurence Fishburne as Holloway and Sterling. In both plays these names received top billing and, one might argue, helped draw Broadway audiences. Yet while Wilson's producers opted for name recognition to protect their financial interests, Wilson was not impressed. He recalled how his own name was presented with little fanfare in New York at the 1984 premiere of *Ma Rainey's Black Bottom*: "If your name has no value, they don't put it up on the marquee; they put the actors' names up there in big letters because it is a business, and that's what it's about. It doesn't matter whether the play is any good or not. If you can get a star in there to do the role, you're going to have people come see it" (interviewed by the author). With *Ma Rainey's Black Bottom*, Wilson was introduced to Broadway's world of dollars and cents and to another dimension of what being a successful playwright entails.

Wilson was not blinded by the limelight of *Ma Rainey*'s success. Although the play eventually received the New York Drama Critics' Circle Award and gave him immense exposure, he managed to remain focused upon his work. His fear of being a "one-shot playwright" forced him to adopt some strategies to secure his longevity in the field. One such strategy was to always have a work in progress, even as he may have had plays running simultaneously on Broadway or making their way across the country's regional theatre circuit. While *Ma Rainey's Black Bottom* was enjoying a successful stage reading at the O'Neill, Wilson admitted that he "had an idea for my next play [*Fences*] . . . and I was more concerned with getting that down on paper than I was with what would happen to *Ma Rainey*" (Nelsen 8). While *The Piano Lesson* made its way from the Yale Repertory Theatre to regional theatre and eventually to Broadway, Wilson had already begun *Two Trains Running*.

Wilson's success at avoiding fleeting stardom was based upon more than simply churning out one play after another. As a result of his close relationship with theatre veteran Lloyd Richards, his own die-hard determination to succeed, and several sound business decisions, Wilson has achieved staying power while far too many of his fellow African American playwrights have left the profession. In light of the recent cutbacks in funding from the National Endowment for the Arts coupled with a sagging economy and ever-present obstacles black dramatists face with small audiences and lack of community support, the label "one-play playwright" has less to do with black dramatists' consistency in writing plays and more with economics and attitudes toward their work.[2] For similar reasons, several well-known names in black theatre who once drew crowds, rave reviews, and Broadway hype for their work have found other lines of work for very practical reasons, chief among which is money.

Ma Rainey's Black Bottom proved to be not only the play that secured Wilson's future as a playwright but also the first full-blown public demonstration of his newly formulated artistic agenda. Added to the play's focus upon Ma Rainey, her band, and the white-controlled recording industry of the 1920s are broader themes that reflect Wilson's conscious concern "to keep all of the elements of the culture alive in the work" (interview). Chief among the African American cultural elements Wilson wishes to preserve is a powerful blues dynamic, which sets an appropriate tone of despair while also affording Wilson's characters buoyancy as they try against devastating odds to survive. As he draws upon this cultural medium that extends "all the way back to Africa and various other parts of the world" (interview), Wilson taps unchartered areas of black consciousness and transforms them into the substance of his dramas about black people.

Ma Rainey is not just about the blues recording industry in pre-Depression America. It blends various properties of the blues dynamic to re-create the emotional landscape of late 1920s Chicago. This blues dynamic is not restricted to the lyrics of the blues singer or notes from a guitar, a piano, or a saxophone. In fact, its presence is so strong in *Ma*

Rainey's Black Bottom that the play can be viewed as a dramatic rendition of a blues song; Wilson's cast of characters embodies the very sentiments that their music imparts. Each endures a life that could easily be summed up in terms of the same disappointments, destitution, and desperation conveyed in the lyrics of the blues songs. Hence, the forces of this traditional part of African American culture motivate character interaction, determine the slow pace and abrupt action of the play, and, to a large extent, shape the play's devastating though inevitable conclusion.

Operating in the play's subtext is a story of real-life blues players who crowded their way into Chicago during the early twentieth century, hoping to trade the backbreaking labor of the South for the rumored "easy life" up North. With their mail-order guitars in tow, they joined crowds of other blacks who either carried their worldly possessions on their backs along dusty roads or packed aboard trains heading north. Hundreds came from farmland in the Mississippi Delta region while others hailed from locales such as Arkansas, Texas, Georgia, and Tennessee. Blues researcher Hugh Merrill notes, "The greatest migration in America took the blues as baggage—from the Mississippi Delta to Chicago and from Louisiana and Texas to California" (11–12).

Those who brought with them the talent to play the blues held a decided advantage over those who were only skilled as farmhands. Music was a possible ticket to financial freedom. Unfortunately only those with tough skin like Ma Rainey could earn a respectable living in the tightly controlled industry. But on many occasions the ability to play or sing the blues could save a performer from starvation and homelessness. Thus, a guitar and a repertoire of blues tunes could provide at least some degree of security once up North. When times were bad, the skilled bluesman could stake out a heavily traveled area on a sidewalk or stroll into a barroom and earn as much as $100 a night playing his guitar and singing any of the popular tunes before blues-crazed crowds.

Chicago's music industry thrived on these itinerant musicians and created a market exclusively for their talents. Recording studios such as Columbia and Bluebird sprang up, and numerous agents were hired to lure wide-eyed farmhands and ex-sharecroppers into record deals. The principle of supply and demand was largely responsible for the eventual popularity of the blues in Chicago around the 1920s. Prior to taking Chicago—and later the entire country—by storm, the genre had been limited to areas such as Mississippi and Texas. However, potential cash profits, hungry audiences, and a healthy supply of fresh talent transported in daily by the Illinois Central and the Gulf and Mobile and Ohio (M&O) railroad lines energized the Chicago music industry and propelled some backwoods blues musicians to fame.

Native Mississippian Muddy Waters (born McKinley Morganfield), known for his off-beat timing and for playing notes that "fell between the cracks," is one of several success stories of the twentieth century blues migrant. Like some other Delta bluesmen, he relocated to Chicago, but through some shrewd maneuvering, he avoided the recording scams. After finding quick employment and a comfortable apartment in Chicago, he went on to make a name for himself with tunes like "Louisiana Blues," "Still A Fool," and "Hoochie Coochie Man." Largely because of him, Delta blues was transformed "from a regional folk music into a truly popular music that developed first a large black following, then a European white following, and finally a worldwide following of immense proportions" (Palmer 16). Although Delta blues eventually attracted a large urban base, its roots remain with the migrants from the South who constituted much of the Chicago audience. According to blues researcher Robert Palmer,

> it was created not just by black people but by the poorest, most marginal black people. Most of the men and women who sang and played it could neither read nor write. They owned almost nothing and lived in virtual serfdom. They were not considered reputable enough to work as house servants for the whites or to hold responsible positions within their own communities. (117)

Despite the historical realities informing *Ma Rainey's Black Bottom*, Wilson disclaims any specific background, preferring instead that the music reflect universal concerns. He notes in a foreword to the play, "Whether this music came from Alabama or Mississippi or other parts of the South doesn't matter anymore" (*MR* xvi). Though Levee alludes to his roots in Jefferson City, Mississippi, and kids Slow Drag about his origins in Fat Back, Arkansas, the emphasis is not upon their geographical differences but upon their mutual plight both as black men in a white-controlled business and as stifled musicians.

If regarded as a blues composition presented as a play, *Ma Rainey's*

Black Bottom becomes infinitely more understandable. Like a blues song or jazz rendition, the play is a slow-building, repetitious, unpredictable ride on an emotional roller coaster. Ma does not appear until well into act 1, yet the goings-on during the prerehearsal session are analogous to a lengthy musical prelude leading up to the vocal accompaniment. Levee's recurring complaints against Ma and the other bandmembers function as the refrain to this blues play; and the competing stories of Ma and her band echo the interwoven improvisations of blues and jazz performers. Corresponding to the emotion-charged lyrics of the blues song are the characters' tortured testimonies of survival. Both Ma and Levee, though constantly at odds with each other, at some point in the play turn inward to reveal the source of their private pain.

Although the blues dominates every aspect of *Ma Rainey's Black Bottom*, also at work in the play are a number of other identifiable elements of African American culture. Either directly or indirectly, some combination of the following themes runs through this and each of Wilson's subsequent plays: black people's need to establish and maintain ties with their immediate families as well as with their cultural ancestors; their mistaken devaluation of their own culture, prompted by a massive exodus from South to North after their emancipation; their heroic struggles and degrading compromises made to achieve economic stability; and the deterioration of their moral, spiritual, and familial values resulting from those compromises and that self-devaluation. To convey each of these major issues effectively in his work, Wilson continues to draw upon the dynamics of the blues, concerned that his audiences—especially the black members—explore both the emotional and historical dimensions of his work and see themselves in the process.

One of the most consistent of these cultural elements surfacing in *Ma Rainey* is what Paul Carter Harrison refers to as "the potency of the African continuum as a psychic and spiritual repository of values and survival strategies" (316). In *Ma Rainey's Black Bottom*, this theme emerges indirectly in the comments made by the self-educated, pseudophilosopher Toledo; in the symbolic polarizations in the band's attitudes toward northern sophistication and southern naïveté, and, ultimately, in the vicious dispute between Levee and Ma Rainey over her "old jug band music" and his more modern, more danceable versions. Yet in the play representations of the African continuum in the play draw harsh criticism and denial from the black men in Ma's band rather than acknowledgment and reverence. To most of them Africa, like life in the South, is a distant world of painful memories and associations; any true measure of advancement, in their view, depends upon how un-African or how unsouthern they have become.

In the larger scheme of Wilson's play, the futility and sheer resignation that define the lives of Toledo, Cutler, Levee, and Slow Drag reflect a kind of cosmic retribution for their blatant denial of their past. Certainly racial oppression and the emasculation it seeks permeate all facets of these black musicians' lives, and racism is largely responsible for their inability to progress. These men are forced to prostitute their wonderful musical talents for mere pocket change and pats on their backs. To make matters worse, they must demand their embarrassingly low pay for playing backup during Ma Rainey's recording session in cash; a black man brandishing a check in 1927 Chicago was automatic cause for suspicion.

Despite racism's role in determining the professional fate of these four black men, *Ma Rainey's Black Bottom* does not portray interracial oppression as the single cause for their plight. In what may be perceived as a reversal of the trend in plays of racial exploitation, the failures of Ma's band seem to stem also from their own ignorance, their own apathy, and their own denial of their past. Thus, the play suggests that if African Americans continue to repress both their African and southern roots, they are destined to live troubled, stagnated lives. In their awkward attempts to compensate for that part of their identity that they have denied, some, like Toledo, adopt alien gods and mimic their ways while others, like Levee, in effect sell their souls to the devil to get ahead in America. Still others, like Slow Drag and Cutler, hide behind light humor or constant denial rather than draw strength from Africa's nationalist possibilities.

Ma's pianist, Toledo, prides himself on being the resident African griot; however, his uninvited lesson concerning an African oral tradition is taken as an insult, not as an earnest attempt to school his unenlightened brothers on some revered African ancestral customs. When the bass player Slow Drag asks the guitarist Cutler for a "reefer," he reinforces his plea by recalling for him a series of activities that they have shared:

> We been doing this [playing in various bands] together for twenty-two years. All up and down the back roads, the side roads, the front roads. . . . We done played the juke joints, the

whorehouses, the barn dances, and city sit-downs. . . . I done lied for you and lied with you. . . . We done laughed together, fought together, slept in the same bed together, done sucked on the same titty . . . and now you don't wanna give me no reefer. (*MR* 31)

As if he has some superior knowledge of African customs, Toledo, who overhears Slow Drag's exaggerated entreaties for marijuana, interprets his strategy as an "African conceptualization. That's when you name the gods or call on the ancestors to achieve whatever your desires are" (32).

But Toledo's teaching methods, hampered by downright uninterested listeners, do not attract the group; instead, he offends them. His condescending air, coupled with his fondness for flaunting knowledge for knowledge's sake, nullifies his unsolicited wisdom. Yet the reasons Toledo's lesson falls upon deaf ears go beyond his faults. Like many others of their race, Toledo's two immediate pupils—Slow Drag and Levee—are convinced that being forced to relate to anything African is similar to being cursed: Levee fumes, "You don't see me running around in no jungle with no bone between my nose" (32).

In its implicit appeal to African Americans to embrace the African continuum, *Ma Rainey's Black Bottom* employs a strategy that has notable precedent in Lorraine Hansberry's *Raisin in the Sun* (1959). Although Wilson admits not having read Hansberry, the strong anti-African sentiments that his characters display echo similar emotions conveyed by Ma's bandmembers. As Wilson does, Hansberry directs the characters' attention toward Africa as they struggle to retain their dignity and to establish themselves in an extremely racist post–World War II America. In *Raisin* Africa is introduced to the Younger family in the form of Asagai, a dashing native African whose presence excites in Walter "that proud and revolutionary spirit which is his heritage" (Hansberry, *Collected Last Plays* 11) and in his young romantic sister Beneatha unexplained yearnings to immerse herself in all things African.

But there is resistance to Africa in *Raisin*, just as in *Ma Rainey*. George Murchison, Beneatha's rich yet romantically uninspiring suitor, echoes an attitude shared by Slow Drag and Levee:

Oh, dear, dear, dear! Here we go! A lecture on the African past! On our Great West African Heritage! In one second we will hear all about the great Ashanti empires; the great Songhay civilization; and the great sculpture of Benin—and then some poetry in the Bantu—and the whole monologue will end with the word *heritage*! (*Nastily*) Let's face it, baby, your heritage is nothing but a bunch of raggedy assed spirituals and some grass huts! (*Raisin* 81)

Like *Ma Rainey*, *Raisin* exposes anti-African sentiments among modern blacks while presenting a strong subtext on the benefits of embracing Africa's culture. Both plays adopt a nonthreatening, nonhomiletic position toward Africa and, by so doing, still manage to reinforce the African continuum.

Characters in *Ma Rainey's Black Bottom* also display a strong anti-southern sentiment typical of many blacks blinded by the false pretenses of the North. Levee, the ambitious yet very belligerent trumpet player, epitomizes this sentiment in his struggle to replace Ma Rainey's "old jug band music" with his jazzed-up arrangements. He scowls at his colleagues, and he repeatedly taunts them with insults stemming from his deep-seated loathing of anything related to life in the South. It surfaces in his instructions to fellow bandmembers on how to adopt his style of music: "Now we gonna dance it . . . but we ain't gonna countrify it. This ain't no barn dance" *(MR* 38). It appears in an early verbal jab at Toledo: "Nigger got them clod hoppers! Old brogans! He ain't nothing but a sharecropper. . . . Got nerve to put on a suit and tie with them farming boots" (40). And again later, he teases Slow Drag: "That's why you so backwards. You just an old country boy talking about Fat Back, Arkansas, and New Orleans in the same breath" (54). While Africa conjures up in Levee's mind images of bones in noses, the South reminds him of clodhopper shoes and sharecropping.

Levee's bitter rejections by both Ma Rainey, who eventually fires him, and Sturdyvant suggest that the gods whom he denounces viciously throughout the play have conspired against him. Earlier, Toledo explains that when an African pleads to the gods for help, their response "depends on if the gods is sympathetic with his cause for which he is calling them with the right names. Then his success comes with the right proportion of his naming" (33). Evidently Levee's mockery of Old World traditions casts him out of favor with such gods.

But there is another deeply personal cause for Levee's cynicism about Africa and the South—a cause that prompts him to simmer in bitter hatred of the South, a cause that teaches him the tactic of humility as a disguise before whites to gain the advantage. When eight years old, Levee witnessed the gang rape of his mother by several local white men from his Mississippi hometown. They had come upon her while his father was away in town. As a young boy he watched these men sexually assault his mother and could not ward off their merciless attack. He also witnessed his father sell his farm to these same white men and eventually lose his life in a scheme that allowed him the satisfaction of killing most of his wife's assailants. Thus, the young black boy learned to hate the South, whose unbridled racism had taken his mother's dignity and his father's life. So Levee does not mentally and physically divorce himself from the South merely out of a selfish desire for fame and fortune up North. Like many other blacks after Reconstruction, he chooses to quit this scene of vigilante justice, backbreaking, undercompensated labor, and perpetual emasculation of black men for the uncertain but beckoning North.

Although Wilson, who gives Levee's personal attitude against the South this personal root, seems sensitive to his concerns and those of numerous blacks who left the South, the playwright considers the Great Migration to be the "great mistake" of his people. Yet this great mistake does not rest heavy on the minds of the play's southern-grown transplants. Toledo still has a few fond memories of farming down South, but he is quick to add, "I done got too old to be following behind one of them balky mules now" (*MR* 93). Slow Drag is excited over the good fortune of Toledo's old friend Nevada, who has managed to get a job operating an elevator in St. Louis rather than "stepping in mule shit" (93).

Levee's struggle to oust Ma Rainey's brand of music and supplant it with his own is one of several variations on Wilson's theme of preserving one's cultural heritage. By this interpretion, Levee's adversary, Ma Rainey, is an agent of the past fighting against all odds to sustain an endangered cultural element. Levee, on the other hand, has foolishly sold his rights to his past for the price of a couple of songs. Ma's music has its basis in the South and conveys the oppression of her southern audience as no other type could. It is firmly ensconced in the psyches of her adoring fans who hail from the clod hills, the tobacco fields, and the cotton fields of places like Georgia, Mississippi, and Alabama. Moreover, her style of singing is not only a product of the South but it also perpetuates certain folk elements of African American culture that extend as far back as Africa. Her singing is at once a symbol of the African continuum and a reminder of the resilience and perseverance of Ma's people. She is their queen.

While Ma Rainey and Levee effectively symbolize the clash between old and new ideals, Levee's avant-garde arrangements are indicative of the actual evolution in musical tastes that took place in the North around the '30s and '40s. During this time the "downhome" blues was very soon eclipsed by newer rhythms of jazz. According to one study of this period, "compared to the rapidity with which jazz changed during the same period of time, Delta blues was practically standing still" (Palmer 133). While earlier forms of blues still enjoyed a large audience among northerners, the more danceable, up-tempo sounds of "brass, clarinet, banjo, guitar, string bass or tuba, and sometimes a piano and/or a set of drums" (134) quickly gained popularity. For example, when Muddy Waters came to Chicago in the early 1940s, he realized he had to modernize his music or become extinct. It was Muddy's sister who warned him, "They don't listen to that kind of old blues you're doin' now . . . not in Chicago" (135). Interestingly, her observation expresses Levee's very sentiments about Ma's so-called jug band music: "The peoples up North ain't gonna buy all that tent-show nonsense. They wanna hear some music!" (MR 65).

The forces of change are ominous in *Ma Rainey's Black Bottom*. Although evolution in the public's musical taste is inevitable, change, as represented by Levee, is not at all positive. Levee is an impetuous, hot-headed, selfish villain, who shows no reverence for an older form of music. He fails to acknowledge the debt jazz owes to the blues and, by the same token, severs all ties with his southern roots. Personal ambition takes precedence. Thus, Levee's actions and attitude enact Wilson's theme of cultural fragmentation. His irreverence, his violence, and ultimately the certain fate that awaits him may all be interpreted as the wages of his sins against his past. After he breaks free of the South as well as Ma's band, self-destruction soon follows.

Added to Levee's potential for destruction is the frustration of a bad business deal. Levee is swindled out of his dreams and winds up a ruined man. His upbeat music, therefore, seems to mock him with its worthlessness as his secret negotiations with Sturdyvant to purchase and promote his song sour. The lie of the North is made visible as Sturdyvant backs out of this arrangement with Levee:

STURDYVANT: I had my fellows play your songs, and when I heard them, they just didn't sound like the kind of songs I'm looking for right now.

LEVEE: You got to hear me play them, Mr. Sturdyvant! You ain't heard me play them. That's what's gonna make them sound right.

STURDYVANT: Well, Levee, I don't doubt that really. It's just that . . . well, I don't think they'd sell like Ma's records. But I'll take them off your hands for you. (108)

The relationship between cultural denial and emotional or financial bankruptcy is unspoken but clear in *Ma Rainey's Black Bottom*. The play unfolds to reveal the gradual disintegration of a group of black men who have warped views of their history. Let loose in an indifferent world without the stability of a cultural base, they lack the confidence to demand more for their lives. The results of their cultural detachment may be seen in a shocking display of blasphemy ("God can kiss my ass" [98]), intraracial bickering and violence, a marked sense of powerlessness around Ma Rainey and her white business managers, an absence of any nurturing influence from family, and an alarming distaste for the past. These are mere shadows of men. Although Levee does possess the warrior spirit needed to aggressively improve his chances in life, he has so many personal insecurities gnawing at him that they overshadow his valiant efforts to excel. Similarly, Toledo can read, articulate his opinion on a variety of subjects, and play the piano with ease; yet he wastes his time taunting others with his knowledge rather than using his talents actively to improve his and their situations.

Unfortunately, Ma's band does not seem to realize that they need more than just their music to survive. Their blues, though doubtlessly genuine, does not inspire them to move beyond their uncertainties. Coded in the sounds of Cutler's guitar and trombone, Levee's trumpet, and Toledo's piano is a desire for individuality and power, yet their music also discloses their hopelessness to make things happen. James Baldwin wrote that "the American Negro can have no future anywhere, on any continent, as long as he is unwilling to accept his past" (*Fire Next Time* 95). His statement confirms Wilson's focus upon the band's continuing stagnation and despair.

Without the slightest concern that he may rile feminists in his audience, Wilson presses forward in *Ma Rainey's Black Bottom* with an uncompromising agenda of reexamining the black experience in America using the voices of black men. From his first cycle play, *Jitney!*, through *Two Trains Running*, the pattern of male-dominated casts continues uninterrupted. During the period when Wilson turned his attention to revising *Ma Rainey* (1981–84), he learned from his friend and business associate Lloyd Richards some tough lessons about the theatre business; but, just as important, the often unyielding Wilson learned when to compromise and when to stand firm. While he acquiesced to Richards on issues such as streamlining dialogue or merging two plays into one, he held fast to his own inclination to write from the perspective he knows best—that of a black man. In *Ma Rainey's Black Bottom* black men outnumber black women eight to two.

While Wilson's male characters dominate center stage, the play's eponymous heroine and its only actual historical personality, Gertrude Rainey, remains not so quietly in the wings. Although she too bears evidence of artistic embellishments, much of her character is based upon what Wilson gleaned from liner notes accompanying her blues albums rather than extensive research into her background. She does not appear on stage until the middle of act 1, and when she does finally appear, she provides only fleeting insight into her private emotional scars. She would seem mere window dressing for the play were it not for her commanding presence, her brash behavior, and the impossible-to-ignore spectacle that her huge frame and her flashy costume create. But since Ma Rainey's reputation is already firmly established as the Mother of the Blues, she requires little fanfare despite her defiant insistence that her nephew go through the ritual of introduction on her new recording.

Born in Columbus, Georgia, on April 26, 1886, the historical Gertrude Pridgett grew to become a blues legend in a time when race and gender mattered very much in America. Wilson's play is aptly named for her, for she provides a powerful symbol of the tensions felt by thousands of African Americans who migrated North. Her popularity in northern cities during the mid- to late 1920s was supported largely by southern blacks, who found in her blues songs solace from the alienation and disillusionment of city life. Her down-home, earthy style, her naughty lyrics, and her rough looks were welcomed by weary southern blacks, no longer impressed by the deceptive glamor of the North. Her blues, therefore, was a gift to her people, for she intimately understood their miseries. In his warm tribute to the blues legend, Sterling Brown roundly commends her for this gift:

O Ma Rainey,
Sing yo' song;
Now you's back
Whah you belong,
Git way inside us,
Keep us strong . . .
O Ma Rainey,
Li'l an' low;
Sing us 'bout de hard luck'
Roun' our do';
Sing us 'bout de lonesome road
We mus' go. . . . (S. Brown 62–63)

What attracted Ma Rainey's black audience were the exclusive invitations she extended to them through her lyrics—invitations to commiser-
ate as well as to acknowledge proudly the existence of their mutual
culture. If they could not reverse their misfortunes, at least they were
able together to grapple with the enormity of them.

Ma Rainey claims that the first time she ever heard what later was
called the blues was during one of several road shows. She explained to
Library of Congress folk-song collector John Work that she overheard a
young woman singing about a lost lover while her troupe performed in
Missouri. Impressed by the sound and emotions of this song, Ma
decided to include this type of singing in her act. Response to Ma
singing the blues was exuberant among her rural black audiences. Soon
she won over northern audiences as well.[3]

Wilson's fictional Ma Rainey is excluded from the cultural debate
about Africa that Toledo instigates and, for a time, avoids the bitter
antisouthern, anti-African, anti-Christian, antiblack sentiments espoused
by Levee. Yet her silence should not suggest that the emotions expressed by various members of her band are alien to her. She is a
defiant but flawed symbol of success in this northern environment.
Judged by the standards of other black women in her profession in
the late 1920s, she clearly outdistances them. Still, she contends with
the same Jim Crow racism and the same callous manipulation by whites
that have crippled her band. Having performed together with Ma
before white audiences in various cities, Cutler and Slow Drag attest to
her poor treatment:

CUTLER: The white man don't care nothing about Ma. The colored folks made Ma a star. White folks don't care nothing about who she is . . . what kind of music she make.

SLOW DRAG: That's the truth about that. You let her go down to one of them white-folks hotels and see how big she is.

CUTLER: Hell, she ain't got to do that. She can't even get a cab in the North. (*MR* 95)

Although Ma Rainey is not caught up in her band's prerehearsal talk, she eventually reveals her hands-down preference for the South and, further, her important role in preserving as well as promoting elements of African American culture. Ma sees the South not as a stronghold of racism and violence, but as a relief from the cool reception she receives in the North. From the hundreds of remote, rural farm areas, she draws her strength, her identity, and her countless fans. Assured of unanimous acceptance among her southern fans, she cautions, "If that don't set right with you Sturdyvant . . . then I can carry my black bottom on back down South to my tour, 'cause I don't like it up here no ways" (63).

Ma Rainey's blues functions as a vehicle for transmitting "the cultural responses of blacks in America to the situation they find themselves in" (Moyers 168). As a means of negotiating a range of emotional responses to the world around them, her music is a continuum of the African tribal drums, the slave chants, and the Negro spirituals of her culture. Thus, her blues music succeeds in doing that at which Toledo fails miserably—establishing an awareness of the bond between Africa and America.

Ma Rainey's Black Bottom presents a crumbling world where a group of black musicians are caught precariously between two cultures: one, they disown; the other, they fear. In an attempt to improve themselves, they have abandoned the southern farmland, have cut their ties with their families and the church, and have vowed never to return to the place of their ancestors. They cling to their instruments as they would their wives or their god and nurse their melancholy in the soothing notes of the blues.

In the early 1920s, blues performers were among an exclusive group of southern migrants with the greatest potential for economic success in northern cities. Yet unfortunately for many, the fruits of their talents and ambitions merely lined the pockets of those who controlled the music industry. Thus, their only means of breaking the cycle of poverty from which they fled too often became someone else's financial gain. Consequently, *Ma Rainey's Black Bottom* is a fictional case study of black people's "deprivation of possibility" (Reed 93). Wilson fashions drama out of the tragedy that blues performers experienced in 1920s America and demonstrates the limitations they faced when the music that was their life's blood was extorted from them.

FOUR

Developing Character:
Fences

James Earl Jones as
Troy Maxson in the spring 1985
Yale Repertory Theatre premiere of *Fences*.
In this scene, Troy is poised to do battle
with death, his ultimate foe.
Photograph by William B.
Carter. Reprinted by permission.

In both *Jitney!* and *Ma Rainey's Black Bottom*, Wilson wrestled with unfocused plots and shallow characters. While his work received popular approval, critics charged that his scripts lacked discipline and that his casts of characters were too crowded to allow three-dimensional explorations of key personalities. For example, one critic points to the imbalance between Wilson's beefy portrayals of Toledo and Levee and his limited development of Ma Rainey (Fisher B22). Another charges that Wilson spent too much time developing a communal bond among the musicians and not enough upon streamlining the content of the play. He also expresses concern that Ma Rainey is vaguely drawn, finding that Theresa Merritt's hard work cannot overcome this seeming deficiency (R. Brown 13).

Wilson wrote *Fences* in 1983 not only to address these concerns but also to prove to himself that he could raise a single character to a much grander scale. Initially he had no plans to write this riveting domestic drama, which ultimately won the most honors of any play in Broadway history, including a Tony for Best Play and a Pulitzer Prize. In fact, having already completed *Ma Rainey's Black Bottom* and *Jitney!*, he had intended to follow his own strategy, which was next to write *Joe Turner's Come and Gone* and then go on to complete *The Piano Lesson*. But Wilson listened to the advice of his circle of theatre professionals who encouraged him to bring some variety to the then well-populated and unwieldy patterns of construction familiar from *Jitney!* and *Ma Rainey's Black Bottom*. As a means of motivating the playwright to try his skills in other directions, they challenged him to write "a more commercial, conventional play with one main character and others supporting him" (Watlington 110). Such a play would test Wilson's skills at vivifying a complex character as successfully as he had drawn the enigmatic, one-dimensional figures of his earlier plays.

While still basking in the confidence gained from the success of *Ma Rainey*, Wilson accepted this challenge, assuring his chorus of theatrical cheerleaders that he could write such a play, but lingering doubt surfaced when he was alone with only a pen, a pad, and his thoughts. He remembered thinking, "After telling people that I knew how to write that kind of play, I asked myself "Do I really know how to write that kind of play? So I wrote *Fences* in answer to the challenge that I'd given myself" (Watlington 110). And just as *Ma Rainey's Black Bottom* quieted those who doubted Wilson as a serious playwright, *Fences* silenced those who feared his dramatic range had become predictable and limited.

In this attempt to write a better play than *Ma Rainey's Black Bottom*, Wilson decided to turn to the black family unit for his material. With the natural unity provided by the family structure, he could more easily focus upon a single character rather than divide the play's emphasis among a gathering of different personalities. Eventually the domestic drama set in "a middle American urban industrial city" (*F* xviii) generated a protagonist as full-blown as any of Shakespeare's tragic heroes or villains. Troy Maxson, the tyrant of a father and the doting yet unfaithful husband, commands a full range of emotions from pity to disgust. His family and all other characters pale beside his boisterous elocutions and selfish codes of behavior.

As was the case with each of his previous history chronicles, *Fences*, set in 1957, grew out of Wilson's desire to revisit the past in an effort to reexamine the behavior of blacks in various conflicted positions. Yet unlike *Ma Rainey's Black Bottom*, *Fences* does not hearken as far back as Africa. Instead, the play presents a portrait of three generations of black men whose roots converge in a brutish sharecropper of the Reconstruction era. His son, Troy Maxson, is a pivotal force; he is a fifty-three-year-old garbage collector of the late 1950s who still can recall ugly images of life under the iron rule of a frustrated, defeated father of the early 1900s. At the same time, Troy tries the best way he knows how to direct the course of his own son's life away from the negative influence of the boy's ancestors. Here, Wilson is concerned with a more immediate cultural heritage—one that involves voices from the past not as far removed as one's African ancestors but relatives who exist more immediately in the mind's eye. *Fences* typifies Wilson's belief that "you should start making connections to your parents and your grandparents and working backwards. We're not in Africa anymore, and we're not going back to Africa. You have to understand your parents and understand your grandparents" (Watlington 106). Apparently, by promoting the wisdom of living ancestors over that of one's African kin, Wilson makes more practical his admonition to today's black youth to sustain the African continuum.

For Wilson the drama of *Fences* is very much his own drama. The central conflict between father and son mirrors the difficult relationship between him and his stepfather, David Bedford, who died when Wilson was twenty-four. Only following Bedford's death, after the two had been at odds for some ten years, did Wilson discover that this man had been genuinely concerned about him and not just determined to hassle him about his decision to quit his high school football team. Wilson was stunned to learn Bedford's past:

> Bedford, it turned out, had been a high school football star in the 1930s, and had hoped a sports scholarship would lead to a career in medicine. But no Pittsburgh college would give a black player a grant and Bedford was too poor to pay his own way. To get the money, he decided to rob a store, and during the theft he killed a man. For the 23 years before he met Wilson's mother, Bedford had been in prison. By the time he was free, only a job in the city Sewer Department beckoned. (Freedman, "Voice" 49)

Wilson had an even more unstable relationship with his German biological father, Frederick Kittel, who had little to do with Wilson's mother, his sisters, brothers, or him. The young boy grew to dislike his white father and eventually identified exclusively with his mother's African heritage; later, the impact of this paternal aloofness on Wilson's life found its way into *Fences*. The playwright's own turbulent passage into manhood with neither financial nor emotional support from his father is reflected in the escalating battle royal between the antagonistic Troy and his defiant son Cory. Of course, certain identifiable aspects of Wilson's past have been altered, but for the most part, the main outlines remain remarkably similar in the play: the seemingly tyrannical father who once served time in prison for murder, who aspired to become a sports legend, who found unfulfilling work as a garbage collector, and who attempted to dictate his son's future. Thematically, however, the most important parallels between Wilson's memory and *Fences*'s conflict are the eventual epiphanies that both Wilson and Cory experience about their fathers' integrity. Both of these young men mature to some extent when they learn the entire scope of their fathers' actions and are led at least to understand the many reasons for the older men's callous behavior.

Troublesome relationships between fathers and their sons are aired often enough in Wilson's plays that drawing parallels between them and the rifts that separated him from his own father and stepfather becomes inevitable. In both *Jitney!* and *Fences*, for example, father figures Becker and Troy Maxson are fiercely proud of their so-called paternal responsibility, yet they both are ashamed of sons who choose not to follow their fathers' examples. Although Cory's failure to hold his job at the local A&P and his ambitions to play college football in no way match Booster's homicide conviction, in their fathers' estimation the sons are both major disappointments.

In addition to drawing from his own life as a basis for the tumultuous relations between Troy and Cory, Wilson also may have been influenced by similar circumstances in Philip Hayes Dean's *The Owl Killer* (1974), a play that he directed while affiliated with Pittsburgh's Black Horizons Theater. He acknowledges that this play had some influence upon his developing ear for the speech patterns of urbanized black migrants. The plot of this work has resonances with the August Wilson–David Bedford relationship. Emma and Noah Hamilton, a hardworking black couple residing in a small midwestern city called Moloch, have raised their two children to adulthood, yet both their daughter, Stella Mae, and their son, Lamar, bring shame to their parents. Stella Mae bears the children of several different men and steals another woman's husband while the son Lamar murders a man and, through the course of the play, is a desperate fugitive. In speeches reminiscent of lectures meted out by Becker and Troy Maxson, Noah Hamilton sounds Wilson's dominant, albeit problematic, theme of responsibility:

> For thirty years that hot oven has been suckin' th' blood outta me. And y'all layin' up on your behind parts ridin' me. Eatin' up my grub an' sleepin' out my bedclothes. Yes, I hated all y'all sittin' 'round while I had to go an' meet that man everyday. How'd you think I felt, knowin' y'all hated to see me comin'? All y'all ever wanted from me was what I was slavin' to get ahold of. That's all you ever wanted from me—a place to lay your head an' somethin' to put in your stomach. Use' to wish th' house would burn down with all y'all in it so I wouldn't have to feed your behinds. Yes, I took that cracker's shit, I had to. Couldn't do no better. 'Cause if I had knock him on his butt you wouldn't have nothin' to eat an' neither would them chaps. (Dean 90)

Variations on this pervasive motif inform Wilson's two fictional father-son relationships and cast some autobiographical shadows as well.

While *Ma Rainey's Black Bottom* represents Wilson's idea of the tragedy that results when blacks cannot gain a piece of the American Dream through their music, *Fences* explores similar devastation effected when the sports arena rejects them as well. In *Fences* Wilson fast-forwards past three decades, moving from the pre-Depression era of *Ma Rainey's Black Bottom* to the pre–Civil Rights era to examine the trials of black family life in racist America. World War II has left indelible scars on the Maxson family, just as racial segregation along with unchecked housing and job discrimination forces them to settle for far less than the American Dream promised to the country's veterans, its laborers, and to its citizens—black and white.

The late 1950s were also charged with the electricity of social change. As in Lorraine Hansberry's *Raisin in the Sun* (1959; set sometime after World War II) and Phillip Hayes Dean's *Sty of the Blind Pig* (1973; set in the period just before the beginning of the Civil Rights movement), the characters are in for profound changes in civil rights legislation, race relations, and overall improved conditions for blacks. Still ahead in the 1960s, thousands would march on Washington to demand fair treatment for blacks under the law, Malcolm X and the Reverend Martin Luther King, Jr. would raise the consciousness of the black masses, and discrimination within areas of housing, education, and employment would be significantly eased.

But the 1950s was a decade that brought significant legal action concerning black-white relations. Although in 1953, a federal district court in Washington, D.C., ruled that the doctrine of "separate but equal" permitted federally aided housing projects to bar Negroes if equal housing facilities were available, that doctrine was unanimously overturned by the Supreme Court in the landmark 1954 decision, *Brown v. Board of Education.* In 1955 the Reverend Martin Luther King, Jr. led Montgomery, Alabama, blacks in a boycott of the city's segregated buses, and in 1959 lunch counter segregation was challenged. In this atmosphere of impending positive changes in the country's racial attitudes, several headline sports stories reflected the continued resistance of white America to accepting racial integration: on October 27, 1954, for example, a Texas Court of Appeals in Austin overturned a state law against interracial boxing while on October 15, 1956, racial segregation of all sports in Louisiana (both for players and spectators) became legally enforceable under a new state law. Undoubtedly, the years extending from the end of World War II to the eve of the

Civil Rights movement witnessed mounting racial tensions. August Wilson manages to capture some of this tension in *Fences*.

Fences is situated at a juncture when vestiges of an old guard are dying away, thus making room for a new order. During the eight-year span of events in the play, the characters experience the impact of several important historical events to which they adapt or of which they become frustrated victims. Although the play proper begins in 1957, Troy's recollections reach as far back as the 1900s when he struggled under the cruel authority of a sharecropper father who was himself a product of the Reconstruction era. As soon as Troy came of age, he became part of the steady trickle from southern farmlands to northern cities.

The play opens as two middle-aged black men make their way home to celebrate another week's end. Troy Maxson and his friend Jim Bono collect garbage for a living. For eight hours a day, they bend, they stoop, and they hoist cans of refuse to the waiting mouth of a huge trash compactor. As he has done each Friday evening, Troy hands over his weekly paycheck to his wife, Rose, who manages their home. Troy and Jim tease each other and look forward to another weekend away from the mental and physical pressures of their jobs.

But Troy cannot put the pressure of his job behind him. Because he continues to witness blatant discrimination on his job and in other aspects of his daily existence, he harbors a deep-seated disgust for the racism of his country. For example, he fumes over the fact that all of his coworkers who lift garbage cans are black, and all who drive the trucks are white. But garbage collecting is one of the few professions now open to Troy. Although a top-notch baseball player during the Negro League's heyday, by 1957, he is too old to play on a desegregated Major League team.

These feelings of being passed over change Troy into a man obsessed with extorting from life an equal measure of what was robbed from him. Despite a seemingly loving and passionate relationship with his wife, Troy finds the "big-legged Florida gal," Alberta, irresistible. He is drawn into a physical relationship with her—one that produces their love child, Raynell. After Alberta dies in childbirth, Troy is left to raise the baby girl but finds that his only recourse is to plead with Rose to care for the motherless infant. Rose accepts this responsibility heroically, but at the same time she drives Troy away from her.

Troy's massive ego affects his son Cory as well. In tense dramatic episodes, Troy and Cory clash over the boy's plans to become a football player. When Cory is convinced by high school coaches that he has a future in football, he is quick to quit his afterschool job at the local A&P. Troy, who has other plans for Cory's future, secretly discourages an interested recruiter from scouting the boy's talents. As expected, Troy and Cory have a major argument, in which Troy encounters more opposition than he has ever gotten from any member of his family. Troy's brain-damaged brother, Gabriel, always worries that Troy is angry at him; Lyons, Troy's son from a previous marriage, avoids confrontation and visits his father only when he wants a small loan; and Rose exists as a mere shadow in Troy's presence until she learns that he has impregnated Alberta. However, throughout the play Cory dislikes his father's tactics and is not afraid to express his dissatisfaction, whether verbally, in the form of snide remarks, or physically, in a brief wrestling match.

The play ends in the 1960s, a decade that will bring significant changes for African Americans. The final scene takes place on the day of Troy's funeral: one of his favorite concocted stories about doing battle with the grim reaper has caught up with him, and he has died while batting the rag doll he tied to a tree in the yard. Previously alienated, the family members respond to Troy's death by tightening their communal bonds at this solemn occasion, and Rose gently convinces her prodigal son Cory to tear down the fences that have long existed between father and son.

Troy dies a lonely man, but with at least the hope that his son Cory would rise above the racism that had made him so bitter. For much of the play, he vividly recalls the hard life he was forced to endure because of the circumstances black men faced in America. Like many other naive ex-farmhands, Troy was surprised at what the North had to offer: "I thought I was in freedom. Shhh. Colored folks living down there on the river banks in whatever kind of shelter they could find for themselves. . . . Living in shacks made of sticks and paper" (*F* 54). While European immigrants in the early 1900s were welcomed into America's workforce—eventually earning (and able to borrow) enough capital to purchase land, homes, and businesses—blacks continued to be regarded as the country's outcasts. According to Wilson, "the city rejected them and they fled and settled along the riverbanks and under bridges" (*F*, "The Play"). Even though thousands like Troy were strapping young men eager to work, they were passed over for the racially preferred

white immigrants. Troy responded to this rejection and to the segregation that kept him from using his talents in Major League baseball by
adopting sheer survivalist codes of behavior: he resorted to stealing,
eventually murdered a man, and, as a result, was sentenced to fifteen
years in a penitentiary. Wilson knows all too well the thin line separat-
ing the fine, upstanding citizen and the prison convict: "Most black
talent is wasted. I'll tell you honestly, if I weren't doing this, I might be
out shooting drugs, or probably in a penitentiary" (Tallmer C4).

Troy is fifty-three-years old in 1957—old enough to become mellow
with the wisdom of past experience, yet too old to realize any more of
his dreams. The real tragedy of his existence is that this middle-aged
garbage man and many others like him could have, at another point in
time, surpassed even the likes of Jackie Robinson or Babe Ruth had he
been allowed to play Major League baseball. Some black veteran Negro
League players, like Troy, were too old to play in the Major Leagues
when teams finally started signing blacks in the late 1940s. Moreover,
the excellent young black athletes who began playing for Major League
teams had to endure a newer, more blatant form of discrimination.
Under threats of mass walkouts from white ballplayers and their refusal
to share accommodations with a black teammate, the first man to
integrate modern baseball, Jackie Robinson, realized that only a special
breed of black man could withstand such sanctioned abuse. In his
autobiography, *I Never Had It Made*, the legendary black baseball player
turned political activist recalls:

> This player had to be one who could take abuse, name-calling,
> rejection by fans and sportswriters and by fellow players not
> only on opposing teams but on his own. He had to be able to
> stand up in the face of merciless persecution and not retaliate.
> On the other hand, he had to be a contradiction in human
> terms; he still had to have spirit. He could not be an "Uncle
> Tom." His ability to turn the other cheek had to be predicated
> on his determination to gain acceptance. Once having proven
> his ability as player, teammate, and man, he had to be able to
> cast off humbleness and stand up as a full-fledged participant
> whose triumph did not carry the poison of bitterness. (40)

It is difficult to imagine that Troy—given his massive ego—would
agree to such accommodationist terms as those accepted by Robinson

and other blacks who broke the color line in baseball. While Troy relieves his anguish and bolsters his ego by touting his superiority over both black and white ballplayers and bad-mouthing the racist status quo, his sights seem to be focused exclusively upon being able to play the game. He does not consider that the early players were recruited in part for their ability to withstand the unending racial politics that followed them onto the field, into the clubhouse, and out on the road. Troy is not just a victim of his times but of his own thinking.

In addition to concentrating on the reluctant integration of the Major Leagues, the time frame of *Fences* draws attention to lingering scars caused by World War II. Twelve years have passed since the end of the war, yet it has ominous ramifications in the play. Troy's brother, Gabriel, suffered a head injury while engaged in combat and, as a result, is reduced to a mentally impaired though lovable fellow. Once a healthy young black man who willingly went to battle in Europe, he is now a transient shifting between Troy's house, a mental hospital, and a two-room flat that he rents from a neighbor. Gabriel's injuries and the minimal compensation he received from the government ($3,000) are further indication of how hostile the country was to black men, even to those who risked their lives while performing their civic duties. Gabriel is taunted by neighborhood children, and when he retaliates, he is locked up by authorities and released only after Troy pays a standard $50 fee. Gabriel has made a costly sacrifice, yet the country does not reward him with honors and medals. Instead he becomes part of its refuse. He is used up not only by his country but also, apparently, by his brother Troy, who claims Gabriel's settlement money and uses it as a down payment on a home but eventually commits him to a mental institution.

Cory personifies a new wave of optimism, but he must first confront and overcome the potentially emasculating dominance of two previous generations of Maxson men. Faced with a father who has grown to regard him as "just another nigger on the street" (*F* 87) and memories of a grandfather who sired children to be field hands, Cory is the hope of a new generation of black men. His unbridled enthusiasm about the possibility of attending college on a football scholarship suggests that he does not yet suffer from the defeatist attitudes that plagued the Maxson men before him. While Troy considers Cory's job at the A&P to be a fitting beginning to a future of similar work, Cory has his sights on much greater goals.

Fences explores the chemistry between black men—between fathers and sons, between brothers, and between lifelong friends. The most predictably turbulent relationship in the play is between a black man and his son. This historical pattern of polarized father-son relations within the black family is reflected in several other domestic dramas. The intensity of the father-son feud in Dean's *Owl Killer* (1974), for example, rivals the charged atmosphere generated by Troy and Cory Maxson. At the center of the dysfunctional Hamilton family is a father so disgusted with having to provide for his offspring that he unwittingly poisons them against him and drives them to murder and prostitution. Unlike Troy, however, Noah has legitimate reason to be disgusted with his only son, who robs a supermarket, mutilates its owner, and finally murders him. Still, the play implicates Noah as the primary cause of his children's destruction.

The friction between John Williams and his son Jeff in Joseph Walker's *River Niger* (1973) may also be blamed upon how the black father gauges "success" in a white-controlled society. The play, which is set in Harlem during the Black Power era, features philosopher, poet, father, husband, son-in-law, and devoted friend John Williams, who has taken to the bottle out of frustration over his unfulfilled ambitions. Although he is not aware of it, he attempts to recapture some of his dreams through Jeff, who he thinks has gone away to become an Air Force strategic air commander.

While the play resembles *Fences* in the heated disagreements between two generations of black men, a major distinction is in how Troy Maxson and John Williams regard the career choices of their sons. Both are aware of the extent to which black men must maneuver their way to the top in white-controlled fields, but because Troy was virtually shut out of Major League baseball, he wants his son to have no part in collegiate sports. John Williams, on the other hand, sees past the rough treatment blacks must endure to excel. When Jeff claims to be embarrassed to wear his Air Force uniform home because he does not believe in the United States anymore (only later confessing to his father that he could not adjust to constant ridicule by white instructors and found the math required in pilot training classes too difficult), John hungers to see him attired in full gear. He views his son's "right" to be an officer as a major accomplishment for all black people and urges him to "recognize that it's another fist jammed through the wall" (Walker 121).

Lonne Elder's *Ceremonies in Dark Old Men* (1969) also has as its backdrop the Black Power movement of the 1960s. Yet the relationship between the shiftless father, Russell Parker, and his nonworking sons, Theo and Bobby, is not a confrontational one; rather all three join forces to prolong their dependence upon their daughter and sister, Adele.

Fences reminds us that the politics of racial hatred that endured long past slavery continues to drive wedges between black men and their sons. Black men frequently lash out at their sons (or other blacks) as alternate targets instead of confronting head-on the emasculating racism or the social and economic pressures they encounter outside the home. Often their defense is that they must "break the spirits" of these young black men in their charge, just as one might discipline a horse to submission. Some, like Troy Maxson, rationalize that their downright mean treatment of their sons prepares them for the similar treatment that awaits them in society. These men let no opportunity pass without reminding their sons that they are the unquestionable authorities in their homes. Troy tells Cory, "You a man. Now, let's see you act like one. Turn your behind around and walk out this yard. And when you get out there in the alley . . . you can forget about this house. See? Cause this is my house" (*F* 86). Troy mirrors his own father's behavior as he vehemently denies his son's coming manhood and continues to relish his powerful roles—as Cory's father, as the sole provider, and as head of the Maxson household. Still other black men have no other reason for alienating their sons than a will to destroy their own loathed images.

Interestingly Troy gets along marvelously with his first son, Lyons, who is an unemployed deadbeat musician. Despite his troubled relationship with Cory, Troy somehow feels that it is best that he humor Lyons to compensate for being a fifteen-year absentee father/convict. While he hands over Lyons's usual $10 loan, the most resistance he can muster is, "Boy, your mama did a hell of a job raising you" (*F* 18). However, it is Cory, the son with boundless aspirations for a lucrative career and a college education, whom Troy opposes more. While on the surface it would appear that Troy is acting in Cory's best interest, his motives reveal an undercurrent of jealousy prompted by a fear that Cory will exceed him on all counts. Troy cannot envision that his son's athletic ability may finance his college education and does not even consider discussing the matter with Rose. Instead, acting in his usual autocratic manner, he maneuvers behind Cory's back to destroy the boy's chances of playing college football. He seems to gloat over this desperate display of authority, although it causes an already distant son to despise him.

But the complexity of Troy Maxson's character makes it difficult to pin on him the simple label "villain." His emphasis upon responsibility to his family gives him another dimension. Like Willie Loman, he has his share of human failings, yet he draws a degree of empathy because he is portrayed as a victim of his times. Society has dealt him blow after blow, yet he somehow sustains his all-important sense of pride and responsibility.

More important, Troy reverses a stereotype found in portrayals of the black family: the conspicuously absent father. The basic conflicts that emerged from such settings, therefore, revolved around the black female as sole head of the household, stoic in her resolve to hold her family together at all costs. Lorraine Hansberry's *Raisin in the Sun* (1959) and James Baldwin's *Amen Corner* (1968) present many of the often dramatized problems of the manless black household. Both the newly widowed Lena Younger and the long-abandoned Sister Margaret experience a sense of incompleteness, yet they accept their new roles and turn more intently to their God and to their children for solace.

For much of *Fences*, however, the nuclear family remains intact. Despite his flaws, this black father plays a dominant role in the family drama, not as a looming memory but as a powerfully present force. Although outwardly he appears hypocritical as he falls headfirst into an extramarital affair, Troy always manages to find his way home, carrying with him his weekly sack of potatoes, lard, and $76.42 paycheck: "It's my responsibility!" he tells Cory. "A man got to take care of his family" (*F* 38). Despite all of Troy's ugly recollections of his father, he is at least proud to pass on the fact that the sharecropper did not have the "walking blues." Ironically, it was Troy's mother who abandoned her eleven children, fleeing from an intolerably mean husband.

Troy Maxson's character is itself an amalgam of blues personalities. He is the "railroad man" who professed his love in one breath, with another explained why he must go, and with another hopped aboard a departing train. He is also a bluesman sunk low in depression of his own making, and whose woman is gone. According to him, despite doing right, he is the one who is constantly wronged. He has the trickster's edge, but the blues better characterizes Troy's actual and perceived circumstances. Although he tries to convey to his family and to his friend Bono the extent of his hurt, words cannot suffice to tell his story. To understand his character, one must go to the music. There, one may find the emotional equivalent of his seemingly irrational, unpredictable, and ultimately destructive actions in the heartrending lyrics of a blues melody. Coded in these lyrics is what Ralph Ellison describes in his review of Baraka's *Blues People* as "a transcendence of those conditions created within the Negro community by the denial of social justice. As such they are one of the techniques through which Negroes have survived and kept their courage during the long period when many whites assumed, as some still assume, they were afraid" (250).

Several episodes in *Fences* are so weighed down in despair that their emotional impact can only be fathomed by the language of the blues. For example, six months after Troy delivers the double blow to his wife Rose—he has had an affair with Alberta, and they have conceived a child—he sits alone on the steps to his home. He has handed over his two-month-old daughter, Raynell, to a now-estranged wife who is away at church preparing for a bake sale; Cory has taken to avoiding his father; and Gabriel has been finally committed to an institution. This is a low moment for Troy; he is utterly alone. But he does not demonstrate his profound sense of alienation by moaning or crying. Instead, he breaks into song about "a good old dog" named Blue.

> Hear it ring! Hear it ring!
> Had an old dog his name was Blue
> You know Blue was mighty true
> You know Blue as a good old dog
> Blue trees a possum in a hollow log
> You know from that he was a good old dog. (*F* 82)

The song not only fills the silence around him but it allows him to focus his pain. To some extent the supreme loyalty and the steadfast nature of this animal have earned Troy's respect. In some ways he and the dog are kindred spirits. But Troy does not finish singing his blues tribute to the old dog turned hero, because his friend Bono interrupts him. Not until the final scene of act 3—the day of Troy's funeral—do we learn the words to the entire folk tune. In a tender moment, Cory and his half-sister, Raynell, honor their father's spirit by resurrecting what has become Troy's theme song. Although virtual strangers, the brother and sister finish their father's tribute to Blue in harmony.

In addition to song, Troy's adaptation of the blues assumes a visual dimension as he stands cuddling his infant daughter outside a home where he is no longer welcome. His child is motherless, and he is womanless, yet he gathers enough strength to appeal to his long-suffering wife: "Rose . . . I'm standing here with my daughter in my arms. She ain't but a wee bittie little old thing. She don't know nothing about grownups' business. She innocent . . . and she ain't got no mama" (78). The degree of desperation in this moment may only be expressed in terms of the emotional depths conveyed by the blues.

According to Wilson, he began *Fences* "with the image of a man standing in his yard with a baby in his arms" (DeVries 25). From the play's inception, he was aware of the amount of dramatic leverage provided by this visually powerful image, born of his desire to prove that, contrary to myth, black men are responsible: "We have been told so many times how irresponsible we are as black males that I try and present positive images of responsibility" (25). But Troy appears not to pose much of a challenge to this myth. Although he heroically acknowledges the infant as his own—"She's my daughter, Rose. My own flesh and blood" (*F* 79)—his idea of responsibility is seen in his decision to hand over the child to someone who apparently is more responsible than he. Indeed, Wilson's perspective on responsibility might appear dubious to those unfamiliar with his decidedly male ethos, which he links to the history of black male-female relations in America. In an interview with Mark Rocha, Wilson states:

> You've got to understand the sociology of it. The transition from slavery to freedom was a cultural shock for blacks. All of a sudden black men had to ask themselves things like, "What is money?" "What is marriage?" Black women, for all their own struggles, were relatively stable. Economicially, they had control of the house. But what were black men supposed to do to make a living? (Rocha 38)

Still, for Wilson or any member of an audience to view Troy's actions as "responsible" depends on focusing not on the responsibility of the distraught middle-aged garbageman for the entire situation but on his responsibility in honoring his daughter and ultimately facing the evils of his own making. That he does not simply flee apparently saves him from the total damnation heaped upon so many black men caught in similar dilemmas.

Given Wilson's passionate empathy for black male characters, an otherwise brazen act is elevated to a sublime moment in *Fences*. When Troy delivers his illegitimate daughter to his wife, his gesture becomes a heroic act as well as the stuff of which blues songs aré made. Troy has used up all of his options and now has to present the emblem of his infidelity to the woman whom he has hurt most. His decision renders him homeless and womanless. His lover is dead, and his son detests him, yet he still musters the energy to confront the demons of his unfulfilled past.

In creating the marvelously complex and contradictory Troy Maxson, Wilson endows him with sparkling dialogue that exemplifies the playwright's steadily improving ear for the speech characteristic of a generation of blacks once removed from the South—contrary to the opinion of a number of critics who think this character is little more than words. "One wishes for less talk and more onstage action," David Lida of *Women's Wear Daily* complains (8). That "talk" is essential, however, as the play's protagonist speaks with rich figurative eloquence even though his economic status places him clearly below the poverty level. The poet in Wilson transforms Troy into the common man's bard who fashions protective armor out of his words to ward against symbolic emasculation.

Troy's entertaining anecdotes and searing monologues only seem incongruous with his station in life: in fact, language has become his most effective defense against victimization. That his own father was essentially a failure and a victim of the ruthless tenant farming system rests heavily upon Troy, for, as a young boy, he witnessed firsthand his father's destruction: "Sometimes I use to wonder why he was living. . . . He ain't knew how to do nothing but farm. No, he was trapped and I think he knew it" (*F* 51). Unfortunately, Troy's predicament is not very far removed from the bleak conditions that doomed his father—a dead-end job and no chance for a better life. Still, Troy's words portray him as the ultimate warrior, even though circumstances suggest otherwise. Expansive rhetoric justifies his wrongdoing, appeases his family, and apparently soothes his conscience.

Troy's fondness for talk is grounded in the African American oral tradition not yet affected by the cultural shock that followed the invention of the television and the spread of modern audiovisual devices. In fact, the Maxsons do not own a television set, and, as Troy explains to Cory, patching their leaky roof will most certainly take precedence over purchasing an electronic gadget. In the absence of such diversions, verbal communication becomes an art form for Troy. Rarely does he spare words when he has an opportunity to dominate center stage. When Rose cautions him against consuming too much liquor, he launches into a speech on death based upon a series of metaphors that provide a window to his character. By invoking the rules of baseball, he familiarizes death's power: "Death ain't nothing but a fastball on an outside corner" (10). By borrowing images from the military, he acknowledges and, to some extent, admires death's persistence: "I looked up one day and Death was marching straight at me. The middle of July, 1941" (11). And by alluding to wrestling, he suggests that he, as if heeding the speaker of Dylan Thomas's poem, will not "go gentle into that good night: "We wrestled for three days and three nights. I can't say where I found the strength from. Every time it seemed like he was gonna get the best of me, I'd reach way down deep inside myself and find the strength to do him one better" (12).

In addition to being a master at metaphors, Troy is skilled at using language to deflect attention from his faults. One of the most dramatically poignant moments in *Fences* occurs when Troy scrambles to find suitable words to explain to his wife of eighteen years that he has fathered a child with another woman: "I'm trying to find a way to tell you . . . I'm gonna be a daddy. I'm gonna be somebody's daddy" (66). He is moving as he justifies his relationship with Alberta, the "other woman": "I can sit up in her house and laugh. Do you understand what I'm saying. I can laugh . . . and it feels good. It reaches all the way down to the bottom of my shoes" (69). He even succeeds at presenting a convincing plea to Rose to take in and raise his orphaned daughter as her own. Apparently language creates a larger-than-life reality for Troy. In each of these situations, Troy's words redirect any feelings of guilt away from himself. He seems free from remorse and actually appears heroic against all charges while a less eloquent man might appear villainous.

Like all of Wilson's plays to date, *Fences* is very much a black man's story. Black women do have appreciable roles in his dramas; however, they seldom are as developed as the men, who freely commune with other black men, whether in a dingy bandroom, on a back porch stoop, at a kitchen table, or in a one-room cafe. Wilson's sharply drawn male characters are, no doubt, also the result of his early devotion to listening to their conversations in the barrooms and tobacco houses of Pittsburgh. As a young, inexperienced poet who admitted that his verse suffered because he knew nothing of the world, he unconsciously absorbed the larger-than-life narratives of these storytellers. Also, deep within the psyche of young Wilson was (and still is) an urge to search for and create the image of a father he never had, one who would fill his son's head with his wisdom and guide him toward a responsible adulthood. As evidenced by Troy, Wilson assembles from the variety of black men that he has encountered a paternal image—by no means angelic, but an image of a father nonetheless.

He offers no apologies for an emphasis that he deems his privilege as a playwright who happens also to be a man:

> I doubt seriously if I would make a woman the focus of my work simply because of the fact that I am a man, and I guess because of the ground on which I stand and the viewpoint from which I perceive the world. I can't do that although I try to be honest in the instances in which I do have women. I try to portray them from their own viewpoint as opposed to my viewpoint. (interviewed by the author)

Wilson's black female characters are also not as fully developed as the black males because they are frequently less vocal during the brainstorming sessions that the playwright conducts in his mind as he lays the foundation for his next play.

Regardless of the process behind Wilson's depictions of his characters, the women's realities are decidedly different from those of the men around them and are limited to those possibilities sustained and promoted by Western culture. Critic and novelist Marilyn French sees a general dualism in the portrayal of women: "This split in principle of nature, the feminine principle, still exists in our perception of actual women; there is the mother madonna, and the whore; the nourisher and the castrator. This split in the feminine principle I call inlaw and outlaw aspects of it" (23). According to French, the outlaw is described in terms of "darkness, chaos, flesh, the sinister, magic and above all, sexuality," while the inlaw suggests completely different values: "nutritiveness, compassion, mercy, and the ability to create felicity" (24).

These two categories can be usefully applied to the women in *Fences*. Consider Troy's mistress Alberta as an "outlaw": she disrupts the Maxson family circle, sundering relationships between husband and wife and father and son as well as the deeply fraternal bond between

Troy and Bono. She represents everything that sticks its tongue out at the responsibility that Troy faces as a family man and as head of the household. She demands nothing of him—not his loyalty, not his money, not even his time. She provides a haven from the chronic concerns of survival weighing down upon the frustrated garbage collector and would-be Major Leaguer, a place where he can simply laugh out loud. Nevertheless, Alberta is not blamed as the "whore," though she is the key to the disintegration of the Maxson family and ultimately to Troy's tragic demise. When Rose finally does learn about Troy's affair, her fury is directed solely at her husband as a willing party, not at Alberta as his temptress. Never physically appearing in the play, known only through conversations about her, Alberta becomes merely a manifestation of Troy's own flawed character.

While the outlaw Alberta appeals to Troy's hedonistic nature, the "inlaw" Rose reminds him of responsibility. She manages the home, wrestles with daily worries over money, and single-handedly tries to keep the Maxson family together. She does all of this while willfully neglecting to establish time and space for her own growth. As her name suggests, Rose thrives amid adversity and stands out from the moral squalor around her. While few might be expected to withstand the amount of humiliation she endures, Rose seems to thrive upon it; she is able to transform a motherless infant into a stable young girl and pull the loose threads of her family together at the play's end.

Rose Maxson lingers half in the shadows during the entire first act of *Fences*, speaking largely in reaction to her husband's exaggerated stories about himself. However, when she finally discovers her voice, she is convincing even as her character transforms. Though before she was the predictable image of temperance, she suddenly becomes a woman who stands eye-to-eye with her egoistic husband: "I been standing with you! I been right here with you, Troy. I got a life too. I gave eighteen years of my life to stand in the same spot with you. Don't you think I ever wanted other things? Don't you think I had dreams and hopes?" (70–71). In one impassioned scene, Rose's entire history rushes forward out of nearly two decades of dormancy. Yet this moment of revelation does not lessen Rose Maxson's extreme altruism. She is so thoroughly and persistently moral that her character becomes more obviously symbolic than realistic. She is her husband's conscience, quite literally his better half. Like Alberta, she is basically an extension of Troy's ego, not one whose own story requires a full hearing. Her eighteen-year suppression of self and allegiance to family perfectly match the mold of the inlaw, for as French describes it, the inlaw prototype "requires volitional subordination[;] . . . it values above all the good of the whole . . . and finds pleasure in that good rather than in assertion of self" (24).

At the same time, Wilson gives this representation of a feminine principle firm grounding in the actual lives of black wives and mothers. Actress Mary Alice, for whom Wilson created the role of Rose and who starred in *Fences*'s 1984 Broadway production, offers some insights into the role.[1] In an interview following one of many celebrated performances, she detailed her initiation to playing the altruistic heroine: "I just started with what had been given by the writer, what Rose says, what is said about her. I suppose I somehow used women that I knew, women I knew in 1957. . . . A lot of who I am is also Rose. I know many women who are waiting, as she says, to bloom, and many will never bloom" (H. Henderson 68).

Among August Wilson's early depictions of women are the irrepressible Ma Rainey and the long-suffering Rose. Although these images of black women suggest that the playwright's sensibilities are informed more by cultural conventions than by realities, in both cases he prevents them from being perceived as purely one-dimensional or as victims. To the contrary, he demonstrates that each woman actively chooses her life and thus preserves an all-important sense of empowerment. Such power allows Ma Rainey to force her white business associates to realize how very integral she is to their moneymaking enterprise and allows Rose to stand her ground against Troy.

Wilson's symbolic depictions of black women such as Rose have their basis in his capabilities as a poet. Also a by-product of his grounding in poetry is a conscious tendency to incorporate powerful metaphors to communicate his plays' larger thematic concerns. He believes this to be an important part of his strength as a dramatist: "The idea of metaphor . . . is a very large idea in my plays and something that I find lacking in most other contemporary plays. . . . I think I write the kinds of plays that I do because I have twenty-six years of writing poetry underneath all that" (interview).

The title image of *Fences*, the third play in Wilson's black history chronicle, very appropriately conveys a number of realities for the black family of late '50s America. It raises issues ranging from economic and professional deprivation to emotional and moral isolation. The fence, which may either inhibit or protect, is both a positive and negative image to various members of the Maxson family. To Rose, who nags Troy about completing this wooden border, the fence promises to keep in those whom she loves, preventing them from leaving the fortress she so lovingly sustains for them. To Cory, however, the fence becomes a tangible symbol of all that stands in the way of his independence. His work on it is merely an exercise in obedience and a reminder that he is not yet a man—at least not to Troy. To Troy, the fence represents added restrictions placed upon him. Thus he half-heartedly erects one section of the fence at a time and completes the job only after accepting a challenge from Bono, who agrees to buy his wife, Lucille, a refrigerator as soon as Troy completes the fence. It takes Bono to explain to him the importance of the fence:

> CORY: I don't know why Mama want a fence around the yard noways.
> TROY: Damn if I know either. What the hell she keeping out with it? She ain't got nothing nobody want.
> BONO: Some people build fences to keep people out . . . and other people build fences to keep people in. Rose wants to hold on to you all. She loves you. (*F* 61)

On a deeper level, Troy sees the fence's completion as a reminder of his own mortality; he senses that he is erecting his own monument. His anxiety about death's inevitability emerges when his longtime friend questions Troy's choice of wood:

> BONO: You don't need this wood [hard wood]. You can put it up with pine wood and it'll stand as long as you gonna be here looking at it.
> TROY: How you know how long I'm gonna be here, nigger? Hell, I might just live forever. Live longer than old man Horsely. (60)

Troy's reluctance to complete the fence seems ominous, for shortly after finishing it for Rose, he dies. The fence, then, becomes a gauge for his life, during which he experiences both literal and figurative incarceration. He is fenced off from society during a lengthy prison term; he is fenced out of the Major Leagues because of racial segregation; and after he initiates the breakup of his family, he is fenced out of his home as well as out of the hearts of Rose and Cory.

Other metaphors that the poet-turned-playwright effectively weaves throughout *Fences* adopt their imagery from the game of baseball. Images of the game loom large in the consciousness of the onetime Negro Leaguer, Troy, who often borrows the behavioral codes of this game to suit various situations in his life. Part of the tragedy of *Fences* is Troy's belief that he would have surpassed current black players and the white Major League players of his youth had he been allowed to play among them. His ego and professional potential have been devastated because he has been cheated out of at least a chance to play Major League ball. As an outward manifestation of the blues he surely feels because of this loss, Troy adopts the language of the game in order to explain the "deprivation of possibility" (Reed 93) that has hurt him so deeply.

For Troy, life is a baseball game riddled with fast balls, curve balls, sacrifice flies, and an occasional strikeout, but too few homeruns. Although the conflict of the ball game lasts for only nine innings, Troy sees himself as being constantly at bat. From keeping death at bay to announcing a "full count" against his defiant son Cory, Troy flavors his conversation with baseball metaphors at every chance he gets. The various rules of the game become his basis for interpreting his actions and another avenue for expressing his blues. His preoccupation with images associated with the traditionally masculine, extremely competitive sport robs him of the candor necessary to handle the delicate relationships in his life. In one of the most intense moments of the play, Troy struggles to explain to his wife that he has not only been unfaithful to her but has also fathered a child outside of their marriage bed: "I fooled them, Rose. I bunted. When I found you and Cory and a halfway decent job . . . I was safe. Couldn't nothing touch me. I wasn't gonna strike out no more. . . . I stood on first base for eighteen years and I thought . . . well, goddamn it . . . go on for it!" (*F* 70). In using this second language, Troy comes to live it. He completely alienates both his son and his wife by forcing upon them his very selfish view of life. Consequently, he cannot see past immediate self-gratification; he cannot compromise, nor can he ask for forgiveness.

Wilson's use of metaphor in *Fences* extends to include Gabriel, Troy's disabled brother. Gabriel's war injury, a severe head wound, required that a metal plate be surgically implanted in his head. The brain-damaged Gabriel fantasizes that he is Archangel Gabriel, whose tasks are to open Heaven's pearly gates and to chase away hellhounds. When Troy is certain of Gabriel's irreversible condition, he claims the $3,000 compensation awarded his brother and uses it to purchase the home where he, Rose, Cory, and Gabriel live.

Gabriel is what Wilson refers to as a "spectacle character" (interview), whose role, as its label suggests, is to command attention and to force both acknowledgment and understanding of issues that are sooner ignored. Here, he serves as a glaring reminder of the crippling injustices black men endure at the hands of their own country. Wilson notes, "This black man had suffered this wound fighting for a country in which his brother could not play baseball." America cannot hide the shame of thousands of black veterans like Gabriel, who sacrificed dearly in the service of their country yet possibly faced homelessness, prison, or the insane asylum upon their return. Gabriel's payment of $3,000 is ludicrously low for an injury that has maimed him for life.

Although Gabriel is not crucial to the central conflict of *Fences*, his presence gives Troy another dimension. In addition to being an embarrassing emblem of America's darker side, Gabriel is also a manifestation of the worst in Troy. He exposes a man who has become immune to the emotions of self-pity and remorse; a man who, after capitalizing on his brother's misfortune, has him committed to a mental institution. Troy has become so devastated by his own deferred dreams that nothing, save pleasing himself, matters to him. He can sign papers to prevent his son from receiving free tuition as a football recruit; he can sign papers to put his brother away indefinitely. To Wilson, Gabriel has a significant function in *Fences*, and he is bothered by critics who dismiss this wounded man as a halfwit:

> They [critics] make me mad when I read the reviews and they would refer to Gabriel as an idiot. . . . Gabriel is one of those self-sufficient characters. He gets up and goes to work every day. He goes out and collects those discarded fruit and vegetables, but he's taking care of himself. He doesn't want Troy to take care of him. He moves out of Troy's house and lives down there and pays his rent to the extent that he is able. (interview)

Unfortunately theatre critics were not alone in discounting the significance of Gabriel to the overall message of *Fences*. Broadway producer Carol Shorenstein, who invested some $850,000 to bring the play to New York, felt that Gabriel's role was superfluous and feared that sophisticated Broadway audiences would roll their eyes at the final scene when he strains to blow his horn to open the pearly gates for Troy. Shorenstein's apprehensions were fueled by a string of negative reactions to Gabriel following performances of the play in New Haven, Chicago, and San Francisco. One critic complained that the ending was "so silly that it was ridiculous!" (Alice, videotaped lecture).[2] In fact, Shorenstein was so worried about making good her investment that she advocated eliminating Gabriel entirely from the script and writing a new ending. With this in mind, she staged a series of meetings with key figures involved in the play and decided—without Wilson's input or approval—to change the ending of *Fences*.[3] Out of these meetings came several alternate endings that were tested on stage, yet none proved satisfactory.

Shorenstein's persistence about eliminating Gabriel affected her working relationship with Richards and Wilson. When Richards, as director, refused to tamper with Wilson's work on the grounds that such alterations would violate its artistic integrity, Shorenstein moved to fire him and replace him with a director who would acquiesce to her suggested changes. At this point, Wilson could no longer contain his anger: "It is your right to fire the director," he told her. "But you cannot hire another director without my approval" (Alice, videotaped lecture). Shorenstein apparently withdrew her campaign and reluctantly took *Fences* to New York, still harboring grave doubts about its potential to succeed and about keeping Richards on as its director. The play opened on Broadway on March 26, 1987, to rave reviews—its original ending intact.

Ironically, none of the suggested changes for *Fences*'s ending turned out to be an improvement over Wilson's original finale. From her perspective as a member of the cast, Mary Alice believed all along that the play's original ending was appropriate, given the depressing turn of events that the audience witnesses. She notes, "The audience was already dealing with the fact that this man that they had experienced for close to two hours was dead, and there's a whole scene that deals with the fact that he is dead. And so what they needed was something that would give them this release, and the original ending provided that" (Alice, videotaped lecture). According to Mary Alice, Gabriel's frustrated attempts to sound his horn, his "slow, strange dance" (*F* 101), his howling/singing, and his last words, "That's the way that go" (101), drew laughter from the audience and raised their spirits just before the curtain fell.

Wilson plays upon the dramatic tension inherent in the spectacle of Gabriel's character, but he also relies upon this highly sensitive man to introduce an identifiable element of African American culture: belief in a spiritual world. Although Gabriel's perceptions of Christianity and images associated with the afterlife are apparently the results of his dementia, he articulates several myths that have their origins in traditional religious beliefs among African Americans. For example, he revives the myth of Saint Peter, so-called keeper of the pearly gates, and keeps alive the fear of Judgment Day: "Ain't gonna be too much of a battle when God get to waving that Judgment sword. But the people's gonna have a hell of a time trying to get into heaven if them gates ain't open" (*F* 47–48).

Gabriel also confirms the existence of a great Judgment Book in which Saint Peter records "everybody's name what was ever been born" (26). Gabriel, who believes he has already died and gone to Heaven, is a privileged soul, for, according to him, Saint Peter has allowed him to see both Troy and Rose's names recorded in the ledger. And, again, according to Gabriel, he sometimes relieves Saint Peter from the eternal task of guarding the pearly gates: "Did you know when I was in heaven . . . every morning me and St. Peter would sit down by the gate and eat some big fat biscuits? Oh, yeah! We had us a good time. We'd sit there and eat us them biscuits and then St. Peter would go off to sleep and tell me to wake him up when it's time to open the gates for the judgment" (26).

Each encounter with Gabriel convinces one to look beyond his surface disability and concentrate instead upon the spiritual and mythical worlds he creates and the realms of possibility that these worlds offer. Gabriel's ability to look beyond the literal is his own means of negotiating an indifferent world, yet it also exemplifies a long-standing Christian belief among African Americans to look toward things-not-seen for salvation. He has adopted both a frame of mind and a vision that get him through the daily drudgery of his condition. This special vision is most evident in the final scene of *Fences*, when the Maxson family prepares to bury Troy. At this time Gabriel experiences "a trauma that a sane and normal mind would be unable to withstand. He begins to dance. A slow, strange dance, eerie and life-giving. A dance of atavistic signature and ritual. . . . He finishes his dance and the gates of heaven stand open as wide as God's closet" (101). As a spectacle character, Gabriel's significance is in providing a flawed icon of African Americans' cultural past. He is a cultural paradox—not taken seriously by those around him yet conveying in his distorted sensibilities the cultural bedrock of generations past and to come.

In addition to the controversy over Gabriel, Wilson has been involved in several other battles involving what he perceives as affronts to the artistic integrity of his work. A man not given to compromise, Wilson found himself embroiled with Paramount Pictures over their reluctance to hire a black director for a proposed movie version of *Fences*. In fact, Paramount initially targeted white director Barry Levinson for the job without expending any appreciable effort to enlist the services of a black director who might be equally or better qualified. Though Paramount owned the movie rights to *Fences*, purchased in 1987 for an estimated $500,000, Wilson still exerted pressure on them to search seriously for and hire a black director. In a passionate essay, "I Want a Black Director," Wilson lambastes both Eddie Murphy for his cavalier comment—"I don't want to hire nobody just 'cause they're black" (A25)—and Paramount Pictures for their apparent insensitivity to the issue. The essay was inspired by a conversation between Murphy and Wilson during which they hashed out the possibility of converting *Fences* into a movie. Wilson's angry response, which opened a tense debate among black directors and movie producers dealing with similar culturally sensitive material, effectively deconstructs Murphy's statement, exposing trends of opportunism and insensitivity that he believes characterize white America's regard for black talent in particular and black culture in general. On one hand, "What is being implied is that the only qualification any black has is the color of his skin"; on the other, "Some Americans, black and white, would deny that a black American culture even exists" (A25).

While Wilson questions Murphy's motives, he simultaneously asserts a fundamental artistic belief that is undoubtedly responsible for his long, amicable collaboration with Richards: "I wanted to hire somebody talented, who understood the play and saw the possibilities of the film, who would approach my work with the same amount of passion and measure of respect with which I approach it, and who shared the cultural responsibilities of the characters" (A25). Although to date *Fences* has not made its debut on the big screen, Wilson seems satisfied that at least he has expressed his artistic concerns to the rarely chal-lenged media giant. Despite profound differences over who should translate *Fences* to the screen, Paramount's $500,000 investment clearly indicates that its backers believe that the play has the potential to attract a wider movie-going audience and make a profit for the company.

Wilson's campaign to exert pressure upon Paramount led to some interesting reverberations among contemporary black directors who saw him as both a hero and a troublemaker. While on a trip to Holly-wood, he was introduced to another side of the furor that he unleashed. According to one black director, who claimed to represent the senti-ments of numerous others who were on the verge of breaking the stereotype limiting black directors to black subjects, Wilson's crusade would keep them unemployed. In a candid conversation, he enlight-ened Wilson on the paradoxical nature of the controversy: "I appreciate what you're doing by wanting a black director, but we've been out here for fifteen years telling these people it don't matter if we're black or not. We're trying to get a job directing 'LA Law,' and we've been telling them it don't matter. . . . Here you come along wanting us to say that it does matter. We can't say that" (interview). Although Wilson was sympa-thetic to this director's plight, he claims that his efforts should not be misconstrued as "carrying a banner for black directors. I am trying to get the film of my play made in the best possible way" ("I Want" A25).

Regardless of the commercial concerns surrounding a possible film version, the play continues to speak to all types of families in turmoil similar to that of the Maxsons, for, among other things, *Fences* is a play about generations. According to Wilson, it addresses the question, "Are the tools we are given sufficient to compete in a world that is different from the one our parents knew?" (Savran 299). Given Troy's unfortu-nate past, frustrating present, and dismal future, the answer to this question is a resounding "No!" Like a dinosaur, Troy has lumbered into a new age when it is not enough for a man to mete out harsh discipline or to bring home his paycheck or to rule over his wife and home. As he approaches his sixties, Troy shows no signs of giving up the crude codes of behavior that prevailed in his father's house, nor is he willing to conform to the new standards set by a world poised for change. Only death merits his respect. On the occasion of Troy's funeral, the members of the Maxson family convene and heal past emotional wounds that have kept them apart. That Troy's death brings together a family that he has torn apart has ironic significance, for, in the terms of his favorite baseball metaphor, it is his ultimate sacrifice play.

While the men in *Ma Rainey's* band collectively create a blues portrait of the black man's predicament in urban America, Troy Maxson singularly embodies the same. This 1950s hybrid husband, father, and brother is a living testament to what oppression of generations of black families has produced. One part of him reflects his sharecropper father's strong work ethic and sense of responsibility while another reveals his defiance against a system that has denied him the chance to elevate both his and his family's circumstances. He wages constant battles on his job and within his home between old ethics and new realities. Thus his character is charged with the tension that results when these two worlds collide.

In an effort to breathe more life into a singular character, Wilson stretches his dramatic skills to create the brutish, loquacious, and domineering, yet pensive, sensitive, and lovable Troy Maxson; in so doing, he silenced those critics who doubted his dramatic range. This character—who represents a large number of black men in his day caught between the difficulties of being responsible in a white-controlled world and being free to pursue their own desires and ambitions—is an indicator of Wilson's ability to move beyond the multiple shallow characterizations in *Ma Rainey's Black Bottom* and *Jitney!*. Clive Barnes, theatre critic for the *New York Post*, found that the play's very human portrayals "transfixed" him during *Fences*'s Broadway opening on March 26, 1987: "Once in a rare while, you come across a play—or a movie or a novel—that seems to break away from the confines of art into a dense, complex realization of reality. A veil has been torn aside, the artist has disappeared into a transparency. We look with our own eyes, feel with our own hearts" ("Fiery Fences" 23). When all of Troy's fears and insecurities associated with being a black man in 1957 clash with the demons of his past, a bluesman of tragic proportion is born. As a result Troy Maxson can hold his own among protagonists such as Miller's Willie Loman, Hansberry's Walter Lee Younger, and Shakespeare's Hamlet.

Without question the dual successes of *Ma Rainey's Black Bottom* and *Fences* garnered Wilson a prominent place in American theatre and, just as important, bolstered his confidence as a serious playwright. The energy he poured into his next play, *Joe Turner's Come and Gone*, his fourth history chronicle, came more from sheer artistic allegiance to

completing his ten-play project rather than from any desire to win again
the accolades heaped upon his previous work. Wilson wanted to sustain
his momentum, even if it meant ignoring some of the hype surrounding
his previous achievements to focus upon a work in progress. In fact, by
the time *Ma Rainey's Black Bottom* had made its way to Broadway in the
fall of 1984, Wilson had already completed *Joe Turner*. And even before
Fences had made its way across the country's regional theatre circuit and
onto Broadway in the spring of 1987, *Joe Turner* was in production at the
Yale Repertory Theatre.

FIVE

Finding One's Song:
Joe Turner's Come and Gone

From left to right:
Bo Ruckner as Jeremy Furlow,
L. Scott Caldwell as Bertha Holly,
Ed Hall as Bynum, Mel Winkler as Seth Holly,
Kippen Hay as Zonia Loomis, and Delroy Lindo as
Herald Loomis in the 1986 Yale Repertory Theatre produc-
tion of *Joe Turner's Come and Gone*. In this scene,
Herald Loomis's foreboding presence
upsets the tenants of the
Holly boardinghouse.
Photograph by William B.
Carter. Reprinted by permission.

Joe Turner's Come and Gone has very little in common with *Fences*. While the domestic drama about the Maxson family might be subtitled "The Anatomy of Troy Maxson," *Joe Turner* presents a kaleidoscopic view of black men and women who are themselves so culturally disoriented that only fragments of their characters are revealed. Thus, the play is a patchwork of episodes in the lives of post–Reconstruction blacks as they attempt to start new lives or, as Wilson puts it, find their song in strange northern territory.

The theme of finding one's song, which permeates *Joe Turner*, is simultaneously a personal and collective ambition for Wilson and for all of black America. In addition to featuring a host of fictitious personalities, the play is informed by aspects of Wilson's private past—a past, that, according to him, traces his grandmother's trek from a racist South to a hostile North. For Wilson as poet and playwright, finding his song means finding an individual artistic voice despite the anxiety of influence. For Wilson as a black man in America, finding his song means going back to the forgotten regions of his African past, bypassing the influence of his father's German ancestry to confront head-on the painful elements of his mother's history as an African woman who lives in America. Hers is the history he claims, but it is a history drawn to the forefront in his work by a selective process of gathering and piecing together images from both imagined and actual experiences. He explains:

> It was my song. It had come from way deep inside me. I looked way back in my memory and gathered up pieces and snatches of things to make that song. I was making it up out of myself. And that song helped me on the road. Made it smooth to where my footsteps didn't bite back at me. All that time that song was getting bigger and bigger. That song was growing with each step of the road. It got so that I used all of myself up in the making of that song." (C. Brown 126)

Wilson's odyssey to find his song is the basis for a larger strategy to help all black Americans to do the same. He invites them to acknowledge their African beginnings via a journey of symbolic healing, one play at a time. *Joe Turner's Come and Gone* is such a play.

The fourth in Wilson's ten-play cycle, it is set in Pittsburgh in 1911 when blacks continued to reel from the disorientation brought on by years of slavery and by an ongoing mass exodus to northern cities.

Accordingly the play focuses upon cultural fragmentation, that is, the emotional and physical effects associated with cultural upheaval and physical relocation. Herald Loomis, the play's protagonist, is one of many lost souls in this environment. As the play opens, he and his young daughter, Zonia, come upon a boardinghouse where he seeks clues as to the whereabouts of his estranged wife, Martha. Seven years earlier, Loomis had become one of the numerous kidnapped farmhands of legendary Joe Turner, who notoriously tricked freed black men into extended periods of forced labor. Now, finally released, he tries to locate his family only to find his wife, Martha, and daughter evicted and long gone from the meager tenant farmer's dwelling where he had left them. He tracks down little Zonia at his mother-in-law's house but wages a long and tiring search for his wife, who has found solace in a distant church.

With the assistance of the celebrated People Finder, Rutherford Selig, Martha, who has taken the name Pentecost in place of Loomis, finally comes to the boardinghouse; she nearly misses her former husband and little girl, who have been recently evicted by the proprietor. Yet when the family does finally meet, only a partial reunion takes place. Martha reclaims her daughter, yet cannot accept the heathen Loomis. To coax him away from what she sees as his life of sin, she launches into a sermon whose text involves being "washed in the blood of the lamb." Loomis, having finally "found his song"—his identity or place in the world—responds by slashing his chest in a heavily symbolic denunciation of her God and affirmation of himself: "I don't need nobody to bleed for me! I can bleed for myself" (*JT* 93).

The time period featured in *Joe Turner's Come and Gone* is charged with the emotions associated with displacement, alienation, and isolation. The historical context out of which the play evolves includes a backdrop of frustrated sharecroppers; hundreds of unemployed, unskilled laborers; countless broken families; and a pervasive rumor of a better life up North. In his attempt to inspire his audiences to redress the history of this period, Wilson introduces the theme of finding one's song as a healing measure. In the face of staggering odds, each character is, in some way, compelled to find something to make his or her life complete. As they search for their songs, they wander for great lengths of time on what seem to be aimless paths.

To create drama out of this very unstable era in black American history, the playwright stretches to encompass four hundred years of African American presence in America and to create a link between past and present descendants of Africa and hundreds of thousands of historically forgotten southern migrants. W. E. B. Du Bois, like Wilson, saw drama in the very existence of African Americans who endured such oppression. In his exhaustive sociological study *Black Reconstruction in America*, he notes, "Easily the most dramatic episode in American history was the sudden move to free four million black slaves in an effort to stop a great civil war, to end forty years of bitter controversy, and to appease the moral sense of civilization" (3). In epic fashion Richard Wright's Twelve Million Black Voices documents the lean years following the Emancipation Proclamation, when freedmen and their families could not escape the system of sharecropping that engulfed them.

When they finally left their dilapidated shacks next to the cotton fields, they headed North to cities like Chicago, Washington, Philadelphia, and, of course, Pittsburgh. Wilson captures these haunting images in a prefatory note to the play: "From the deep and the near South the sons and daughters of newly freed American slaves wander into the city [Pittsburgh]. Isolated, cut off from memory, having forgotten the names of the gods and only guessing at their faces, they arrive dazed and stunned, their hearts kicking in their chest with a song worth singing" (*JT*, "The Play"). For many blacks, the decision to migrate up North was not a spontaneous one. Concerns about leaving behind homes, jobs, loved ones, and familiar surroundings were carefully weighed before striking out on such a life-changing journey. Also, potential migrants faced pressing questions about the gradual and often painful process of relocation. For example, they had to decide whether to uproot an entire family at once or send one relative up North to assess employment and housing possibilities; if conditions proved favorable, remaining family members would follow.

Joe Turner's Come and Gone is the product of Wilson's keen powers of observation, which allow him to make art out of a patchwork of personal impressions. He describes the development of *Joe Turner*: "In imagination I knew, for instance, that they had outhouses as opposed to toilets, so that's in there. They had horses as opposed to cars, so Seth comes in and says 'Henry Allan tried to sell me that old piece of horse he got.' Things like that." (Barbour 12). Joan Fishman notes that in creating the premise and set for *Joe Turner*, Wilson "took elements of one real life, Bearden's, and combined them with elements of other real lives, and he created a drama" (136). For example, the play's boarding-house setting, along with other elements of Pittsburgh local color that appear in the play, was influenced by *The Twenties* (n.d.), Bearden's series of paintings depicting certain images of his childhood stay in the steel town with his maternal grandmother. Moreover, Reuben, the young boy in *Joe Turner* who grows attached to his deceased friend's pigeons and reneges on a promise to free them, is based upon Bearden's life as a boy; the character grew out of Wilson's ideas of how the young Bearden may have responded to this environment. Further details of the plot closely resemble Bearden's actual experiences in Pittsburgh:

> Bearden lived in this house [his grandmother's boardinghouse] in the mid-1920s. It was here that he met Eugene, a sickly child who taught him to draw. Bearden's grandmother was pleased with her grandson's interest until she discovered that the bulk of the artwork was drawings of the nearby brothel where Eugene lived and his mother was employed. Bearden's grandmother immediately moved Eugene into her home, and he brought with him his collection of pigeons and doves, which Eugene made Bearden promise to free when Eugene died. This occurred one year later. (136)

From the play's inception, Wilson knew that *Joe Turner* would not be like any of his previous works. In fact, he came to the project determined "to create the sense of a whole other world" and to do so by "looking at the familiar in a new way" (Powers 54). This inclination toward what the Russian Formalist Viktor Shklovsky called "defamiliarization"[1] here entails regarding the past as an alien landscape littered with fragments of nightmarishly familiar experiences—some real, some imagined. In fact, he likens his experience writing the semi-naturalistic boardinghouse drama *Joe Turner's Come and Gone* to

> walking down a road in this strange landscape. What you confront is part of yourself, your willingness to deal with the small imperial truths you have accumulated over your life. . . . You've got that landscape and you've got to enter it, walk down the road and whatever happens, happens. And that's the best you're capable of coming to. The characters do it, and in them, I confront myself. (Powers 55)

The playwright selectively gathers disjointed images from this expansive range of his memory and tries to contain them within a suitable dramatic framework.

The makeup of *Joe Turner* is an eclectic combination of familiar and unfamiliar signposts that lead Wilson to areas of his consciousness previously partitioned off because of the pain of their memory. These include a W. C. Handy album, a real-life outlaw named Joe Turner, a folk song of lament, a Romare Bearden collage called *Mill Hand's Lunch Bucket* (1978), Wilson's then ongoing poetry series titled *Restoring the House*, and his mission to write a play that showed African American characters who were to be clearly identified as African people. Although Wilson does not assign any particular order to this seemingly unrelated list of components, together they create a unified, convincing portrait of what life for blacks was like in post-Reconstruction America.

The seeds for *Joe Turner* germinated as Wilson listened to a W. C. Handy album: *W. C. Handy Sings His Immortal Hits*. He explains,

> There's a cut on the album where Handy says, "The story of the blues cannot be told without Joe Turner. Joe Turner was the brother of Pete Turner, governor of Tennessee, who oppressed Negroes into peonage. He had a chain with forty links to it. And the men would be late coming home from their work in the fields. And someone would say, 'Haven't you heard? Joe Turner's come and gone.' " (Barbour 10)

It was Joe Turner's name, not that of his brother the governor, that became legendary down around Memphis after the Civil War. Because he extorted manual labor from a kidnapped workforce of former slaves, Joe Turner was seen as a convenient metaphor for focusing upon cultural fragmentation, the disintegration of the black family, and the plight of the black man as social pariah: "When I became aware of this song somehow it fit into the play. Because the seven years Loomis is with Joe Turner, seven years in which the world is torn asunder and his life is turned upside down, can in fact represent the four hundred years of slavery, of being taken out of Africa and brought to America" (Powers 54).

The words that make up the title of Wilson's boardinghouse drama were frequently uttered by grieving women from the Memphis area who, at the turn of the century, were left to fend for themselves and their children after Joe Turner had made off with their men. The statement "Joe Turner's got my man and gone" simply acknowledged this crime and expressed resignation in the face of a white man whose desire for free labor could so disrupt their lives. The cries of these wives, sisters, mothers, daughters, and lovers form an appropriately solemn blues context for W. C. Handy's recording and provide an even larger emotional landscape for Wilson's play about cultural fragmentation.

Joe Turner's Come and Gone was not the original title of Wilson's play for the 1900s. The boardinghouse scene depicted in Bearden's collage *Mill Hand's Lunch Bucket* so intrigued him that he initially adopted this very same title for his play. Later, having listened to Handy's blues ballad, he changed his mind. For Wilson, the attraction of the Bearden collage was an isolated figure of a black man seated at a table with a look of "abject defeat." Mesmerized by the implications of this man's expression, he was moved to wonder about the circumstances that caused such resignation. He thought to himself, "Who is this man and why is he sitting there and what are the circumstances of his life? That became Herald Loomis" (Powers 53). These questions became Wilson's inspiration for imagining other characterizations and evoking a mood of desolation for his play. *Joe Turner* also owes a structural debt to the collage, for it reflects the seemingly incoherent patchwork that is Bearden's hallmark.

Joe Turner's plot was largely determined by a series of poems that Wilson was then working on, *Restoring the House*. The story line of this saga in verse was a free black man's quest to locate his sold and deported slave wife. Though there are several significant differences, this is an interesting approximation of the plot of Charles Chesnutt's popular work of fiction, "The Wife of His Youth" (1899)—husband and wife are separated during slavery, and one spouse sets out in search of the other after their emancipation. The search motif, which was a focus of Wilson's poetic venture, provided an important ingredient in the play.

While *Joe Turner's* archetypal theme of search—what Wilson terms "finding one's song"—recalls the quest in Chesnutt's work, the play's emphasis upon facing demons of one's past parallels a contemporary novel, Toni Morrison's *Beloved* (1988). Both works feature tormented protagonists who go to great lengths to atone for a terrible past; and both Sethe and Loomis come to acknowledge that in order to go forward, they must revisit those pasts—no matter how horrifying. Although Sethe faces a hell arguably of her own making, Loomis is apparently the chosen medium for thousands of tormented slaves whose stories for centuries lay submerged beneath the currents of the Atlantic

Ocean. The thematic similarities are not entirely coincidental, though one critic observes that *Joe Turner* is "eerily close—almost a companion piece—to *Beloved*" (Winer 7). Wilson admires Morrison's work and, on occasion, has paid homage to her for writings that are firmly rooted in the black tradition.

Wilson regards *Joe Turner* as a textbook for modern audiences, for in it he strives to demonstrate certain positive African characteristics, which his central character Herald Loomis must accept before achieving mental or spiritual emancipation. Wilson's motive for writing this disturbing story of spiritual and cultural alienation is that "somewhere, sometime in the course of the play, the audience will discover these are African people. They're Black Americans; they speak English but their world view is African" (Powers 53). Since *Ma Rainey's Black Bottom*, he has stated directly as well as demonstrated in his work his firm belief that Africa should remain a powerful influence in the lives of African Americans.

August Wilson is far from the first black writer whose work calls for a spiritual return to Africa. This appeal may be traced as far back as *The Interesting Narrative of the Life of Olaudah Equiano, or Gustavus Vassa, the African* (1789), whose transplanted author nostalgically enumerates customs of the virtuous and highly civilized African people from which he had been forcibly taken. The "African continuum," although a recently coined phrase, not only inspired the cultural nationalist fervor of the 1960s but also was important to the New Negro of the Harlem Renaissance. During this literary era, Langston Hughes wrote "The Negro Speaks of Rivers" (1925), a work that highlights ancestral ties among members of the African diaspora:

> . . . I bathed in the Euphrates when dawns were young.
> I built my hut near the Congo and it lulled me to sleep.
> I looked upon the Nile and raised the pyramids above it. (4)

Likewise, the words of noted historian, writer, and collector Arthur Schomburg in 1925 very aptly describe August Wilson's mission as a black dramatist of the 1980s and 1990s:

> The American Negro must remake his past in order to make his future. Though it is orthodox to think of America as the one country where it is unnecessary to have a past, what is a luxury

for the nation as a whole becomes a prime social necessity for the Negro. For him, a group tradition must supply compensation for persecution, and pride of race the antidote for prejudice. History must restore what slavery took away, for it is the social damage of slavery that the present generations must repair and offset. (231)

Apparently Wilson's literary predecessors of both the 1920s and the 1960s saw that a symbolic return to Africa was imperative to the cultural health of black Americans.

The African continuum also became instrumental in the Black Arts movement and Black Theatre movement of the mid-1960s and early 1970s, when it was advanced by framers of the cultural nationalist agenda for black Americans. Writers, critics, and activists, such as Amiri Baraka and Larry Neal, saw that a linkage with Africa in the art, music, and writing of black people was crucial to their liberation from Western influence. Nationalist writer and critic Neal explains in his essay "The Black Contribution to American Letters": "Among black Americans today, the nationalist impulse gives rise to romantic longing for the pastoral innocence of the African past. Increasingly writers and artists are turning to the folk culture for inspiration and new formal ideas" (781).

No doubt Wilson, who came to maturity during this period as an adherent of this movement, carries with him smoldering embers from an earlier cultural nationalist ideology. The continuing concern about using an identifiably African frame of reference is at the very foundation of *Joe Turner* and has been consciously incorporated into a number of the play's features. Wilson has subtly included elements of an African worldview, such as a reverential regard for the spiritual world, a belief in sacrificial rites, an anachronistic conjure man, and an exceptionally high regard for storytelling. With Africa as an ever-present backdrop, *Joe Turner* is a decided departure from his three previous chronicles of the black experience in America. While *Jitney!* and *Ma Rainey's Black Bottom* follow predominantly naturalistic story lines, *Joe Turner* rests on a "more mystical than realistic base" (Powers 50). Indeed, of all of Wilson's drama to date, this two-act play offers the most pronounced demonstrations of the African continuum—what Paul Carter Harrison, in his afterword to *August Wilson: Three Plays*, calls "a psychic and spiritual repository of values and survival strategies that authenticates experience and fuels the imagination for a creative achievement capable of promoting personal renewal and collective healing" (316). The African continuum is the force that drives *Joe Turner* and challenges Wilson to find a dramatic form flexible enough to encompass the four hundred years blacks have been in America.

However, this task has also drawn the play's most negative criticism. A number of critics think that *Joe Turner*'s structure is a poor match for the playwright's overly ambitious saga. One notes that "the play seems to crack at times with the very force of its contents" and wonders if Wilson "has yet been able to create a form that can contain his volcanic subject matter, or whether the breaking, spillover effect is what he intended" (Marshall 240–41). Another observes, "Wilson's elemental power continues to overwhelm the basic structure of his dramas. His efforts remind you of a large man trying to squeeze into a suit two sizes too small. Every now and then, you hear the fabric ripping" (Richards, "Tortured Spirit" B12).

What these critics deem to be Wilson's difficulties with structure are more likely the results of his sensitivities as a poet. He refers to his poetry background as "the bedrock of my playwriting. Primarily not so much in the language as it is in the approach and the thinking—thinking as a poet, one thinks differently than one thinks as a playwright" (interviewed by the author). In particular, he sees this difference reflected in his use of metaphor, as evidenced in *Fences*.

In *Joe Turner* an effective demonstration of Wilson's dependence upon metaphor is his decision to situate the action within a boardinghouse. To be sure, the choice is historically accurate for 1911. Out of sheer necessity, Pittsburgh during the early 1900s became a city of numerous makeshift dwellings. The lure of the city's steel industry brought hundreds of southern black men and women into town by foot and by rail, where they quickly exhausted its available housing. Some companies established for their employees bunkhouses conveniently located near their work, while others struck business agreements with local black families to house the overflow of hired laborers. Those migrants who looked for their own housing or arrived too late frequently had to settle for substandard conditions. According to one study,

> The severe shortage of rental units that blacks could occupy in the Pittsburgh area also gave rise to several new types of housing for the incoming southern blacks: railroad cars converted to

bunkhouses; basement dwellings; boathouses on the Mononga-
hela River; warehouses; make-shift shelters hastily built in previously uninhabited ravines and hollows. (Gottlieb 69)

Bertha and Seth Holly are typical of those black families in Pittsburgh during this time who opened their homes to boarders. However,
they owe nothing to local steel companies for their business operation;
this boardinghouse was passed down to Seth by his father. Thus, he and
his wife can establish their own rates for room and board and collect
100 percent of the money due them. The dwelling seems pleasant
enough and well run by the husband and wife team. Meals are provided
according to schedule, and rules of behavior are made known and
strictly enforced. Seth routinely reminds his tenants, "It's two dollars a
week for the room. We serve meals twice a day. It's two dollars for room
and board. Pay up in advance" (*JT* 14). He also is quick to caution
them: "Your business is your business. I don't meddle in nobody's
business. But this is a respectable house. I don't have no riffraff around
here" (48).

More important than its historical verisimilitude, this representative boardinghouse is also an effective metaphor for Wilson's thematic concerns about cultural fragmentation among African
Americans. As he does in *Jitney!*, and later in *Two Trains Running*, the
playwright devises a well-populated setting to allow a kaleidoscopic
view of a certain cross-section of black America. Featured tenants include an enraged ex-member of Joe Turner's workforce, an abandoned
wife, a fresh young guitar player, and a conjure man, each nursing some
emotional wound yet hopeful for change. Their comings and goings,
witnessed by Bertha and Seth, reveal a diverse people uprooted from
their homes—by force or by choice—in search of jobs, love, or their
personal identities—their song.

Bertha and Seth's boarding establishment, despite the stigma of
impersonality often associated with such a dwelling, is an oasis on the
emotional landscape that Wilson explores. Although the tenants in this
motley group are paying customers, they receive much more than room
and board for their weekly rent. In addition to the maternal warmth
they reap from the even-tempered, compassionate Bertha, they are
provided a sanctuary where they mull over their insecurities and contemplate their destinies in this new land. This way station or gateway to
the North prepares them for the cultural shock that awaits them. Thus,

the Hollys' Pittsburgh boardinghouse of the 1900s, like the numerous ones that actually existed in this steel town, plays an important sociological role in the shifting landscape of black America.

The characterization in the play also demonstrates Wilson's preference for the figurative. Thus Herald Loomis, the play's most enigmatic character, rises to the level of archetypal Everyman in his quest to locate his wife.[2] He is not just an errant ex-southern farmhand: Loomis embodies all of the lost souls of his people—those dispersed by slaveholders and those divided due to the massive relocation to the North. His quest for his wife, then, becomes every black person's search for his or her ancestral beginnings, or song. When he and daughter Zonia stumble upon the Hollys' boardinghouse, his subsequent verbal eruption becomes a symbolically profound disclosure of his mission.

Herald Loomis is Wilson's poetic focus in *Joe Turner*, the elaboration of the image first glimpsed in the Bearden collage *Mill Hand's Lunch Bucket*. Garbed in a large wool coat and dark hat, Loomis evolves from the static figure on Bearden's canvas to a personification of the pain and disillusionment of an entire race. On one level he is weighed down by the tragic stories of millions of his slave ancestors who died during the Middle Passage and slavery and who apparently have chosen him to vent their rage. On another, he is a man who, despite his apparent naïveté, has become literally a pariah among his family and his culture. Paul Carter Harrison's descriptions of him capture the duality of his symbolic resonance. He finds him to be "a spiritually crippled—if not mad—man, whose true identity even is questionable"; figuratively, he is "the trickster as redeemer [who] arrives formless at the way station of itinerant travelers, his identity shrouded in a liminal zone between bondage and liberation" (312).

As the symbolic equivalent of black America at the turn of the century, Herald Loomis also reveals the changing place of Christianity in the lives of former slaves and the progeny of slaves. The tension between certain residual African religious ideas and Christian doctrines to which his slave ancestors were exposed by their masters detonates in him an explosion of opposites. When the smoke settles after several of Loomis's cataclysmic, shockingly blasphemous displays against the "white man's god," he discovers that the power of salvation resides exclusively within him: "I don't need nobody to bleed for me! I can bleed for myself" (*JT* 93).

Without his song, frustrated, disillusioned, and alienated from his family and from society, the social outcast Loomis is easily coaxed into drawing his own blood as a brazen challenge to his wife's God, who has grossly failed him. In performing this act, Loomis echoes August Wilson's oft-repeated belief that "God does not hear the prayers of blacks" (Reed 95). This conviction is demonstrated, to some extent, by each of the male protagonists in his cycle of plays. Moreover, Loomis's sacrilegious gesture undermines the Christian belief in Jesus Christ's crucifixion as the ultimate sacrifice undertaken for all humanity. By implication, the blood shed by Loomis marks the crucifixion as a broken agreement. Sensing abandonment and betrayal by this God, Loomis assumes responsibility for his own salvation in a quick stroke of his own knife. Thus, Loomis's self-inflicted wound offers an unmistakable commentary upon African Americans' frustrations with the inherent lie of Christianity as it has been impressed upon them by white America.

The original version of *Joe Turner's Come and Gone* puzzled pre-Broadway audiences; the play seemed to them not to resolve the source of Loomis's conflict. *Fences*'s obscure ending similarly had riled its Broadway producer and quite a few theatre critics. During *Joe Turner's* rehearsal for the 1986 production at Yale, Wilson, Richards, and several other observers noted that the script ended with a lingering question as to whether Herald Loomis "finds his song." What audiences needed, according to Richards, was a more emotionally rewarding catharsis after they had learned of this man's lengthy incarceration and had witnessed his frustrated search for his wife for much of the play. Yet it was not until Wilson sat through several intensive rehearsals of the play that he discovered a solution to Loomis's one-sided portrayal, unsatisfying depiction: "I came up with the idea of ending the first act with him on the floor unable to stand up. When he stands at the end, you can read that as him finding his song" (Savran 297).

Although Wilson was able to devise a resolution to suit his director's tastes, the new portrayal and new lines still did not satisfy his critics. According to their judgment, having Loomis stand up solved only a small portion of the play's problems; it was Loomis's lack of credibility that minimized the dramatic impact and muddled the significance of the play's most climactic moment in act 1, scene 4 when he suffers from what one reviewer calls "symptoms of a drug addict" (Suavage 23) and another deems "a cyclonic paroxysm of spiritual torment" (Rich, "Panoramic History" C15). In particular, Wilson's critics charged that "the new ending does not make dramatic sense" (Richards, "Tortured Spirit"

B12) and that "the audience cannot relate any of this to a human experience" (Scherer B10). They reasoned that the distance between Loomis and the audience that Wilson establishes early on in the play—with the frightening image of him as a darkly clad, potentially maniacal intruder—lessens their capacity to empathize with him and understand the degree of his torment. Thus, during the riveting scene between Loomis and the conjure man, ambiguity and confusion dominate the theatregoers, who are more prone to view his convulsions as a dramatic non sequitur or *deus ex machina* rather than a resolution to his conflict.

The issue critics raised concerning Loomis's alienation from the audience is but another example of the gap between Wilson the conformist and Wilson the refreshingly independent writer. Although he has made several alterations to his work for clarity at the insistence of Richards, in many instances he has been adamant about retaining scenes as well as characters just the way he initially fashions them. Thus, criticism notwithstanding, the definitive version of *Joe Turner's Come and Gone*—considered by *The Washington Post* as "bold theatricality" (Richards, "Tortured Spirit" B12) and by *The New York Times* as his "most profound and theatrically adventurous" (Rich, "Panoramic History" C15)—still features Loomis thrashing about on the floor of the Hollys' boardinghouse in a wrestling match with his own demons of the past as well as those of all before him who perished during slavery. That Loomis earlier could avoid them only because he had no past is an important aspect of the play's theme of finding one's song, one that Wilson considers crucial enough to magnify even at the expense of losing or distancing his audience.

While this final version of *Joe Turner* leaves both readers and audiences with fewer questions, it still is significantly open-ended. Admittedly oblivious to earlier writers of tragedies, Wilson pays little attention to the Aristotelian convention calling for a reversal of fortune for the tragic protagonist. In the final turbulent scene of *Joe Turner*, Loomis and his ex-wife, Martha, engage in a verbal confrontation that reaches its climax when Loomis, in a graphic attempt to denounce her God, slashes his chest, smears blood over his face, and exclaims, "I'm standing! I'm standing. My legs stood up! I'm standing now!" (93). Apparently Wilson sees this as not merely self-sacrificial parody but as a major epiphany for a man who, for so long, has been defined by forces other than his own. Unfortunately, according to some critics, Wilson demonstrates this realization more clearly in his accompanying stage notes than in Loomis's startling actions. Wilson interprets the spectacle most eloquently:

> Having found his song, the song of self-sufficiency, fully resurrected, cleansed and given breath, free from any encumbrance other than the workings of his own heart and the bonds of the flesh, having accepted the responsibility for his own presence in the world, he is free to soar above the environs that weighed and pushed his spirit into terrifying contractions. (*JT* 94)

As has become Wilson's trademark, *Joe Turner* steers away from a simple moral or neat resolution. Instead, the playwright is, as usual, an instructor who carries his students to the threshold of awareness but leaves them there to ponder. This artistic strategy continues to be the source of much debate between Richards and Wilson. While Wilson stands firm about maintaining the original integrity of his work, Richards is faced with the job of translating it to suit the needs of audiences on one hand and financial backers on the other. A blend of subtle imposition, compromise, and obstinacy has generally served them well in these endeavors. In this instance, Broadway audiences were not impressed. In fact, the play had a comparatively short season (March 27 to June 26, 1988) at the Ethel Barrymore Theatre. This lackluster reception was due not so much to the lack of a celebrity among its cast (as in *Fences*) but upon the play's difficult premise. Many audiences simply found Wilson's psychic protagonist and mystical flourishes over their heads and left the theatre more confused than enlightened. But Richards makes no apologies for audience reactions to the play. He explained that *Joe Turner* "took you deeply into a place where you had never been before. It made you work, and there are people who go to the theater who don't like to work" (Rothstein, "Round Five" 8).

The conjure man, Bynum Walker, who figures prominently in the cataclysmic scene that has been the focus of both praise and condemnation, provides another example of Wilson's symbolic characterizations. The anachronistic voodoo man—Wilson's more modern rendition of the African healer—directs Herald Loomis toward a major epiphany of self-renewal and self-sufficiency. Bynum is a key figure in *Joe Turner*, the personification of Africa revisited. Yet as a rootworker and African healer residing in a Pittsburgh boardinghouse in the 1900s, he also is an example of a "leftover from history"—what one *New York Newsday* writer calls "a link to an Africa that separation has confused and mutated into a special American thing" (Winer 7). During much of the play, this self-possessed, talkative, hauntingly clairvoyant man is tolerated by fellow boardinghouse tenants, appearing more as a harmless lunatic than one whose spells and potions merit any serious attention. He is often preoccupied with incantations and minirituals involving pigeons, bloodletting, and exotic dances. Moreover, he is confident that his roots are powerful, bragging to a heartbroken female tenant that he can fix it so her man will not only return to her but will stray no more. To the boardinghouse proprietor, Seth Holly, Bynum is a deranged lunatic bent on frightening away rent-paying customers and trampling his vegetable garden during daily sacrificial rituals involving pigeons. To the proprietor's wife, he is a slightly senile yet tolerable old gentleman who simply needs a place to stay. Other residents regard him as part of the furniture, occasionally winning a moment of their attention.

But Bynum Walker's role in *Joe Turner* is far more crucial than the reactions of his neighbors would indicate. Notwithstanding Seth Holly's opinion of him as an obvious mental case, Bynum is a pivotal character in the play. Even more than the spiritually dispossessed Herald Loomis, Bynum is the key to understanding the play's emphasis upon finding one's song by reconnecting with Africa. Like Gabriel, his analogue in *Fences*, he reflects Wilson's defamiliarization strategy: he is cast as an ineffectual prophet surrounded by disbelievers. Emphasis is consciously shifted from conjurer as bearer of potions and magic spells to conjurer as spiritual healer, binder of severed relations, and human bridge to Africa's past.

Just as with Charles Chesnutt's portrayal of the lovable trickster Uncle Julius in *The Conjure Woman* (1899), the elements of deception surrounding Bynum's character are double-edged. On the surface his insistence upon performing sacrificial rituals on the premises of a boardinghouse affirms his lunacy. Initially, this quasi-comedic conjurer seems to promote the perception that Africa is hopelessly out of sync with the concerns of 1911. Audiences are at first not challenged to alter their impression of Bynum as comic relief rather than conveyor of anything of serious value. Instead, the Bynum who appears early in *Joe Turner* reinforces lingering inclinations to caricature voodoo practice and to doubt the sanity of anyone who engages in it.

Indeed, Bynum's role in *Joe Turner* develops from the foundation laid by this comfortable stereotype of the minstrel-like conjure man.

His Afrocentrism is revealed gradually, as if in stages. Thus, in following his character's evolution, the especially perceptive audiences can peel back layers of misconceptions about the importance of the African tradition he represents. Bynum unfolds by degrees, gradually, luring the audience toward an understanding of his nature as a character who is grounded in the practices and beliefs of his African ancestors. He goes from performing unexplained rituals with pigeons, to learning the secret of his own healing potential to working roots to fix a broken marriage, and finally to exorcising Herald Loomis of images associated with the horrors of the Middle Passage.

According to Wilson's stage notes, Bynum functions in the play not as an eccentric but as a perfectly sane African healer. His description— "a short, round man in his early sixties" (*JT* 4)—strategically suggests his birthdate to be somewhere around 1850, about a decade before the outbreak of the Civil War. In 1911 such a man would conceivable have accurate recollections of the customs and values of his slave ancestors. Thus Bynum may be regarded justifiably as the spirit of Africa existing on the fringes of a more modern though less receptive black society, just as the boardinghouse exists on the fringes of the more modern though less receptive white society. Such a view of Bynum may explain why he is dismissed by other characters in the play as an embarrassment— someone to be avoided or pitied rather than honored.

It is not coincidental that the character whom Bynum irritates the most is the northern-born boardinghouse owner Seth Holly, who considers himself superior to "all that mumbo jumbo nonsense" (1). He tells his wife, "Ever since slavery got over with, there ain't been nothing but foolish-acting niggers" (6). He later tells Bynum, "I ain't never picked no cotton. I was born up here in the North. My daddy was a freedman. I ain't never seen no cotton!" (70). This apparent superiority claimed by Seth is grounded historically in condescending attitudes held by northern blacks—and, by extension, Western thought—in regard to newly freed slaves who clung to the customs of their slave ancestors. Thus Seth and Bynum may be seen as representing longtime polarities between those African Americans who acknowledge ancestral ties with Africa and those who totally disavow any connection with the continent and its people.

As foil to the African healer and conjure man, Seth is embarrassed by his people's African and southern origins. Unlike Bynum, who struggles to bring Loomis to realize his obligation to his ancestors, Seth prides himself on how much he has evolved from his African past. He brags of his northern distinction while considering Bynum and the clodhopper-wearing southern farm worker Loomis embarrassingly primitive. He distances himself from Bynum early in the play, proclaiming,

> I know Bynum. Bynum ain't no mystery to me. I done seen a hundred niggers like him. He's one of them fellows never could stay in one place. He was wandering all around the country till he got old and settle here. The only thing different about Bynum is he bring all this heebie-geebie stuff with him. (35)

Seth expends a great deal of his energy trying to demystify Bynum's actions and to silence the echoes of Africa that he represents.

Despite Bynum's deceptively low-key role in the play, he ultimately prevails as the only one who can lead the disillusioned Loomis to the healing realization of his African identity. When Loomis lapses into a trance and recalls a haunting vision of bones coming from the water, Bynum automatically assumes the role of spiritual leader, gently prodding him with questions that draw out of him the entire experience:

> Loomis.: I done seen bones rise up out the water. Rise and walk across the water. Bones walking on top of the water.
> Bynum.: Tell me about them bones, Herald Loomis. Tell me what you seen. (53)

Among the entire group of boarders, only Bynum can communicate with Loomis while he is in this possessed state. With this African healer's help, Loomis learns that these bones are images from his past begging to be acknowledged as his song. Wilson explains this troubling vision as "Loomis's connection with the ancestors, the Africans who were lost during the Middle Passage and were thrown overboard. They are walking around here and now and they look like you because you are these very same people. This is who you are" (Powers 54).

Bynum attributes his powers as a conjure man to lessons learned from his deceased father. One day while alone on a road in Johnstown, he is led to a mystical reunion with his father by an elusive figure he calls Shiny Man, a godlike being whose body emanates brilliant light. This Shiny Man takes Bynum on a journey to a place that can only be described in hyperbole, much like paradise or heaven, but abandons

him once they arrive. In a narrative remarkably reminiscent of the
African folktale, Bynum recalls encountering his father amid larger-
than-life surroundings:

> I wandered around there looking for that road, trying to find
> my way back from that big place . . . and I looked over and seen
> my daddy standing there. He was the same size he always was,
> except for his hands and his mouth. He had a great big old
> mouth that look like it took up his whole face and his hands
> were as big as hams. Look like they was too big to carry around.
> My daddy called me to him. Said he had been thinking about
> me and it grieved him to see me in the world carrying other
> people's songs and not having my own. Told me he was gonna
> show me how to find my song. (*JT* 9–10)

Bynum's elaborate vision fuels his lifelong quest to locate Shiny
Man. To him, locating the godlike Shiny Man will signify not only that
he has honored the wish of an immediate ancestor but also that he has
found his own song, his own place in the world, his own talent for
healing. That Bynum finds his source of strength and direction by
reconnecting with his father—albeit in a dream vision—suggests that
untapped wisdom is just within reach for those in tune with their past.
Given Bynum's sense of urgency about this search, his motives in soliciting
the services of Rutherford Selig, a self-proclaimed People Finder, are
understandable. Like numerous other inhabitants of Pittsburgh, he
presses a dollar bill into Selig's hand in hopes that he will one day return
with news of the whereabouts of this very important missing person.

To understand how Bynum's quest for Shiny Man fits into Wilson's
larger agenda, one must step back from the play as one would from an
impressionistic painting. One must first understand that Shiny Man is
the African alternative to what August Wilson calls "the white man's
God." He explains in an interview,

> Amiri Baraka has said that when you look in the mirror, you
> should see your God. If you don't, you have somebody else's
> God. So, in fact, what you do is worship an image of God which
> is white, which is the image of the very same people who have
> oppressed you, who have put you on the slave ships, who have
> beaten you, and who have forced you to work. (Moyers 178)

This elusive deity who overwhelms Bynum and leads him to the spirit of his deceased father apparently answered Bynum's own spiritual probings. Shiny Man, therefore, personifies Wilson's alternative to oppressive images that he associates with Christianity.

In the greater scheme of Wilson's decade-by-decade revision of African American history, Bynum is a chief player. This initially misunderstood conjure man is the catalyst for Wilson's historical approach to the troubling record of African American experience in the United States. In *Joe Turner* he is the only character empowered with the ability to forge ties between Africa and America. Only the African healer and rootworker possess the antidote to the cultural fragmentation that slowly devastates his fellow boardinghouse neighbors. As a conduit between Africa and America (past and present), he conjures up fields of experience whereby African Americans can counter their present cultural alienation by drawing upon the wisdom of their ancestors.

Bynum's quest for Shiny Man parallels Loomis's search for his identity and, by extension, becomes every black man's search for affirmation in a world with few gods and even fewer monuments to his past. As conjurer, Bynum's far-from-insignificant role is to bring about "a collective African unconscious" (Rich C15) by moving "within and through . . . the mask of minstrelsy to ensure survival, to operate changes, to acquire necessary resources for continuance, and to cure a sick world" (Baker 47).

Wilson's black female characters also become larger-than-life images or metaphors in his rendition of life during Reconstruction for newly freed slaves, ex-sharecroppers, and tenant farmers. At the same time, *Joe Turner* reflects realistically the influx of black women who made their way to Pittsburgh during this migration north. Some came to the city after their husbands had relocated there, found employment, and sent for them. Some came at the invitation of other relatives or friends in a practice called "chain migration." Others took their chances by coming with no prospects for employment or lodging. While many single black women made the trek without incident, others en route to Pittsburgh alone were not as lucky. In addition to the inherent dangers a lone female traveler faced, many were simply physically and emotionally ill-prepared for the journey.

The road to Pittsburgh was not especially friendly to black female migrants, and the scarcity of lodging once they arrived in the city was just as devastating. One study offers an example: "One woman with three children left her husband in Georgia during World War I to come to Pittsburgh. She ended up living in one damp room, using an outdoor water supply, trying to nurse her sick children back to health while she took in washing to earn money" (Gottlieb 47). Fortunately such hard-luck stories were balanced by reports of a number of tough black women who came to the North alone, found work and shelter, and settled down comfortably there. One such woman "moved from Virginia to Homestead [a section of Pittsburgh]. Though her brother and some of her southern friends already lived in the area, she lodged with strangers in Homestead and soon found a job there as a restaurant cook" (47).

Equipped with knowledge of his hometown's history and demographics, Wilson fashions an array of black women migrants to Pittsburgh who, like the male characters, find their way to the Hollys' establishment and are also in search of their songs. In these female portrayals Wilson continues to advance a larger figurative meaning. Powerfully suggested by the errant courses these women choose is a pervasive breakdown of the black family unit. For differing reasons these women have become missing pieces to various historically divided black family portraits. Another component conspicuously missing is the husband and father. In *Joe Turner*, he is either kidnapped from his family by a lawless white man, conditioned to avoid serious relationships with women, or so accustomed to flight that he just walks out the door when trouble befalls his marriage. Black men and black women suffer a breakdown in communication in this play, which underscores the disorientation caused by slavery, the migration north, and decades of systemic apathy or active antagonism against the interests of the black family. Whether these men and women just miss each other, cross paths for brief encounters, or engage in obsessive pursuits of their mates, their efforts are futile. With the notable exception of Seth and Bertha, who have a seemingly stable union, these men and women appear incompatible and, in fact, emotionally sterile.

Of the group, Molly Cunningham best typifies the huge population of single and independent black women coming into Pittsburgh during the early 1900s. While Mattie Campbell, Martha Pentecost, and Bertha Holly affirm more conventional ideas of the period about black women's roles in domestic settings, Molly represents a breed of women whose definition is not tied up with the home and family. Extremely cautious of relationships with males, she exudes independence and a healthy concern for self. While Mattie and Martha profess emotional dependence upon their men, Molly prefers to be free of such bonds: "Molly can make it nice by herself too. Molly don't need nobody leave her cold in hand. The world rough enough as it is" (*JT* 65).

Unlike the self-effacing Mattie, Molly is quick to let the men around her know that she is in control. In addition to looking like what Wilson describes as "a kind of woman that 'could break in on a dollar anywhere she goes' " (47), her strong opinions on issues make women who choose the domestic life appear to have bartered away their freedom. On having children, she declares, "Molly Cunningham ain't gonna be tied down with no babies" (63). Her feelings about men are equally plain: "I don't trust these men. Jack or nobody else. These men liable to do anything" (62). She adds, "I don't trust nobody but the good Lord above, and I don't love nobody but my mama" (63). Molly is both cautious and strong-willed, but she is not a total loner. She tells Seth before she agrees to take one of his rooms, "I like me some company from time to time. I don't like being by myself." She combines a survivor's sound judgment and principles, yet she keeps herself open to the possibility of sexual intimacies with the menfolk.

Mattie Campbell is quite the opposite of the fiercely self-sufficient Molly Cunningham. Traveling alone, the emotionally distraught Mattie comes to the Pittsburgh boardinghouse searching for her husband, who has abandoned her. Up from west Texas, the couple had resided in Pittsburgh for three years before their marriage deteriorated. Now Mattie, who seems unable to accept the desertion, hopelessly follows the trail of the long-gone Jack Carper. Having witnessed the deaths of two of his babies within two months of their births, he was convinced that she was the victim of a "curse prayer" or hex. According to Mattie, "He just got up one day, set his foot on the road, and walked away" (22). No longer confident of her ability to keep a man, she petitions the resident conjurer for advice. Her stay at the boardinghouse, then, is merely a brief respite from her obsessive odyssey to find Carper.

Like Mattie Campbell, Martha Pentecost temporarily enjoys a relatively stable domestic life, yet she too is forced by circumstances beyond her control to become, technically, a single woman again. Both are without structured home environments; both are without their men; and both desperately search for their songs to fill these voids. But there the similarities in these women end, for Martha's life has followed a distinctly different pattern. *She* is the party who abandons the marriage, and her husband is the one driven to locate her. After spending several years awaiting her husband's return, she deals squarely with the growing likelihood that Loomis will not find his way home again. Following a period of mourning, Martha rebounds emotionally and spiritually to become a devout member of her church. As Loomis becomes a memory, she becomes an increasingly fervent religious convert. The schism between Martha and Herald Loomis is one of the most troubling failures in this play about cultural fragmentation, yet neither husband nor wife is to blame for their inability to reconnect. Unfortunately the forces of history have caught up with the two, adding them to the countless other black families forever separated.

Of the trio of women in *Joe Turner* who offer variations on the domestic theme, Bertha Holly best exemplifies marital harmony, the calm so lacking in the lives of the culturally detached black women around her. Her twenty-seven-year marriage to Seth is a refreshing contrast to the various broken relationships they witness daily. In addition to Seth's even temper, his unquestioned fidelity, and his obviously high regard for Bertha, the marriage seems to endure because she has not neglected her individuality; she is comfortable with who she is. Also, because of her ready supply of compassion and keen perceptions about human behavior, she seems to remain safely immune to the emotional sterility that surrounds her own marital haven. She tells the weary Mattie Campbell,

> You get all that trouble off your mind and just when it look like you ain't never gonna find what you want . . . you look up and it's standing right there. That's how I met my Seth. You gonna look up one day and find everything you want standing right in front of you. Been twenty-seven years now since that happened to me. But life ain't no happy-go-lucky time where everything be just like you want it. You got your time coming. You watch what Bertha's saying. (75)

Bertha's role in *Joe Turner* goes beyond providing clean sheets, warm meals, and wise counsel for her customers. In the context of the boardinghouse's figurative importance to these migrating patrons, she becomes the symbolic matriarch whose role is to nurture each of the troubled souls in her care—not simply with food, but with broad sympathy for their individual circumstances. This almost divine role allows her to see good in even the most despicable persons in her charge and to defend them against both warranted and unwarranted attacks. For example, she deflects her husband's worries over Bynum's morning pigeon ritual near their garden with "Bynum don't bother nobody. He ain't even near your vegetables" (2). She again calms down her husband after Loomis's blasphemous outburst with "Leave him alone, Seth. He ain't in his right mind" (52).

The women migrants of *Joe Turner* are a microcosm of the real-life black women who shared with black men the road to Pittsburgh during the early 1900s—not just as wives looking to rendezvous with husbands for a better life, but as dislocated, dispossessed sisters desperately seeking their songs as well as their identities and independence. Each of these women who come to the Holly boardinghouse could very well be the promise of some black family's existence and stability. Yet their strong presence also points to a women's liberation movement already underway decades before the more publicized furor of the 1960s. While some regret their manless circumstances, others brag of their independence and meet head-on the challenges that living the single life as a black woman in the North entails.

The strange landscape that Wilson excavates in *Joe Turner* is littered with remnants of a dreaded past, yet it also contains directives to a more positive future. In any case, according to Wilson, the past must be reexamined before any kind of meaningful healing is to occur. The play, then, serves as Wilson's song and all black people's song. It is also a journey back to areas of a personal and collective past whose profound truths cannot be contained within the conventional dramatic form. Out of necessity, then, the playwright alters an otherwise naturalistic setting to create a vehicle more suitable for conveying his ideas on the fragmenting of black America at this important historical juncture. The familiar becomes the unfamiliar, and the past encroaches upon the present in a tale of missed connections, reunions, and false starts.

In addition to the rugged terrain of this strange landscape, *Joe Turner* offers a redemptive subtext. Once the weary migrants face their respective demons in this way station, they at least are positioned toward the future rather than hopelessly bogged down in the mire of a past that they would sooner forget; they find their songs. Having witnessed the past out of which they and their ancestors have emerged, each, like Loomis, will be able to "say my goodbye and make my own world" (90).

SIX

August Wilson as Teacher:
The Piano Lesson

Lou Miles as Wining Boy
in the Yale Repertory Theatre's
winter 1988 premiere of *The Piano Lesson*.
In this scene, Wining Boy sings
"The Wandering Man Blues."
© by Gerry Goodstein.
Reprinted by permission.

Well on his way toward completing his ten-play chronicle, Wilson has grown increasingly didactic in his approach. The fifth installment, *The Piano Lesson*, which garnered the playwright a second Pulitzer Prize in 1990, continues the trend. The impulse that drives each of these plays is Wilson's desire to change attitudes about the importance of one's culture and heritage. To achieve this end, he manipulates various aspects of drama to create potential learning situations. While the point of *Joe Turner's Come and Gone* seems indistinct to some, in *The Piano Lesson* Wilson simplifies the play's message with a solitary instructional prop—a 135-year-old piano that is simultaneously the Charles family heirloom and a unifying device for the play. This dominant device is made the center of the play's conflict as well as its symbolic core. As in *Joe Turner*, Wilson uses metaphor as a teaching device in *The Piano Lesson*; however, this metaphor is not in competition with as many other obviously symbolic forces. Thus, understanding what it represents does not require as much "work" (as Richards observes in an April 1990 *New York Times* interview with Mervyn Rothstein). Moreover, in *The Piano Lesson* Wilson softens his approach to convincing playgoers that his characters ought to be recognized as Africans, a goal that had frustrated him and baffled *Joe Turner's* audiences. The effect of Wilson's sharper focus is a more immediately recognizable lesson on what to do with one's cultural heritage.

Wilson himself learned many a valuable lesson in the tough streets of Pittsburgh, where alcoholics and vagrants conducted daily classes in "street smarts." Later, he basically taught himself black culture as he reacted against the predominantly white high school he left at fifteen and as he identified with his mother's black heritage. Wilson knows that he is very fortunate to have survived Pittsburgh's streets and to have learned the value of understanding his roots. He has since committed his art to demonstrating to other blacks the important role their own culture plays in their advancement. Apparently Wilson's own education—the rudiments of his formal schooling and his voracious appetite for reading black literature and studying all forms of black culture—along with his personal quest to define his racial boundaries contributes to the didactic thrust of his work.

The Piano Lesson is charged with confrontation and debate. Just up from Mississippi, Boy Willie sweeps into his sister Berniece's home with aspirations of selling a truckload of watermelons along with the Charles family piano, which sits undisturbed in her parlor. He is on a mission to collect enough money to buy several acres of land back home and believes that selling the piano would assure him sufficient capital to return and finalize a deal he made with a prospective seller. However, his greatest obstacle—aside from a truck that breaks down every few yards and his pitifully inadequate preparation for moving the weighty piano—is his sister, who adamantly refuses to sell the family heirloom. Debate ensues, and the argument over the fate of the piano widens an already existing gap between the siblings.

But the object of this heated discussion is more than simply a piano. For Berniece, the instrument represents those members of their family who were centuries ago bartered in a deal made between its original owner, Robert Sutter, and a poor white farmer who wanted it as a gift for his wife. It represents her father, who lost his life because he removed the piano from the Sutter home and gave it to some of his own relatives. It represents her mother, who, after her husband's death, incessantly polished its surface and asked the young Berniece to play the instrument in her father's memory. As a result of years of carrying this emotional baggage, Berniece develops a phobia about playing the piano, choosing instead to train her own daughter to make use of it. The piano's emotional and monetary values are elevated even further by the images carved on it. These, which bear the likenesses of several Charles family ancestors, were made by Berniece and Boy Willie's paternal grandfather, who was a wood craftsman of considerable repute in his day.

Despite his sister's refusal to sell the piano, Boy Willie maintains that he can reap more practical good from the otherwise useless object by investing his share of the sale in a small plot of land. With impeccable logic, he rationalizes against Berniece's less forcibly argued position. He recalls how his sharecropper father had started out in life with little or nothing, and he pledges to honor him by making practical use of his legacy. Like the obsessed Walter Lee of Lorraine Hansberry's *Raisin in the Sun*, Boy Willie wants to use the family heirloom to purchase a piece of the American Dream.

Boy Willie and Berniece are not alone in their claim on the piano. Also apparently bent on retrieving the disputed instrument is a pesky ghost of the piano's former owner. This phantom, as local legend would have it, is the spirit of one of several men who hunted down Papa Boy Charles, their father, and burned the boxcar that he and several hobos had hopped, killing all on board. But even after

Sutter's mysterious drowning death in his own well, he still lays claim to the piano; he has taken up residence in Berniece's home near it and from time to time suddenly appears or tinkles its keys.

The climax of the play involves a confrontation, an exorcism, an epiphany, and a reunion. The ghostly visits to Berniece's home become so frequent and annoying that she eventually solicits the help of a minister—her boyfriend, Avery—to exorcise it, but it is not until Boy Willie engages Sutter's ghost in a brief wrestling match that the Charles family experiences any sense of relief. After the bout Berniece's apprehensions about playing the piano disappear along with the ghost. During an epiphanic moment in the play's concluding action, she gravitates toward the piano, sits down, and begins summoning her dead ancestors by striking the ivory keys she had previously shunned and chanting a litany to all of her relatives who died in its service. At this point an unspoken truce is called between the sparring siblings. Each instinctively knows what will be the piano's destiny. Boy Willie softens his belligerent tone with his sister and uncle and makes plans to leave Pittsburgh on the next train.

The Piano Lesson is Wilson's second play inspired by a Romare Bearden collage. Just as *Mill Hand's Lunch Bucket* provided Wilson's creative stimulus for writing *Joe Turner's Come and Gone*, so *The Piano Lesson* did the same for his play of the 1930s. This work, however, does not mimic the sometimes explosive, seemingly random plotting or the large cast of its predecessor. Instead it is a lesson carefully focused on two related questions: What do you do with your legacy, and how do you best put it to use? These questions came to Wilson's mind as he studied the Bearden work displaying a little girl, her teacher, and a large piano during what appears to be a practice session. The shared activity and the suggestive positions of the two characters—the little girl seated at the piano and her teacher hovering over her with an authoritative air—inspired the play's dramatic conflict and two female roles in his *The Piano Lesson*. Wilson recalls,

> So I got the idea from the painting that there would be a woman and a little girl in the play. And I thought that the woman would be a character who was trying to acquire a sense of self-worth by denying her past. And I felt that she couldn't do that. She had to confront the past, in the person of her

brother, who was going to sweep through the house like a tornado coming from the South, bringing the past with him. (Rothstein, "Round Five" 8)

The lessons in *The Piano Lesson* are more complex than they first appear. In considering what one should do with a legacy, the play reveals more than one teacher and more than one lesson. For example, the teacher-pupil relationship portrayed in Bearden's collage models the relation between Wilson and his audience. *The Piano Lesson* thus becomes the playwright's self-authored textbook of culture and history, instructing playgoers about the black experience in America. Also, each of the cast of characters teaches both directly and indirectly, as their words and their actions signal their regard for their legacy. Some reject it outright while others embrace and protect it. Doaker Charles, for example, much like the African griot, is a reservoir of knowledge about Charles family history. He is quite conscientious in recapitulating the events of the piano's long and turbulent past.

Having decided upon the play's basic premise and at least an outline for Berniece and her daughter Maretha, Wilson further envisioned that the piano in the collage was suitable for conveying "the idea of linkage." He noted, "It promoted a link to the past, to Africa, to who these people are" (Rothstein, "Round Five" 8). Just as in *Ma Rainey*, *Fences*, and *Joe Turner*, the importance of ancestral linkage to the South and, by extension, to Africa is an underlying message in *The Piano Lesson*. At the core of Wilson's didactic strategy is discovering one's black identity by reading various signs that frequently go unnoticed. Thus Berniece at first only partially addresses the pervasive questions on the purpose and best use of a legacy. She believes that the piano is a monument to her ancestors, which, by right, ought to be preserved, but for much of the play, she has not worked out in her mind what her role is beyond playing warden of the 135-year-old icon. Her own pent-up frustrations and suppressed fears after the deaths of her grandfather, her father, her mother, and her husband not only keep persistent suitor Avery at a distance but they also have brought her life to a virtual standstill. "I just stay at home most of the time. Take care of Maretha" (*PL* 79), she tells Lymon. But the impatient Avery tries to put an end to her self-imposed limbo. He asks,

What is you ready for, Berniece? You just gonna drift along from day to day. Life is more than making it from one day to another. You gonna look up one day and it's all gonna be past you. Life's gonna be gone out of your hands—there won't be enough to make nothing with. I'm standing here now, Berniece—but I don't know how much longer I'm gonna be standing here waiting on you. (68)

When she sits down at the piano in the final scene, Berniece discovers for herself and reveals to others that playing the ancient emblem is equivalent to reclaiming charge of her life. Playing the piano releases her from her personal turmoil as she summons the spirits of her relatives: "I want you to help me Mama Esther . . . I want you to help me Papa Boy Charles . . . I want you to help me Mama Ola" (107). This act also provides a nonverbal response to the play's two pressing thematic questions.

In contrast to his sister, Boy Willie knows full well what to do with his legacy and is determined to put it to use; he has both definite and immediate plans for the piano. These selfish designs and impetuous actions are instructive; they should agitate black Americans who regard without feeling or simply ignore vestiges of their past in their desperate pursuit of an American Dream that has historically excluded them. But Boy Willie is not entirely heedless of his past. The way he sees it, his plan to use the piano in his quest for property is, in fact, a way of honoring his deceased father:

> I take my hat off whenever somebody say my daddy's name. But I ain't gonna be no fool about no sentimental value. You can sit up here and look at the piano for the next hundred years and it's just gonna be a piano. You can't make more than that. Now I want to get Sutter's land and I can go down and cash in the crop and get my seed. As long as I got the land and the seed then I'm alright. I can always get me a little something else. Cause that land give back to you. I can make me another crop and cash that in. I still got the land and the seed. But that piano don't put out nothing else. You ain't got nothing working for you. Now, the kind of man my daddy was he would have understood that. (51)

Implicit in Boy Willie's argument is Wilson's belief that owning land is essential, especially for already marginalized black Americans. Yet while his ambitions do make practical sense, he, too, only partially grasps the complex lessons of the piano.

Actor Charles Dutton portrayed the depths of Boy Willie's uncompromising character in three significant productions: in 1988 at the Yale Repertory Theatre, in 1990 on Broadway, and in 1995 in the CBS Hallmark Hall of Fame television adaptation. For a third time Dutton stepped into a role tailor-made for him by August Wilson, who is a friend as well as professional associate, to challenge his acting skills to the utmost.[1] Wilson saw that Dutton's energy and dramatic range made him ideal to play Boy Willie; his performance was described by one critic as "a study in perpetual motion" (Rothstein, "Star" C17) and by another as "a whirlwind sweeping across the stage" (Greene 36). Having portrayed Levee in *Ma Rainey's Black Bottom* and Herald Loomis in *Joe Turner's Come and Gone*, Dutton has become quite familiar with the themes and style of Wilson's work. The ease with which he stepped into these roles also has much to do with the empathy he feels for Wilson's marginalized black male protagonists, characters who are familiar to him: "At different points in my life, I've experienced the kind of men and women in August's plays. I knew Levees. I knew Doakers. I knew a Wining Boy (Greene 38).

The primary lesson in *The Piano Lesson* emerges from observing an extremely tense dilemma, and audiences could easily split down the middle over the piano's fate. In fact, until convinced otherwise by director Lloyd Richards, Wilson was satisfied with that outcome. He admits, "To me, it wasn't important. The important thing to me was Boy Willie's willingness to engage the ghost in battle. Once you have that moment, then for me the play was over. But I found out that it wasn't over for the audiences, which kept saying, 'Yeah, but who gets the piano?'" (Rothstein, "Round Five" 8). But Richards found Wilson's original ending problematic, muddling the play's message. Richards had to persuade the playwright that in order for the play's major lesson to be realized, he must answer the obvious question. Thus, before the play reached Broadway in its final (and ultimately published) form, Wilson was subjected to more of Richards's subtle guidance in the form of probing questioning: "There are a lot of wonderful stories here. But which one do we want to tell? How do Berniece and Boy Willie's stories fit together? What role does the piano play? Why did Berniece stop playing the piano? What happens to the piano after the play ends?"

(Freedman, "Leaving His Imprint" 38). Such questioning does not seek immediate answers but invites reflection on possible improvements.

While Wilson liked the idea of an open-ended final scene with the curtain falling as Boy Willie wrestles with the ghost of the piano's former owner, Richards's concerns went beyond the text to the audience: "The fact is you have to have a resolution to the evening for the people who are sitting there. So we looked and tried things—various things to find a resolution to the play. Until then, I devised a finish that we never considered an ending. But it was a finish for the evening while we were still working on the end" (Shannon, "From Hansberry to Wilson" 129). Richards noted that given the high cost of the average theatre ticket and the added expense of a babysitter, parking, and so on, the theatregoer at least deserves a play with a satisfying ending. According to Richards, "The play was missing a lot in terms of its thinking and filling out, and it hadn't found its conclusion yet. We've really had to build it up" (Migler 139). By the time the two men had reached an agreement on how to fine-tune *The Piano Lesson*, Richards had become what one writer calls "an implant specialist" (139). Convinced by Richards's prodding, Wilson rewrote the final scene, extending the action beyond the wrestling match to reveal that Boy Willie rescinds his claim on the piano. Thus the new ending reveals that this powerful icon is to remain in his sister Berniece's home as a testament to their slave ancestors:

> BOY WILLIE: Wining Boy, you ready to go back down home? Hey, Doaker, what time the train leave?
> DOAKER: You still got time to make it.
> (MARETHA *crosses and embraces* BOY WILLIE.)
> BOY WILLIE: Hey, Berniece . . . if you and Maretha don't keep playing on that piano . . . ain't no telling . . . me and Sutter both liable to be back.
> BERNIECE: Thank you.
> (*The lights go down to black.*) (PL 108)

The debate between Wilson and Richards over *The Piano Lesson*'s ending underscores Wilson's emphasis as a playwright, which is more on provoking thought than on providing solutions. Consequently his repeated assertion that his plays are based upon little, if any, research is credible. His relative disinterest in analysis, then, explains why *The Piano Lesson* does not specifically respond to the pervasive economic woes unfolding outside Berniece's door. Though set during the early Depression years and during the height of the black migration north, when breadlines, widespread unemployment, insufficient housing, and a crippled U.S. economy were afflicting Pittsburgh—just as other urban areas—Wilson's work diverts attention from the larger picture to focus upon one extended black family's cultural rather than economic health.

As in *Joe Turner*, the revisions that Wilson made to his conclusion may have satisfied his director, but *The Piano Lesson* still sustained its share of scathing reviews. Chief among Wilson and Richards's nemeses was former Yale School of Drama dean and *New Republic* critic Robert Brustein, who in a highly critical essay published in May 1990 denounced *The Piano Lesson* as "the most poorly composed of Wilson's four produced works," questioned Lloyd Richards's professional and financial priorities in working with Wilson, and labeled their collaboration " 'McTheater'—the use of sequential non-profit institutions as launching pads and tryout franchises for the development of Broadway products and the enrichment of artistic personnel" (28).

Brustein also took issue with the three-hour length of a single performance of *The Piano Lesson*. In fact, he is not alone in this complaint. *New York Times* critic Mervyn Rothstein notes, "Conventional wisdom on Broadway is that a serious play should be two and a half hours long because audiences will not sit still for more" ("Round Five" 8). While Richards chose not to respond to most of Brustein's charges, he took special offense at this one. He countered, "Does that rule apply to *Merchant of Venice*? I hear it runs more than three hours. Has anybody spoken to Mr. Shakespeare lately about doing something about it?" Wilson was equally annoyed, threatening "to write a five-hour play" (8).

Despite Richards's public defense of Wilson's long scripts, much of his advice to his protégé during private conferences was to delete superflous lines and sometimes entire scenes. *Fences*, for example, was notoriously long before Richards convinced Wilson to downsize it for a more manageable production. According to Richards, *The Piano Lesson* also suffered from bloat. His first step in approaching this problem was to convince a stubborn Wilson that something needed to be eliminated without jeopardizing their relationship. Wilson recalls,

> I sent him a draft of *The Piano Lesson*, and he called me up and said, "Well, I read it. I think there are one too many scenes in

the second act." He didn't say, "I think this particular scene. . . ." He said, "There's one too many scenes in the second act." I said, "Oh, okay. I'll look at it. This has got to be the scene Lloyd is talking about as this is the only one that's expendable." And, sure enough, I found it was better. I cut it out. He was right. (Barbour 13–14)

The short-lived media flurry over Brustein's charges did not interrupt Richards and Wilson's collaboration or affect the reception of their work. *The Piano Lesson* went on to earn Wilson a second Pulitzer Prize. Like *Fences*, the play surmounted great skepticism over its unconventional ending to become an acclaimed success, both critically and commercially.

In *The Piano Lesson* Wilson teaches through the examples set by his characters. Rather than dwell upon the political and economic realities of the 1930s for black Americans, Wilson shows his audience how these hardships affect individual members of the Charles family and others who come into Berniece's home. To some extent each character, with the notable exception of Doaker Charles, responds to the effects of the Depression and displays the cultural fragmentation and alienation so prevalent in *Joe Turner's Come and Gone*. The multiple threats to the preservation of this black family—the Depression, the migration north, and the resulting damage in their connection to the past—may be measured indirectly by examining both the various jobs Wilson assigns the characters and their respective work ethics.

Blacks were doubly disadvantaged during the Depression, for they had long endured economic hardship disproportionately. One study of the period accurately characterizes them as "Always last hired and first fired":

> Blacks suffered sooner, longer, and more profoundly than whites the disastrous effects of the vast economic dislocation of the 1930s. In the South, the cotton economy was hit so hard that the number of Black tenant farmers and sharecroppers decreased by some two hundred thousand from 1930 to 1940. Industrial workers North and South were laid off or displaced by whites. By 1932 fifty-six percent of Blacks were unemployed. (Barksdale and Kinnamon 476)

The majority of the black men in *The Piano Lesson* are marginal members of a society that has squeezed them out of its workforce. Consequently they resort to moneymaking tactics such as selling watermelons, hauling (and stealing) wood, or participating in other schemes for quick profit. While Boy Willie also relies on some fairly shady means of raising funds, he does so for what he considers to be an honorable reason: investing in land. That he tries to utilize the only resource available to him suggests that he, unlike Lymon or Wining Boy, still possesses the warrior spirit. Although Boy Willie lacks a steady income that could finance his endeavor and enable him to avoid confronting his sister over the piano, he holds onto his dream until he is given good reason to let go.

The lessons of *The Piano Lesson* continue as Boy Willie's accomplice is introduced. Lymon, instead of embracing his past, chooses to sever all ties to his roots in Mississippi. On the surface he reinforces several prevailing stereotypes of black men who migrated from the South: forever in trouble with the law, averse to hard work, fond of flashy clothes, devoid of personal ambition, driven by sexual lust, and essentially limited in vision to the here and now. Lymon buys a truck in Mississippi so that he can sleep undetected by the law; he is on the run from a Mississippi white man named Stovall. After he and Boy Willie are ambushed while hauling wood and subsequently jailed on false charges, Stovall pays Lymon's $100 bail in exchange for a promise of $100 worth of labor from him. But Lymon shocks authorities by refusing: "I'd rather take my thirty days" (*PL* 37). After being forced to accept Stovall's arrangements, Lymon is released but soon after disappears, unwilling to honor the judge's orders. His mission up North with Boy Willie, then, is merely an opportunity to get out of Mississippi where his family roots lie and where he is a wanted man. "They treat you better up here" (38), he claims naively.

Despite Boy Willie's insistence, Lymon has no intention of returning to the South, where he faces certain reincarceration at the notorious prison camp known as Parchman Farm. What he fears most is the work expected of him there. "They work you too hard down there. All that weeding and hoeing and chopping down trees. I didn't like all that" (39). He even complains about his short detail as waterboy there: "That water was heavy" (39). The North for Lymon is all that the South is not: the easy life, quick money, lots of uninhibited women, and no white vigilantes on his trail. Finding honest work is never as high a priority for

Lymon as donning a fine suit of clothes and carousing in the Pittsburgh night spots, looking for women.

Perhaps not so immediately obvious as these faults are the redeeming qualities of this cultural transplant and fugitive from the law. Like many of the black men whom Wilson portrays, Lymon has the potential to be fully productive, yet growing up in an indifferent and racist South has markedly limited his aspirations and made him a mass of paradoxes. Although he purchases a flashy green suit, matching shirt, and shoes from Wining Boy, he does so with money he earns honestly by working with Boy Willie. Although he engages in much womanizing while in Pittsburgh, he still has much respect for women and hints to Berniece that he might seriously seek her affections. Although he seems to have an aversion to hard work, he picks and loads watermelons along with Boy Willie and assists him in selling them. Although he refuses to return to Mississippi, he is motivated not just by his wish to avoid the law but by his belief that blacks are treated better up North. Like hundreds of southern black men coming into the cities before and after him, the deceptive lure of the North draws him; but also like them, he is certain to be consumed and discarded by this same society to which he feels such misguided attraction.

The North also did not fulfill the dreams of Boy Willie's blues-plagued uncle, Wining Boy. Music has failed this onetime piano-playing man, who now turns to liquor to buffer the pain of his unsuccessful life. Like Herald Loomis, he is cut off from his cultural base and, as a result, lives a tormented existence. But, unlike Loomis, Wining Boy willfully rejects family ties in favor of liquor, juke joints, and a life on the road.

Wining Boy's disgust with playing the piano is another demonstration of Wilson's belief that the most poignant drama emerges when blacks cannot find success in sports or music, the only arenas open to full black participation. But being good at playing the piano is not enough for Wining Boy. In fact, he seems ashamed to claim piano playing as his profession. Instead, he blames the piano for the sorry course his life has taken: "All you know how to do is play that piano. Now, who am I? Am I me? Or am I the piano player? Sometime it seem like the only thing to do is shoot the piano player cause he the cause of all the trouble I'm having" (*PL* 41). Ironically, the same instrument that eventually reunites the Charles family is Wining Boy's nemesis, symbolizing that which disintegrates his family, keeps him constantly relocating, and indirectly drives him to drink.

At fifty-six, Wining Boy realizes that he cannot find happiness forever entertaining in various bars and gambling joints. Once married but thrown out by his wife, Cleotha, who refused to tolerate his rambling, Wining Boy becomes an alcoholic. He seems restless by nature. With his mysterious "sack of money" in one hand and a bottle of liquor in the other, he travels a road much like the one *Joe Turner's* Herald Loomis took in search of his song. Up North he now lives the blues that he so frequently played throughout the South. As Wilson notes, "He is a man who looking back over his life continues to live it with an odd mixture of zest and sorrow" (*PL* 28).

One character who has not given up is Berniece's persistent suitor Avery; he sees tremendous opportunity in the cultural institution of the black church. Thus, like Boy Willie, he opts to use his legacy to gain a degree of financial security. His ambition is to construct a church, assemble a congregation, and minister to them with Berniece at his side as his wife. Yet as an aspiring black minister, Avery is subject to the unkind stereotypes traditionally assigned to this often caricatured profession. Although he seems genuine enough in his religious conviction, he is perceived as a comical figure by the men he encounters. Even Berniece seems at times to not take him seriously, as she continues to keep him at arms' length. As the play's other black men see him, Avery is a thinly veiled version of themselves—street-smart con men who would willingly play any role that gives them an economic advantage. Therefore, they refuse to believe that Avery was "called" to the ministry, choosing instead to believe that, like them, Avery has found a lucrative scheme to support himself. Wining Boy sees it this way: "Ain't nothing wrong with being a preacher. You got the preacher on one hand and the gambler on the other. Sometimes there ain't too much difference in them" (30). Sharing this disregard for all men of the cloth, Boy Willie asks, "How you get to be a preacher, Avery? I might want to be a preacher one day. Have everybody call me Reverend Boy Willie" (43).

Avery has also found employment in Pittsburgh as an elevator operator in a downtown skyscraper. But he is not satisfied with the meagre pension plan, annual Thanksgiving turkey, and annual ten-cent-per-hour raise that this job offers. And although Avery seems to be in control of his life, he still has to kowtow to white officials at the local bank where he hopes to secure a loan: "Oh, they talked to me real nice," he tells Doaker. "I told Berniece . . . they say maybe they let me borrow the money" (96).

Avery, Boy Willie, Lymon, and Wining Boy represent the various approaches black men adopted to negotiate life in the North. Regrettably only Avery and Boy Willie aspire to do anything useful with their legacies. Avery sees that by building a church and serving as minister he will be set for life, and he comes to Pittsburgh prepared to conform to the system and establish a home there. Unlike Boy Willie, he is working within and around the myriad societal constraints placed upon black men of this day. In his hopes to be a minister and husband, he follows a safe course to assure that he does not offend the powers that be and jeopardize his plans to settle down and prosper in his new environment. Boy Willie, in contrast, has no use for the North and leaves the South to drum up capital to invest in land back in Mississippi. Lymon comes to escape the hard labor that is the staple of life for black men in the South and to partake of the so-called good life. The eternally restless Wining Boy has already run his course in the South as a piano player and gambler and now resigns himself to wandering about and drinking.

Of the entire group of black men in *The Piano Lesson*, Doaker Charles, the level-headed referee between Berniece and Boy Willie, has what was for black men in the 1930s the most reliable and best-paying job available. He is a full-time railroad cook who, because of the transient nature of his job, resides with his niece in Pittsburgh when he is not aboard a train. Apparently his job has helped mold him into a wise and self-sufficient man who is accustomed to keeping strife in proper perspective. As the forty-seven-year-old uncle of the feuding siblings, he brings much-needed calm and reason to their debate. He also is not a burden to Berniece, for he prepares his own meals, looks after his clothing, and adds a welcome masculine presence to his widowed niece's home. Twenty-seven years of railroad work have left Doaker content; unlike his restless brother Wining Boy, he seems satisfied with how he has lived his life. He shows no signs of anxiety about a lack of money or about his single life. He keeps a liquor bottle stashed away somewhere, yet—again unlike his brother—he appears to limit his drinking to rare occasions.

As a railroad cook Doaker is a member of a very honorable group of black men: the Pullman porters who serviced various railroads during the Depression. According to a recent study based on interviews with black former railroadmen, "Black men, from their point of view, saw the Pullman Company as a way up and a way out of poverty. Many men say it was 'the only game in town,' and it was a relatively prestigious game. As one porter remembers it, 'It was good job for a black man' " (Santino 7). Although Doaker's particular assignment is to cook, others are responsible for a wide range of duties, including shining shoes, making beds, and generally catering to the all-white passengers' every need. Since the supply of black railroad employees was originally tapped from slave labor, there was a lingering tendency among the white passengers these black men encountered to act like masters. Yet given the choice between standing in breadlines to feed themselves or their families and acting the part of obsequious servants, numerous black men chose the latter while adopting various means of deflecting the racism that seemed an inevitable part of the job.

Such antidotes included harmonizing and storytelling. Scenes of male bonding among Doaker and his rowdy company turn into raucous sessions of competitive storytelling, singing, or light-hearted games of the dozens. For example, while Lymon, Wining Boy, and Boy Willie sit around the kitchen table talking casually, their conversation soon leads to a railroad song about the advantages of marrying a railroad man over a farming man:

> When you marry, don't marry no farming man oh-ah
> When you marry, don't marry no farming man well
> Everyday Monday, hoe handle in your hand oh-ah
> Everyday Monday, hoe handle in your hand well
> When you marry, marry a railroad man, oh-ah
> When you marry, marry a railroad man, well
> Every Sunday, dollar in your hand oh-ah
> Every Sunday, dollar in your hand well. (*PL* 40)

The Piano Lesson, like many of Wilson's plays about the black experience, emphasizes male bonding. As early as *Jitney!*, his exploration of black men employed as jitney drivers in a Pittsburgh station, he focuses on their relationships. He investigates, from a black man's point of view, the chemistry that exists among a traditionally oppressed group as they try to survive in America without sacrificing either their dignity or their masculinity. They are by no means oblivious to women, yet the sometimes unexplained camaraderie that they develop in each other's company is crucial in their lives.

It takes little to get Doaker talking about trains. When prompted by Boy Willie, he muses, "They got so many trains out there they have a hard time keeping them from running into each other. Got trains going every whichaway. Got people on all of them" (19). Doaker has another opportunity to display his fondness for narrative when he volunteers to relate the long and turbulent history of the piano. He crams into a few minutes the changing fortunes of a piano that has affected several generations of Charles family members from slavery to the 1930s. He seems to savor telling the story and embellishes it with verbal flourishes of his own. He recalls,

> So Sutter lined up his niggers and Mr. Nolander looked them over and out of the whole bunch he picked my grand-mother . . . her name was Berniece . . . same like Berniece . . . and he picked my daddy when he wasn't nothing but a little boy nine years old. They made the trade off and Miss Ophelia was so happy with that piano that it got to be just about all she would do was play on that piano. (43)

Doaker is steeped in the rich folklore that evolved among this exclusive class of black railroad men. Many a fabricated tale or trickster story had its beginnings on the long rides from station to station. Taken as a whole, these rhetorical exercises reveal not just these men's capacities for constructing entertaining narratives but they also speak to the dominant cultural milieu for blacks at the time of their inception. According to Santino,

> The stories the porters share are cultural artifacts: they tell us something about the men that tell them, the times of which they report, and the perception of those times by the men who live them. The stories are cultural products—different men recount the events in different ways. . . . Pullman porters are good storytellers: theirs was and still is (among the retired men today) a primarily oral culture. Making of their past a good, well-performed story is itself a prized activity and a valued capability. (61)

An expert storyteller himself, August Wilson taps into a rich vein of the black oral tradition by including this black railroad man. But Doaker's significance goes beyond his rhetoric. Although his relatively calm bearing in *The Piano Lesson* may suggest otherwise, he represents yet another version of the warrior spirit. In a sense, his profession forces him to adopt a measure of Avery's conformity, but it also compels him to use a great deal of Boy Willie's cunning. By necessity he can transform instantaneously into the ultimate trickster, pampering and smiling at white passengers to nearly double his salary in tips while laughing with other black employees about his wiles. And they resisted with more than their wits. Under the leadership of fellow Pullman porter A. Philip Randolph, these proud black men eventually unionized to become the Brotherhood of Sleeping Car Porters, an organization that succeeded in overturning numerous unfair labor practices and inequities in pay for black railroad employees.[2]

The different ways in which the men of *The Piano Lesson* support themselves shed some light upon their personalities, and it is also important that the sole black female character, Berniece, also works. Her apprehensions arise not just from her obsession over the piano but from her status as a thirty-five-year-old widowed, single parent who also happens to be a black woman living in 1930s Pittsburgh. With money from her wages as a maid and from whatever rent she collects from her Uncle Doaker, she supports a household and raises a young daughter. By comparison she seems better off than the typical black woman of her day, enjoying a home and a steady income, yet her status as a widow assumes tragic proportions within the context of the times and is deemed especially unfortunate in the eyes of the men around her.

Berniece is not identified by her occupation so much as she is by the fact that she must work at all: this is regarded as a kind of unnatural experience that no young, reasonably attractive woman should have to endure. Only women who cannot marry have reason to go into the workforce. Doaker concurs with these societal dictates. He tells Wining Boy, "If she go ahead and marry Avery . . . he working everyday . . . she go ahead and marry him they could do alright for themselves. But as it stands she ain't got no money" (*PL* 58). He pities his niece for having to leave for work so early in the morning to clean house "for some bigshot down there at the steel mill" (58), and, at every opportunity he gets, lectures her on the advantages of marrying Avery.

But though she is managing a home and raising a daughter during the Depression on a maid's wages, Berniece does not see marriage as her only recourse. Marriage, to her, is not the same convenient arrangement that her boyfriend Avery envisions it to be. She is frankly offended by such insinuations. She fumes,

You trying to tell me a woman can't be nothing without a man. But you alright, huh? You can just walk out of here without me—without a woman—and still be a man. That's alright. Ain't nobody gonna ask you, "Avery, who you got to love you?" That's alright for you. But everybody gonna be worried about Berniece. (*PL* 67)

To be sure, Berniece's ideas about men, marriage, and her independence may seem anachronistic when one considers the 1930s setting of *The Piano Lesson*.

In his role as teacher/playwright, Wilson has expressed a commitment to integrating as many aspects of black culture into his work as possible. He explains, "I try to actually keep all of the elements of the culture alive in the work. . . . I purposely go through and make sure each element of that is in some ways represented—some more so than others in the plays, which I think gives them a fullness, and a completeness . . . that this is an entire world" (interviewed by the author). In addition to emphasizing the rich black oral tradition that thrived among black railroad men, he turns our attention to another oral legacy of black culture—ghostlore. In *The Piano Lesson*, the ghostly specter of Robert Sutter refuses to relinquish his claim on the piano as well as an unspoken related claim on these descendants of slaves once owned by the Sutter clan. Not just a figment of imagination or hallucination, this spirit of the former 300-pound white landowner is a confirmed presence in Berniece's home as he is witnessed by each member of the Charles family.

Belief in the supernatural among blacks, especially in the rural South, has supported a large body of folk narratives that reveal much about relationships between slaves and their masters in early America. Chiefly used by white slave owners to deter insurrection and escape, ghost legends stimulated the slaves' imaginations and, as expected, evoked abject terror in would-be runaways.[3] Psychology and fear were the chief means of discouraging movement among slaves, especially during the night when visibility significantly decreased. Even after slaves were manumitted, ghostlore continued to be a tool used by white southerners who wished to stem the exodus of their black labor supply. As folklorist Gladys Fry notes, "The system of control had one primary aim: to discourage the unauthorized movement of Blacks" (44).

The Great Migration is at its peak during the time of *The Piano*

Lesson. As evidenced by frequent arrivals and departures in Berniece's home and recurring conversations about rambling, restlessness, train rides, and letters from relatives and friends, the black population in the 1930s is undergoing an unprecedented cultural upheaval and dislocation. Despite the upward mobility suggested by this mass movement, many blacks, like Berniece, still could not free themselves from thoughts of their brutal life in the South. Jim Crow followed them to their destinations, assumed a different form, and continued to oppress them.

Wilson wishes to dispel this lingering anxiety, which he personifies in the ghost of Robert Sutter. Thus one of his chief concerns in *The Piano Lesson* is that this spirit be duly exorcised from Berniece's home—not just to ease those who are terrified about its repeated appearances but to lift the invisible control that the Sutter family still enjoys over their lives. According to Wilson, it is essential that Boy Willie challenge this ghost head-on. Contrary to Richards's emphasis upon the fate of the piano as the play's more significant resolution, Wilson believes that an all-out confrontation with this ghost is the essential point of the play. This explains the abrupt ending in the script's original version; once Boy Willie engages the ghost in a wrestling match, "the lights go down to black." Wilson recalls, "I wanted Boy Willie to demonstrate a willingness to battle with Sutter's ghost, the ghost of the white man—that lingering idea of him as the master of slaves—which is still in black Americans' lives and needs to be exorcised. I wasn't so much concerned with who ended up with the piano, as with Boy Willie's willingness to do battle" ("How to Write" H17).

The history of Robert Sutter's ghost becomes the stuff of legend in the hands of seasoned storytellers like Wining Boy and Doaker. As Gladys Fry observes, "Rumor was the method used not only to circulate the falsified story as legitimate news, but to expand and exaggerate the account as it was verbally transmitted from one excited person to another" (63). To the surviving brothers of the murdered Boy Charles, perpetuating the saga of the Ghost of the Yellow Dog is an art form. A boxcar on the Yellow Dog railroad was the final resting place for Berniece and Boy Willie's father. It was here where he, along with four hoboes, perished in a fire deliberately set by an irate Robert Sutter, who sought personal retaliation for Boy Charles's involvement in repossessing the celebrated piano. According to rumor, the spirits of these five men returned to avenge their murder by pushing their murderers one by one, down into their wells to their deaths. Doaker expertly lays out the details of this larger-than-life tale:

> Must have got mad when they couldn't find the piano cause they set the boxcar afire and killed everybody. Now, nobody know who done that. Some people say it was Sutter cause it was his piano. Some people say it was Sheriff Carter. Some people say it was Robert Smith and Ed Saunders. But don't nobody know for sure. It was about two months after that that Ed Saunders fell down his well. Just upped and fell down his well for no reason. People say it was the ghost of them men who burned up in the boxcar that pushed him in his well. They started calling them the Ghosts of the Yellow Dog. (45–46)

While Doaker attributes the explanation of the drownings of Robert Sutter and Ed Saunders to rumor, Wining Boy brings the story closer to home. He claims to have actually heard the voices of the Ghosts of the Yellow Dog on several occasions and details how he personally sought advice from these spirits on improving his life and apparently got it while standing "right there where them two railroads cross each other" (34–35). Wining Boy takes the ghost narrative from the realm of the spiritual to the real. In doing so, he reflects a popular pattern in the evolution of folklore: "Suggestibility increases as credibility decreases" (Fry 63).

The instructional platform that Wilson establishes in *The Piano Lesson* is almost three decades removed from the call to arms that Amiri Baraka issued in his fever-pitched description of Revolutionary Theatre of the 1960s. Then, black theatre was a catalyst to shock the country's blacks into both awareness of and action against their victimization. Then, the lessons presented to black audiences included graphic displays of antiwhite, anti-Western emotion. In 1964 Baraka (then LeRoi Jones) wrote:

> The Revolutionary Theatre must teach them [white men] their deaths. It must crack their faces open to the mad cries of the poor. It must teach them about silence and the truths lodged there. It must kill any God anyone names except Common Sense. The Revolutionary Theatre should flush the fags and murderers out of Lincoln's face. . . .

Our theatre will show victims so that their brothers in the audience will be better able to understand that they are the brothers of victims, and that they themselves are victims if they are blood brothers. And what we show must cause the blood to rush, so that pre-revolutionary temperaments will be bathed in this blood, and it will cause their deepest souls to move, and they will find themselves tensed and clenched, even ready to die, at what the soul has been taught. ("Revolutionary Theatre" 211, 213)

This revolutionary temperament surfaces but is clearly redirected in Wilson's work in general and in *The Piano Lesson* in particular. He avoids the hardcore agitprop that characterizes black theatre of the turbulent 1960s and replaces it with more soul-searching theatre—that which invites black audiences to take a closer and more personal look at how they have fared in America's exclusionary history. *The Piano Lesson* shows the Boy Willies and the Bernieces, who are preoccupied with coming to terms with the forces shaping their family's history and with deciding to accept the inherited responsibility of sustaining their legacy. Wilson examines a neglected area of concern for black Americans' present and future well-being: their cultural past.

Wilson told one interviewer, "I think *Piano Lesson* is my best play" (Savran 298). He told another, "I'm growing as a playwright and I'm learning more about the possibilities of theater. I'm also becoming more comfortable with poetry in drama—I'm a better poet than a play-wright—and so I think I'm really finding my true voice" (Hawley C2). This fifth play in Wilson's proposed ten-play project displays a decep-tive ease that suggests that Wilson has, indeed, found his true voice. The skill with which he integrates elements of black culture into a play also charged with confrontation represents a decided advance over the prob-lems of construction that plagued his initially divided script for *Ma Rainey's Black Bottom*. He continues to create powerfully realistic dia-logue that reflects the pressing concerns of blacks during unusually harsh economic times. And in *The Piano Lesson*, his use of metaphor becomes a potent teaching tool that masterfully augments his dramatic vision.

SEVEN

Going Back to Pick Up the Ball:
Two Trains Running

Larry Fishburne as
Sterling and Ella Joyce as
Risa in the spring 1990 premiere
of *Two Trains Running* at the Yale Repertory
Theatre. In this scene, Sterling and Risa
mask their true emotions by
pretending to be kissing cousins.
© by Gerry Goodstein.
Reprinted by permission.

August Wilson came into manhood during the turbulent 1960s, a decade that holds special meaning for a culturally and politically conscious writer. He was twenty-three years old at the height of the Black Power movement in 1968. Fully engaged in its cause, he, along with other politically charged artists, utilized his talents to communicate a philosophy of black cultural nationalism. However, for many artists and activists alike, the fervent crusade for racial justice and cultural affirmation that seemed so pervasive then has given way to a less abrasive but an apparently less effective agenda. As one who was very much a part of it, August Wilson can recall with pride his role in the earlier cultural movement. He does not set himself apart from the angry young playwrights of the early 1970s, such as Ed Bullins and Amiri Baraka. He admits, "I think it was an absolutely great time, much needed, and I'm sorry to see it dissipated. . . . It was all a part of the people's lives; they had been given a platform" (Powers 52). However, his current work does not feature the Clays or the Walker Vessels, who spew violent rhetoric and profanity and advocate the deaths of their white oppressors. Instead of assailing white America's conscience, his characters seem preoccupied with discovering, acknowledging, and grappling with both their collective and individual pasts in order to move their lives forward. Their focus is upon overcoming the effects of cultural fragmentation and renewing their strength by reclaiming the African continuum. Thus, Wilson renders more cerebral, more three-dimensional accounts of the black experience within—not apart from or outside of—the context of America.

Set in 1969, *Two Trains Running* (1990) presents the debris of an explosive era in black awareness. Its very premise suggests what happens when there are no heirs to carry on the legacy established by past black activists, too many of whom now exist only as martyrs. Wilson expresses this sense of loss in his play for the 1960s by invoking a familiar football analogy—"going back to pick up the ball": "There's a character in *Two Trains Running* [Aunt Ester] who says 'If you drop the ball, you've got to go back and pick it up. There's no need to continue to run because if you reach the endzone, it's not going to be a touchdown. You have to have the ball' " (interviewed by Bond).

According to Wilson, current generations of blacks seem to have abandoned the hard work and sacrifice of their ancestors, paying only lip service to what was their elders' raison d'être. He also laments the cultural emptiness that plagues black youth. Nowhere is this more obvious than in the commercial bonanza stemming from Spike Lee's 1992 film Malcolm X. Sweatshirts, caps, and a variety of paraphernalia bearing the familiar "X" have become virtually a uniform for many of the same black youth who appreciate little and know even less about their past. Although Malcolm Little's famous "X" originally signified a disavowal of his so-called white name and a celebration of his African roots, in the hands of moneymakers it also became a faddish craze and an emblem of unreflective militance.

Wilson's theme for *Two Trains Running* addresses the misplaced values of today's youth by imploring them to "go back and pick up the ball." Although its metaphor is borrowed from sport, the theme has extremely serious cultural as well as economic implications for black Americans. In particular, it strengthens Wilson's plea to them to look to the African continuum as inspiration for their cultural preservation and their continued advancement. It is also an appeal to black Americans to continue to confront white America and to demand that which they deserve as citizens, whether that be equal opportunities for employment, comparable pay, or simply fair and humane treatment. In addition to its cultural implications within the context of the play, the simple phrase "going back to pick up the ball" describes the politics of economics—an area in which blacks have historically been cast as victims rather than as benefactors. Even more than cultural redemption, then, *Two Trains Running* is a play about the economic survival of black Americans and the many entrenched oppressive forces with which its characters often collide as they choose among luck, violence, and fair play.

Wilson's play for the 1960s is a static, two-act succession of stories about the bleak circumstances blacks face in Pittsburgh and, more generally, in America. The text of the play for the most part comprises testimonies of various members of the motley group of personalities who frequent Memphis Lee's Home Style Restaurant. *Two Trains Running* affords Wilson the opportunity to demonstrate knowledge gained while he worked as a short-order cook after he relocated to St. Paul from Pittsburgh. At one point he supported a wife, a daughter, and himself working as an $88-per-week cook at Little Brothers of the Poor on East Lake Street. He also spent time in similar popular locales, such as Butler Drug and Aunt Nora's restaurants. The experience taught him a number of rituals associated with the restaurant business: for example, how owners pay their workers, how they replenish supplies, and how they regard customers and employees. Clues to Wilson's experience as a former cook also surface in his impeccably accurate price listings for entrees popular in a '60s restaurant that caters to a black clientele.

But Wilson learned more than how to tend a griddle at Little Brothers of the Poor. As Ishmael Reed observes, "Wilson's job as a cook and dishwasher gave him a front-row center seat for the rich verbal entertainment and instruction—and incidentally also account for his frequent and accurate descriptions of soul food" (95). The restaurant, like the bars, the poolrooms, and the tobacco shops, became another substitute classroom for the young, street-smart Wilson.

The year is 1969, and the atmosphere is charged with emotional fallout from the recent death of Martin Luther King, Jr. and a local preacher/prophet, and blacks are still reacting to the 1965 slaying of Malcolm X. Short ribs sell for $2.45 a serving, James Brown and Aretha Franklin enjoy their respective titles as "Godfather" and "Queen" of soul, and the United States is embroiled in racial turmoil and still stuck in the quagmire of the Vietnam War. When mutual commiseration is not enough to uplift the blues-ridden lives of these customers, they turn to playing the numbers and visiting Aunt Ester, a sage reportedly 322 years old, whose extraordinary longevity and surreal presence cast her as a preternatural phenomena rather than simply the warm and wise elderly woman that others believe she is.

This soon-to-be demolished restaurant is positioned across the street from West's funeral parlor and Lutz's Meat Market. Its regulars include Memphis, the restaurant's caustic owner who refuses to settle for anything less than $25,000 from the city for his restaurant (which it plans to raze as part of a downtown revitalization plan); Holloway, a onetime house painter but now the self-made historian of the group; Wolf, a professional numbers runner; Hambone, a mentally retarded man who is obsessed with getting a ham that was promised him for a paint job completed some nine and a half years ago; Sterling, a naive ex-convict fresh out of the penitentiary and hungry for work; West, a wealthy mortician who once doubled as a numbers runner and bootlegger but now owns a posh funeral parlor where he displays for an adoring and curious public the body of a highly influential religious leader; and Risa, an attractive young waitress who has mutilated her legs with razor cuts to deflect unwelcomed attention from men.

Two Trains Running troubles some who see the play as a missed opportunity to delve more deeply into the historical realities of the decade it features. Similar criticism was levied against *The Piano Lesson*, which sidestepped the pervasive woes of the Depression in favor of focusing on the story of a family. Ironically what some critics, such as *Los Angeles Times*'s Sylvia Drake, see as a "problem" (F1), Wilson regards as marking his intent to avoid "what *white* folks think of as American history for the 1960s (Rocha 26). He explains that "the point of the play is that by 1969 nothing has changed for the black man. People talk about King and Malcolm, but by 1968, as it says in the play, both are dead" (27). Emphasis is shifted, therefore, from rehashing the rhetoric of the larger social and political arenas of the 1960s toward a more personal exploration of the emotional landscapes of individual characters. *Two Trains Running* tells the separate stories of black men and black women who try to find their song without first acknowledging from whence they have come.

Although *Two Trains Running* is set in 1969, the play is basically a smoldering reaction to a series of unforgettable cataclysmic events that occurred in 1968. The tone of America's internal woes was set by back-to-back assassinations that year of key civil rights figures—Reverend Martin Luther King, Jr. and Senator Robert Kennedy. Following King's shooting on April 4, riots broke out in 130 American cities. In the wake of massive looting, burning, and violence, federal troops were dispatched to several cities, including Washington, Baltimore, and Chicago. Also following King's murder, the Black Panther party gained power as a watchdog group to ward off ongoing injustices against blacks. A sign of racial tension in America seen around the entire world was the image of three black American athletes accepting their 1968 Olympic medals while they wore black gloves and raised clenched fists to demonstrate defiance against rather than allegiance to the United States.

Among other things, 1968 was an election year, but in an address to the nation, President Lyndon Johnson shocked his party and the American public by declining to seek a second term. Under fire from both anti–Vietnam War protesters and civil rights activists, Johnson had had his fill of the presidency. In Chicago the Democratic National Convention turned into a free-for-all where special interest groups ranging from Yippies to Black Panthers vied for the spotlight and wreaked havoc on the proceedings.

In 1968 America was also embroiled in controversy from abroad. In Vietnam, American troops murdered over one hundred villagers in what is now known as the My Lai Massacre. Early in the year North Korean communist soldiers seized the U.S. Navy spy ship Pueblo in international waters. One U.S. soldier was killed, and eighty-two were taken as hostages. Also by early 1968, the Vietnam War had taken a grisly toll. Of the 500,000 troops and personnel stationed in Vietnam, 16,000 had been killed and another 110,000 had been wounded.

Plenty happens in the late 1960s—violent racial upheavals in urban areas, assassinations of political leaders, and chaotic antiwar protests— yet audiences and critics alike frequently charge that nothing happens in *Two Trains Running*. Clearly their frustrations suggest that they are accustomed to the neatly resolved, almost predictable well-made play; however, *Two Trains* offers few easy solutions. Despite the unprecedented events of 1968, a strange calm hangs over Memphis's diner. Like O'Neill's wounded group in *The Iceman Cometh*, they have witnessed and participated in the madness, yet they have chosen to withdraw from it. In this case, Memphis's customers and his sole employee show little change because, as they see it, America is back to business as usual—especially as it relates to the concerns of its black citizens. Wilson explains the apparent economic, social, and political detachment of the characters in *Two Trains* in terms of an analogy: "In 1968, the relationship of blacks to white Americans was not that much different than the relationship of slaves to their masters. It was like a day off on the plantation. Nobody was working. There were no jobs. There were all these people with families but no means of support, because society didn't have any use for them" (Dworkin 8).

Two Trains, like all of Wilson's chronicles, invites audiences to reexamine a black worldview. To accommodate them Wilson adopts a strategy not unlike that which scholar-critic Stephen Henderson outlines in his important essay "Saturation: Progress Report on a Theory of Black Poetry." Henderson asserts that the poet or writer

> considers the communication of this "Blackness" to be significant and his [the audience] reception of it to be significant, whether he agrees or not. This communication of Blackness may be related to theme, or what is commonly called the subject or meaning of the poem or it may be related to the structure of the poem—the way it is put together. With regard to theme, saturation may occur when the theme is simply, obviously, and naturally black. (7–8)

Henderson's theory provides a useful means of describing Wilson's mission as a playwright: he attempts to communicate blackness by "saturating" his work with an abundance of elements from an identifiably black culture. These interrelated signs of blackness are as varied as the food his characters eat, the locales they frequent, the stories they tell, the language they use, and the gods they believe in. As one *Newsweek* writer observed in a review of *Two Trains*, "What we witness is not a play about the '60s, but a form of oral history, in which we're invited to eavesdrop on the timeless continuum of the African-American experience" (Ansen 70).

Wilson's communication of blackness in *Two Trains Running* is foreshadowed by the play's title, which is taken from a railroad love song composed by blues singer McKinley "Muddy Waters" Morganfield. The lyrics to "Still A Fool" (1951) draws on an oral tradition that may be traced back to "rail connections between Northern industrial Pittsburgh and Southern rural Mississippi" (Rosenburg D7). In this blues song, a black man is caught in a love affair with "another man's wife." He contemplates catching a train, but none goes in the right direction.

> Well now it's two, there's two trains running.
> Well ain't narry one ho—going my way.
> Well now one run at midnight and the other jes fo' day.
> It's running jes' fo' day.
> Oh, lawd, sho' 'nough 'tis.
> Oh well . . .
> I been crazy.
> Yes, I been a fool.
> I been crazy ho—all of my life.
> Well, I done fell in love with another man's wife
> With another man's wife.
> Oh, Lawd, sho' 'nough I done.
> Oh well. ("Still A Fool")

Railroads had a great impact upon the sociology, demographics, and, at one time, the economics of black life. The train occupies a special place in the folk culture of black Americans and serves as a favorite metaphor of the blues singer, for it was one of several agents that affected the emotions of thousands of oppressed and depressed people. For example, it indirectly contributed to splintering the black family by cutting short otherwise promising relationships between black men and black women, and by facilitating the constant relocation of those who were desperately seeking work or just plain restless.

One of the play's most vocal characters shares a special connection with the train. For thirty-six years Memphis Lee has plotted how he would return to the South to avenge himself against white persecutors who took his land and drove him away. To Memphis, the train represents his only link with his past in Jackson, Mississippi. Its noisy presence continues to remind him that his peace of mind depends upon his decision to go back to pick up the ball—that is, to set straight the record of his past. This means retrieving his land, punishing his persecutors, or both. He tells Holloway, "I'm going back one of these days. I ain't even got to know the way. All I got to do is find my way down to the train depot. They got two trains running every day" (*TT* 31).

The title *Two Trains Running* also suggests what one theatre critic calls "parallel opposites: life and death, African spirituality and American materialism, tradition and practicality, separation and integration, Malcolm X and Martin Luther King" (Rosenburg D7). Perhaps the most dominant theme intimated by this title is that the present generation of black Americans must choose between holding fast the virtues of their cultural heritage and seeking by any means necessary money for sheer survival. While blacks remain under the lion's paw of economic oppression, the dual concerns of culture and economics understandably do not receive the same priority. Although the raging debate in *The Piano Lesson* ends in a triumph for culture within the Charles family, the characters in *Two Trains Running* tend to favor more immediate economic payoffs. What may seem like irresponsible or lackadaisical approaches to life, therefore, are instead means developed for coping in a society that continues to foster economic slavery. Comments made by the seemingly onmiscient Holloway support this observation:

> People kill me walking around talking about niggers is lazy. Niggers is the most hard working people in the world. Worked three hundred years for free. And didn't take no lunch hour. Now all of a sudden niggers is lazy. Don't know how to work. All of a sudden when they got to pay niggers, ain't no work for him to do. (*TT* 34)

One of the most frequent reservations expressed about *Two Trains Running* concerns its lack of momentum.[1] The blues aesthetic, which is the force underlying much of Wilson's work, has considerable relevance to the play's nearly arrested movement. The play's lax tempo and unconventional structure imitate the often unhurried, repetitive, and sometimes amorphous form of blues music. It is important to note that, for Wilson, emphasis is upon evoking a particular mood, not upon conforming to abstract principles of the well-made play. When he depicted Ma Rainey, whose fans endearingly dubbed her "Mother of the Blues," he had her express a similar regard for the limitless emotional potential of the blues: "You don't sing to feel better. You sing 'cause that's a way of understanding life" (*MR* 82). *Two Trains Running*, like *Ma Rainey's Black Bottom*, is best viewed as a dramatic rendering of a blues song; form and structure are secondary to catharsis.

Also, because the substance of *Two Trains Running* is conveyed largely through conversations about the past, very little action transpires. Indeed, during the course of the play's succession of stories few major developments occur. Hambone's landlady finds his scarred body sprawled across the bed, and the restaurant owner Memphis Lee learns that Pittsburgh city officials agree to pay him the entire $25,000 for his establishment. A love affair between ex-inmate Sterling and waitress Risa stirs the action a bit, but despite a steamy kiss and suggestions of marriage, any future plans the two entertain seem hopelessly stalled. It is a seemingly small action, Sterling's decision at the end of the play to ransack Lutz's Meat Market and snatch a ham for Hambone's casket, that best conveys one of the play's most urgently pressed themes: "going back to pick up the ball."

The nonstop personal narratives in *Two Trains Running* also reflect a culture that has traditionally honored vocal expression. Wilson had earlier provided a striking practitioner of this time-honored cultural form in Troy Maxson, one of his most talkative characters. But the multiple tales in *Two Trains* also allow Wilson to reintroduce the art of listening, a skill that he himself mastered in the bars, restaurants, and tobacco shops of Pittsburgh during his early adult years. Mesmerized by the stories of old black men, Wilson would listen carefully to learn the secrets of their long endurance, wishing that he could be as fortunate. This ability to listen would also serve Wilson well as a poet and later as a playwright struggling to find appropriate substance for his work and trying to write realistic dialogue. He soon discovered that his ear provided the very essence of his creative skills.

Audiences who expect the wealth of stories that are told in Memphis's cafe to wind up as parts of a neatly arranged plot soon discover that this is not to be. By deliberately emphasizing the stories themselves, not plot and action, Wilson forces the audience to listen differently and invokes an atmosphere reminiscent of African tribal customs. Director Lloyd Richards likens the two-way process of talking and listening in Wilson's work to "sitting at the feet of elders. Somehow, around the tribal fires the wise men talk" (Erstein E1). Similarly, critic Paul Carter Harrison sees much evidence of the black oral tradition coming into play. He describes the verbal calisthenics that go on among the majority of Wilson's characters, such as those in *Two Trains Running*, as "telling stories that enlarge the time and space of reality by weaving a circuitous course of parenthetical anecdotes, asides, and utterances into a coherent pattern that encourages unanticipated tensions which amplify the coded signification inherent in the story" (301).

These are not just Wilson's incorporation of a black cultural tradition but they are also, for several of the characters, a remaining source of power. In a world where economic concerns prevent black men like *Fences*'s Troy Maxson from sustaining family ties and where a lack of money is perceived as an affront to their manhood, talk becomes "the only vehicle of redemption" (Courtemanche 3). Sterling depends upon talk alone to capture Risa's affection; Memphis cloaks his insecurities behind a barrage of words; and Hambone's protest amounts to the often-repeated two-liners "He gonna give me my ham! . . . I want my ham!" (*TT* 63–65.)

The retired painter Holloway has an important role in the storytelling sessions in *Two Trains Running*. He is a modernized version of the African griot, carrying bits and pieces of the histories of just about every character in the play. As a regular in Memphis's cafe, Holloway is undoubtedly privy to much local news, but his knowledge goes beyond overheard conversations to a kind of guarded omniscience. He may easily be stereotyped as one of those old men unencumbered by the demands of daily work or rigid schedules and fond of hanging about bars and barbershops where debates are common. However, Holloway's function is to ensure the historical accuracy of the stories around him. For example, when Memphis complains that Sterling does not want to work, Holloway lectures the rude owner on the background of the black man's work ethic and thereby vindicates the unemployed Sterling: "If the white man could figure out a way to make some money by putting niggers to work . . . we'd all be working" (*TT* 35). Holloway sees a long-standing connection between the slim chances blacks have for employment and their precarious status within the white power structure. He underscores this via a rather involved analogy about the white man's practice of "stacking niggers" that demonstrates how, alone, blacks are virtually worthless to the white man; but employers can use the slave owner's strategy of achieving wealth by assembling an oppressed and underpaid black workforce. This victimization of the powerless echoes the sentiment that *Ma Rainey's Black Bottom*'s Toledo expresses in his speech about leftovers from history.

Wise to the ways of life and of the white man and eager to school any naive listener, Holloway becomes the voice of decades—even centuries—of the black experience. He can be counted on to add a philosophical edge to any discussion around him; no subject escapes his keen commentary. Appearing to have been anointed the group's unofficial sage, he volunteers his wisdom to help their troubled psyches at least keep some healthy perspective. For example, he attempts to soften the blow of Hambone's death by avoiding talk about the deceased and addressing instead the larger concepts of love and death: "You got love and death. Death will find you . . . it's up to you to find love" (*TT* 102). Holloway clearly perceives American racial politics, foreseeing the paranoia among whites when one just "us[es] the word[s] nigger and gun" (85). He explains, "[Y]ou say the word nigger and gun in the same sentence and they'll try and arrest you. Accuse you of sabotage, disturbing the peace, inciting a riot, plotting to overthrow the government and anything else they can think of" (85–86).

Holloway has invested in the economic system that rejects his comrades and can now look forward to a regular income. Although middle age has slowed him down considerably, he once painted houses for a living. Like Memphis, he is one of those old men who found a way into the economic game that excluded many other black men. On the day that he is conspicuously absent from his regular perch in the cafe, he has gone downtown to apply for Social Security payments. Now, without fear of poverty, he can afford to sit around Memphis's place daily doling out wisdom while witnessing others wrestle with hard times.

A chief irony in *Two Trains Running* is that, although the play is essentially a succession of stories, eagerly related, one character does not participate. Risa, Memphis's catatonic black waitress whose history begs to be told, remains a mystery. Unlike Hambone, whose conversation is severely limited because of his mental handicap, Risa simply refuses to reveal any of her background. Instead, she makes herself an ugly emblem of protest against male definition of women; she takes a razor blade to her legs as a symbolic gesture of defiance against sheer lust. August Wilson himself provides few clues to the root cause of Risa's masochism. When questioned about her motives, he sighed, "Well, I wish I could talk more about her than I can. For me the scarring of her legs was an attempt to define herself in her own terms rather than being defined by men. . . . [B]asically for me it was her standing up and refusing to accept those definitions and making her self-definition" (interviewed by the author).

Wilson's own uncertainty about Risa may at first seem difficult to accept. After all, he created her character and determined her circumstances in the play. Although he plucks Risa from among the imaginary characters parading across his imagination during a brainstorming session, as sometimes happens with other characters whom he chooses, he does not recognize her. His initial understanding of characters is like a blank tablet, which gradually fills as he "listens" to their stories. "I always say whatever the material dictates; that's what I will follow," he explains (interview). Though his method of selecting characters seems random, he sets them within a vividly imagined past that grounds their stories and gives their characters more than one dimension.

Despite *New York Times* critic Frank Rich's alarm over Wilson's "inability to make more than a thematic conceit out of this lone woman" ("August Wilson" C13), Wilson believes that Risa offers some insight as to why Memphis's common-law wife of twenty-two years leaves him without so much as shaking his hand (*TT* 4). Cast as Memphis's foil, Risa provides far more information about Memphis's background than she does about her own apparent history of victimization. For if the bristly restaurateur's constant verbal assaults on Risa are any indication of his regard for women, then there is little wonder why he remains a single man. Clearly, to him, Risa is the epitome of incompetence—someone to be dominated, manipulated, and scolded. He seems ever ready to admonish her even at the slightest infraction of her duties: "Risa, get on back there and get to work. You ain't got time to be standing around talking" (18). Although it is, at first, difficult to get past Memphis's scolding, a pattern of either misogyny or extreme naïveté begins to emerge and to give clues about his failed relationship.

According to Wilson's design, Risa is also to be considered the allegorical Everywoman. That is, she "has to carry all of the women's stories in the play" (interview). Viewed this way, Risa's scars are to be perceived as emblems of defiance and independence for all black women in America. Yet during the entire course of *Two Trains Running*, not once does Risa convincingly affirm her position as a wronged black woman. Even at seemingly opportune times, she refuses to be drawn into lengthy discourse about her mutilation. "You wouldn't understand" (99), she tells Sterling as he tries to comprehend her.

Contrary to Wilson's expressed plans for Risa, she seems to find meaning only through her relationships with each of the men in the play. Ironically the little that is revealed about her past seeps into the play through conversations between certain men who claim to know merely portions of her story or through her unexplained emotional attachments to others. One is left feeling that there is much more to this woman and regretful that *she* does not get to tell it.

Holloway describes her narrow escape from being committed to a mental institution and her eventual conversion to the doctrines of Prophet Samuel. He prides himself in knowing Risa: "I know Risa. She one of them gals that matured quick and every man that seen her since she was twelve years old think she ought to go lay up with them somewhere" (32). His perceptions seem to be accurate: Memphis, Wolf, and Sterling define Risa mostly in terms of her sexuality. She is a physically attractive woman who ought to be honored that men ogle her form and desire her body. Memphis notes, "[A]ny man be glad to lay up next to that every night" (31). Even Wolf, the numbers runner, claims to have lusted after Risa for a period of time. He reveals, "I know all she need is a man. Somebody to make her feel like a woman" (32).

But it is Sterling who expresses the most earnest emotions about Risa. He is in love with her. Although his chances of supporting a wife are dreary at best, he wants to marry the "teasing brown angel" he claims God has sent him. In his hopes of demonstrating how very unnatural her attitude toward men is, he goes beyond the predominantly sexual appeals made by his friends: "Risa . . . you in the world, baby. You a woman in the world" (100).

Risa's unexplained attachments to the late spiritual leader Prophet Samuel and a mentally retarded regular in the restaurant affectionately called Hambone shed even more light on her personality. Both men enjoy Risa's special allegiance, though her ties to them remain essentially a mystery. As a proud dues-paying member of Prophet Samuel's First African Congregational Kingdom, Risa is quick to defend his legacy against sarcasm. Exactly what Prophet Samuel means to Risa is never fully divulged in the play.

While Prophet Samuel may provide Risa's character with a spiritual dimension, Hambone serves as a testament to her compassion. Her maternal concern for this mentally unstable man—reminiscent of the compassion displayed by Bertha Holly, the boardinghouse mother/proprietor of *Joe Turner's Come and Gone*—casts her as the embodiment of altruism. Knowing that her routine kind gestures toward Hambone will anger the restaurant owner, she continues to give him coffee, a warm bowl of beans, or a wrap to shield his body from the cold. She frequently intercedes on Hambone's behalf to ward off Memphis's verbal attacks against him. When Hambone is found dead, she laments the pauper's funeral that awaits him, preferring instead to "lay him out in a gold casket" (92).

Risa's character pales in the all-male environment of *Two Trains Running*. Lacking a voice, she becomes an object of interest for various men who not only crowd into the play their own accounts but claim her story as well. While the men tell competing tales of economic woes and of missed opportunities, she silently endures an obviously painful past. Harry Elam cites Hortense Spillers's assertion that "in a very real sense black American women are invisible to various public discourse" (74) as a possible explanation for Risa's position in the play. He considers her "an 'outsider-within' the male world of Memphis's restaurant" (167).

As it stands—despite Holloway's wealth of advice and Wilson's thematic thrust—for two of the characters, Wolf and Sterling, retrieving the symbolic dropped ball is simply not practical, especially after they concede that those in the white power structure who establish the rules keep changing them to bar blacks from economic inclusion. These same interests control the country's banking system and, through exclusionary practices in granting loans for houses and businesses, have reduced these men to the unpredictable and dangerous pursuits of gambling and numbers running. Like Troy Maxson of *Fences*, they give up their dreams and do whatever is required to survive. As grown black men with no demonstrable skills to put them into a legitimate workforce, Sterling and Wolf flirt with dubious means of acquiring money that keep them only one step ahead of the law.

Wolf exudes the air of a professional as he conducts his numbers racket out of Memphis's restaurant. Shut out of mainstream financial operations, he has established a popular and, for many, a respectable enterprise among his Pittsburgh clientele. He defends the legitimacy of his business with the shrewdness of a financial wiz. Thus he is quick to enlighten Risa, who believes what he does is a waste of time and a poor use for money: "It's the same thing as putting money in the bank. This way you might take out more than you put in . . . but Mellon [the bank's owner] ain't gonna let you do that. The numbers give you an opportunity. If it wasn't for the numbers all these niggers would be poor" (*TT* 3). Memphis Lee, who several years back won enough money to purchase his restaurant, agrees with Wolf's assessment. He too is a firm believer in the economic salvation that playing numbers offers black people. He notes,

> It wasn't till I hit the numbers eight or nine years ago that I got to the point where I could change clothes everyday. See, most niggers around here can't do that. The only way they can do that is to hit the numbers or get lucky in a crap game. The ones that are working . . . the only way they can do anything is to wait on their income tax return. Half the time the government cheat them out of that. (3)

Unlike the still hopeful Boy Willie of *The Piano Lesson*, Wolf has been forced to work outside the same American Dream that eludes them. Consequently, Wolf may be seen as a now-disillusioned version of Boy Willie; no doubt most of his dreams also have been deferred. For despite Wolf's ability to eke out a living in the numbers racket, he still is a low man in this illegal operation controlled by others. Even though he may appear to wield at least some authority, he must still abide by rules set by the all-white Albert clan. This truth is painfully revealed when Wolf is faced with telling the penniless Sterling that his winnings are to be cut because "every nigger in Pittsburgh played 781" (63)—the same number Sterling and Risa concocted. Going so far as to consider purchasing a gun to protect himself and asking his friends to break the news to Sterling first, the unfortunate Wolf reveals just who has the power.

This stranglehold that the white power structure continues to have on blacks in the late 1960s has victimized Sterling most. Like the persistent ghost of Robert Sutter that attaches itself to Berniece and Boy Willie's piano, the ghost of white oppression refuses to loose its hold. Its politics of selfish economics continues to devour would-be productive citizens, such as Sterling, and discard them as wretched statistics. Forced to watch from the sidelines, some, like Sterling, grown weary as spectators, reach out and grab some of the material comforts of life that would otherwise forever be out of their reach. Sterling robs a bank for this very reason: "I was tired of waking up everyday with no money. I figure a man supposed to have money sometime. Everybody else seem like they got it. Seem like I'm the only one ain't got no money" (54).

At the beginning of *Two Trains Running*, Sterling has just been released from a five-year prison sentence, but his continued freedom is contingent upon finding steady employment. Since he has no marketable skills and since jobs are at a premium for everyone, he finds no work as he scrounges about Pittsburgh looking for various odd jobs. Unhappily, the signs all point to Sterling eventually returning to jail, a place that has been a temporary home for a surprising number of black men like himself. Wolf underscores this bleak truth: "[J]ust walk down the street and ask people . . . every nigger you see done been to jail one time or another. The white man don't feel right unless he got a record on these niggers" (54).

Sterling's story best epitomizes the root causes of epidemic levels of violence, crime, and incarceration that blacks face in a more modern version of slavery. *After Hours* theatre critic Elleanor Courtmanche observes, "A vicious cycle is at work—you need economic power to get political power, but the work ethic, as the route to that power, reveals itself after all as being in the interests of the white status quo" (3). Sterling's story also demonstrates how little value is assigned to his life and to the lives of others like him who must pander to the whites controlling virtually all the country's institutions—banks, prisons, local governments, and, ironically, organized crime. The same system that spends thousands of dollars in attempts to rehabilitate its inmates and reposition them in society seriously considers lengthening his stay simply because he is a star football player within its sports program. The same system that withholds him from society for five years releases him to resume his squalid life with a better chance of returning to prison than of finding gainful employment. Even from birth, Sterling has been an unwelcome statistic. Given up by his own mother and ultimately becoming an orphan, he tells a heartrending story of a very erratic childhood. There is no mention of a father in his recollections, yet he does acknowledge some sort of bond with an orphanage worker whose death hastens his steady decline into criminal activities.

Sterling is a strangely off-beat character. Far from presenting the hardcore image one might expect, he appears painfully naive—almost childlike. But his revealing tales of a solitary battle to survive—being orphaned at an early age, being shuffled off to various living arrangements, and of being put away from society for five years—help explain his off-the-wall comments. The stories shed light on his stunning advice to Memphis on getting top dollar for his restaurant: "You got insurance? If you got insurance you could burn it down" (58) or his unscientific observations about the moon: "I be looking at the moon. Seem like it's getting closer and closer. You ever notice that? You look up and see if it ain't getting closer. . . . I don't go outside when it's a full moon. There be at least three or four people killed that night. I believe it's the end of the world" (88). Even more fantastical is Sterling's whirlwind romance with waitress Risa, whom he seriously intends to marry though he lacks even a prospect of a job, and the shadow of prison life still looms over him. Like the sullen trumpeter Levee of *Ma Rainey's Black Bottom*, who, at eight, witnessed his mother's rape and later his father's murder at the hands of vicious whites, Sterling is a product of a sick society. It has left him apparently off-balance psychologically, a man not taken very seriously by those around him.

Despite the tragic circumstances of Sterling's life, he is far superior to those who snub him; he still has the warrior spirit needed to challenge the white power structure, no matter what it does to wrong him. Wilson thus has fashioned him as a thinly veiled disciple of Malcolm X, who stirred young black men of the 1960s out of complacency and into an ever ready state of rebellion. As the avowed cultural nationalist preached, the black man's willingness to shed blood for their cause was the ultimate test of his manhood. Wilson recalls his own reactions to Malcolm's challenging accusation "You're afraid to bleed":

> As a 20-year-old black male, sitting in Rob Penny's living room listening to the album [containing Malcolm X's speeches], hearing these words, your heart leapt in your chest and the muscles of your throat strained to shout, as one man actually did, "We'll bleed!" To which Malcolm responded, "I said you're afraid to bleed." And the voice came louder, gathering its strength from countless others who must have felt the same, "I said we'll bleed!" ("Legacy of Malcolm" 89–90)

The willingness to bleed, like a number of other resonant themes Wilson uses to characterize the black man's struggle in America, surfaces in several of his works. Troy bleeds when he is stabbed during a fateful brawl. Loomis bleeds when he wounds his chest with a knife. Sterling bleeds when he cuts his hand on Lutz's glass casing while trying to retrieve a ham for Hambone.

Wilson presents Sterling's forceful and decisive move to get Hambone's recompense, and the blood he shed in the process, as reflections of the revolutionary temperament that thrived during the 1960s Black Power movement. Then, black playwrights in particular portrayed the ideal revolutionaries as "new kinds of heroes—not the weak Hamlets debating whether or not they are ready to die for what's on their minds" (Jones, "Revolutionary Theatre" 214–15). That Sterling does not just talk but acts in defense of Hambone's fight for justice makes him kindred to a long line of young black men willing to bleed and even die for their cause. Although Sterling clearly violates so-called rules by which white America keeps black America in check, he is shown to be acting rationally and perfectly within his rights.

Judged according to Wilson's view of justice for blacks, Sterling indirectly triumphs in the bank robbery over those who victimize him as he affirms his irrepressible warrior spirit. Wilson's no doubt controversial sanction of crime and violence as a means of equalizing justice in America for blacks echoes the similarly controversial ideology he shared with fellow revolutionary activists of the turbulent '60s. Thus, the way he sees it, one's willingness to go back to pick up the ball overshadows whatever else is done or said in the process; *actions*, not words, are of paramount importance. Wilson explains, "For Sterling, given his circumstances, robbing a bank is not simply a criminal act. It can be seen as a noble and heroic thing, a gesture of resistance to the options society offered him" (Dworkin 8). He is one of those characters who, as Wilson notes, "demonstrate a willingness to battle. Not all of them are in the penitentiary, but some, because of that spirit, find themselves on the opposite side of the society that is constantly trying to crush their spirit" (Moyers 179).

Both Memphis Lee and Hambone also display remarkable degrees of that same warrior spirit in wresting from the white power structure that which is due them. Although they are on opposite ends of the economic spectrum and their respective stories seem antithetical, neither is willing to accept the label "victim," and each regularly confronts his opposition to repeat his demands. Memphis Lee's story goes back thirty-seven years to Jackson, Mississippi, where he once farmed land he owned. But local whites, envious of his status as a landowner, ran Memphis off his land, killed his mule, and set fire to his crop. Despite this, Memphis resolved to rise above their harassment, and, though he had no immediate alternative but to abandon his property at that time, he left knowing better how to deal with whites. When Jim Stovall's henchmen went so far as to mutilate and kill his mule, he at once concluded,

> okay, I know the rules now. If you do that to something that ain't never done nothing to you . . . then I know what you would do to me. So I tell you what. You go on and get your laugh now. Cause if I get out of this alive I know how to play as good as anyone. Once I know the rules. Whatever they are. I can play by them. (*TT* 73)

Memphis prides himself in the lessons he learned from these ugly past episodes in his life—lessons that he credits with his current success as sole owner of a Pittsburgh business. For Memphis, perhaps the most important result of these past confrontations is that he now "know[s] how to deal with whites. . . . Down from where we come from you learn how to deal with white folks quick" (70). Buoyed by his hard-earned knowledge of whites, Memphis summons both his warrior spirit and his political savvy to wage and win an ongoing fight to get every bit of the $25,000 compensation for his restaurant.

Although Memphis does not shrink from confrontation, he has no use for the group politics in vogue, such as rallies, sit-ins, or soap-box speeches. He has grown disgusted over the years at the faddish, insincere nature of such forms of protest among his people and prefers instead a much less trendy and collective means of demanding fair treatment. He lambastes the then popular Black Power concept, asserting, "I don't know how these niggers think sometimes. Talking about black power with their hands and their pockets empty. You can't do nothing without a gun. Not in this day and time. That's the only kind of power the white man understand" (42). For the cynical Memphis, a proposed birthday celebration for Malcolm X represents unchanneled energy left over from the man's death. He also detests one of the more popular slogans of the '60s: "black is beautiful." He sees the statement as an affirmation of an inferiority complex among blacks rather than as a positive assertion: "Sound like they trying to convince themselves. You got to think you ugly to run around shouting you beautiful" (43).

Memphis's cynicism is an outgrowth of the numerous clashing ideologies of this politically charged era. One also hears in his frequent condemnations the voice of Wilson, who also chose to demonstrate his nationalist fervor with little fanfare. Despite the flurry of consciousness-raising activities, Memphis notes that no singular effective strategy had been adopted to protect the civil rights of black Americans. Thus, ignoring the hype, Memphis is a firm believer in the gun and common sense as the black man's most effective negotiating devices. While *Ma Rainey's Black Bottom* (some forty years earlier than the action of *Two Trains Running*) depicts an era when black musicians did not have the benefits of civil rights legislation to protect them, *Two Trains* demonstrates the irony that as of 1969 essentially little has changed for blacks in general. Indeed, the abundance of political concepts available to blacks during the '60s paradoxically did more to promote dissent than to instill solidarity. Blacks were faced with choosing between the physical confrontation espoused by Malcolm X and the passive resistance of Reverend Martin Luther King, Jr., between assimilation and separatism, and between the black church and the Black Panther party. Though some may argue that the number of choices suggested a type of progress, others, like Memphis, view the increasing clamor and multiplication of factions with disdain.

Even more than either Sterling or Memphis, the mentally retarded Hambone best highlights the postrevolutionary spirit of going back to pick up the ball. In his persistent nine-and-a-half-year effort to get a ham that the neighborhood's white butcher owes him for painting a fence, he epitomizes the resolve of an entire race of people who have been just as adamant about receiving from America what is, by right, theirs. Hambone's circumstances roughly parallel those of thousands of black Americans from slavery on, who worked faithfully only to discover that they were not to be compensated. But unlike the slaves, whose very lives were at stake should they revolt, Hambone resorts to what is for him the most appropriate means of protest. Each morning he greets his adversary with the irksome reiteration, "He gonna give me my ham!" Although his near decade-long persistence does nothing to sway the butcher, he ultimately wins the respect of all who know of his ordeal. After his mutilated body is found lying across a bed where he lived, Hambone suddenly is transformed from a reluctantly tolerated, mixed-up fellow to a martyr for the cause. Wilson sums up Hambone as "Black America standing patiently outside the door saying, 'Boss, you oughtta let us into this thing; you oughtta let us participate' " (Dworkin 8).

Hambone is another of Wilson's "spectacle" characters. For Wilson such characters become forceful metaphors; their significance to the play may be measured in terms of the multiple and profound figurative interpretations they make possible. Like the piano in *The Piano Lesson* or the boardinghouse in *Joe Turner's Come and Gone*, Hambone's very presence raises some important issues about black culture; but, more important, he conveys the valiant efforts of those who persevere in spite of awesome disadvantages.

Unlike his precursor, the mildly retarded Gabriel in *Fences*, Hambone has no clear history—a fact that makes his case all the more disturbing, for, much like thousands of culturally alienated black Americans, there is no record of his prior existence. This lack of a past record is noticed only after Hambone dies and Memphis Lee's crowd considers notifying his next of kin. At this point even the resident historian Holloway can provide no information, admitting that he knows little about him: "Hambone ain't had no people. Most anybody know about him is he come from Alabama. Don't nobody even know his right name" (*TT* 90).

Wilson considers Hambone's role in *Two Trains Running* to be extremely important, since his presence, as well as his death, in some way affects the majority of the other characters. For example, Hambone is the eerie alter ego of Memphis. Just as Hambone repeats his demands for a ham, Memphis regularly insists that he plans to return to Jackson and reclaim land illegally taken from him. Thus, Memphis's displeasure with Hambone is essentially displeasure with himself. Also, while alive, Hambone makes an indelible impression upon Risa, who has marred her legs to keep lustful men away from her. Although she is virtually an enigma, Hambone manages to expose a tender side of her otherwise stoic personality. She exuded a tender, maternal concern for this man and, frequently against Memphis's decree, showed him compassion. For other characters, Hambone's death precipitates certain changes. He turns the floundering Sterling into "the man of action." "Without Hambone you don't have a Sterling," Wilson explains (interview). In addition, Hambone's death so affects Memphis that the usually hostile restaurant owner contributes fifty dollars toward flowers in Hambone's honor. While once he frowned upon giving Hambone even a bowl of beans, now—especially after succeeding in getting $25,000 for his restaurant—he is moved to generosity.

Hambone is not a chief player in the economic games of his day, but he is a persistent one, as much of his life is dedicated to demanding compensation for what is misjudged as a token endeavor. Because of his insignificance on the economic scale, he is easily ignored or dismissed by the financially more powerful in their selfish fights to survive. His heartrending circumstances cast a troubling light upon the inhumanity that results from an obsessive regard for money. His untimely death sends shudders through the regulars of Memphis Lee's restaurant, disturbing the daily preoccupations of blacks blinded by dollar signs and the numbers.

West, the successful local mortician, is somewhat of an aberration from the theme of pervasive economic struggle in *Two Trains Running*. Of all of Memphis's clientele, he is the most affluent, yet unlike Hambone, Memphis, or Sterling, he has no nemesis to expel from his past. He is one of a few characters immune to the admonishment, "Go back to pick up the ball." The past has little appeal for him, and he glimpses back only to ponder whether his beloved deceased wife is in heaven. Furthermore, West has no real quarrel with the white power structure, since his source of wealth is the lucrative service he renders to Pittsburgh's black community. By perfecting the fine art of satisfying his customers, West wins their loyalty and thus enjoys a virtual monopoly as the director of funeral services for every deceased member of the black community. According to Holloway, West's popularity is such that his business is almost overwhelmed with customers: "West was burying niggers so fast you couldn't keep up with them. Every nigger in Pittsburgh at some time or another was walking up handing West some money. He done buried their cousin . . . their uncle. Their mother" (*TT* 52).

Although West sports tailor-made suits and owns a fleet of Cadillacs, he has not always been financially secure. A onetime gambler, bootlegger, and numbers runner, he was no "Johnny B. Goode" (52) according to Holloway. In fact, the only appreciable difference between his circumstances and those of the many who are not as fortunate is that West learned early that illegal rackets would soon lead to his demise. His decision to venture into the funeral business took him safely away from the criminal element. While his previous livelihood depended upon games of chance, West now enjoys a steady income based upon the certainty of death.

According to Wilson, West's character was originally intended to be "the specter of death" (interview). But this vision that the playwright hoped to capture never quite took form. Although dressed in an ominous black suit, black gloves, and black derby and constantly associated with death, West becomes more the opportunistic entrepreneur who is merely in the business of burying people rather than the personification of death. His chief concerns are maintaining profit margins and decreasing overhead while steering clear of any business deal that does not yield significant financial gain. For example, he apparently considers his cash offer of $15,000 for Memphis's business both a benevolent and savvy gesture: "Now, I told you I'd give you fifteen thousand dollars for it. Cash money. We can go down to the bank right now" (*TT* 38). He also cannot be convinced by Risa to bury Hambone gratis in a bronze or silver casket rather than in the usual government-subsidized welfare casket, complaining "I don't get them free, woman. I call the company and order the casket, they send me the bill . . . I got overhead" (92).

Although West's character never quite matches Wilson's original conception, he remains important in calling attention to some long-standing folk beliefs about death still honored among blacks as late as the 1960s. Believing that "death is such an integral part of life" (interview), Wilson seeks to weave it into the fabric of *Two Trains Running*, especially in the character of West. In previous plays, such as *Fences*, death occupies a prominent place and earns the respect of even the most irreverent individual. That it commands similar respect in *Two Trains Running* is indicated by residual folk expressions preserved by these black city dwellers. Over the years West has obliged many of their superstitions about the dead. As is customary in some parts of Africa, for example, many requested that certain items once esteemed by the deceased be placed in the casket along with the corpse. These range from baby dolls to fresh vegetables. Even though West disapproves of these various tokens, he understands that such loving gestures by family members of the deceased reflect their unspoken belief in the afterlife. Of course, paying homage to the spirit goes against the beliefs of one who is by inclination and training clinically objective about death—"They don't understand about dead folks. Dead folks don't know nothing" (37). But the financially astute West realizes that as long as the grieving family is comforted, he stands to keep their business.

The adage "death demands dignity" aptly describes West's philosophy for a successful funeral service, for despite his professional objectivity, he still acknowledges with reverence death's awesome power: "You can live to be a hundred and fifty and you'll never have a greater moment than when you breathe your last breath. Ain't nothing you can do in life compared to it" (61). Like the throngs of mourners and oglers who tramp through his parlor to see the deceased Prophet Samuel, West senses that death is more than a cessation of life. He, too, is possessed by a morbid sense of admiration for this corpse and, for that matter, anyone who has access to death's mystery. Unfortunately, it appears that the people of this poor, working-class black community have few, if any, living heroes and therefore are inspired only by members of the spiritual realm: Prophet Samuel, Malcolm X, Hambone—and, arguably, Aunt Ester.

For many of the characters in *Two Trains Running*, going back to pick up the ball or reclaiming their cultural legacy is simply not a high priority. When they examine their lives, they find a chronic spiritual hunger that torments them. Yet, unlike the Charles family in *The Piano Lesson* or Herald Loomis in *Joe Turner's Come and Gone*, they are not compelled to appease it. They seem focused upon daily survival and satisfying their immediate needs and do not look to their ancestors for support. Theirs is a cultural fragmentation that cannot be mended by the material gods that they serve nor by the human gods they hail. The so-called white man's God has, by their account, never been their ally. Therefore, they have had to create their own sacred images.

Such psychic emptiness, together with overwhelming despair among these individuals, spawned three alternate spiritual entities in *Two Trains Running*: Prophet Samuel, Malcolm X, and Aunt Ester. Unfortunately, these choices of spiritual leadership reflect the widespread dissension among blacks of the 1960s as well as their serious lack of unity. References to the political and spiritual resonance of the black church are conspicuously absent in the play, and an emotional wasteland threatens to take its place. Also, in the final analysis, none of these substitute gods is all things to all people; in fact, as Wilson shows, belief in any of them requires changing one's moral consciousness and suspending common logic.

Even after his death, Prophet Samuel is able to attract hordes of people—the hopeless, the desperate, or simply the curious. While alive, he enjoyed a popular ministry based upon a mixture of showbiz antics, con artistry, and an immodest display of religiosity: he wore robes, went shoeless, and, with much fanfare, baptized converts in a nearby river.

His ascent to power among blacks in the area of his ministry is the stuff of legend as told by Holloway. Several years back, when the then "Reverend" Samuel faced certain indictment for income tax evasion, he made a single visit to Aunt Ester. After that, his circumstances were dramatically reversed. The bank official who initially sought prosecution against him dropped all charges after witnessing a display of "Prophet" Samuel's newly acquired power. While the banker was under the threat of financial ruin, Prophet Samuel led him to believe he had powers to reverse the stock market's drastic decline and thereby won a powerful, lifelong ally. According to Holloway, that was when Prophet Samuel "went big" (26).

To his followers, Prophet Samuel is another symbolic god of economic prosperity, having stumbled upon a formula that ensured their allegiance and their dollars. Like West, he gave the people a service that they desired and told them what they wanted to hear, but beneath this mask of widespread appeal lurks greed and callousness. More important, both West and Prophet Samuel are the flawed products of this black community where heroes are at a premium.

The posthumous allure of murdered activist Malcolm X also draws a huge following among residents. However, in Wilson's hands, the attraction toward Malcolm X as martyr is significantly dampened by talk of ineffectual rallies in his honor and of fickle crowds. Memphis scoffs at the idea of a birthday celebration for Malcolm X to be held some four years after his death. He recalls how several years earlier Pittsburgh's black community banded together to protest the shooting death of a local black resident, but as time passed, they forgot about the once-celebrated cause and actually voted into political office the same policeman charged with the shooting. As a measure of his disgust for such hypocrisy, which he believes will emerge again, Memphis tears from his wall a sign advertising the coming event. Unlike Memphis, Sterling actually looks forward to the planned celebration, but his interest is in the opportunity it affords him to date Risa, not in its prospects for raising his black consciousness. He furthermore trivializes the whole affair by discussing it in his characteristically naive way: "It was real nice. They said all kind of stuff I ain't never thought about before. It made sense though. Hey, Risa, tell him, didn't it make sense? I said I was gonna get me a soapbox and put it out there and tell all the people who wasn't there what they said" (70).

Despite his acknowledged respect for Malcolm X, in *Two Trains*

Running Wilson does not portray the philosophy the slain leader advanced as the redemption of economically and culturally disinherited blacks. Instead, he focuses upon the misguided fervor that has led to gross commercialization of Malcolm's memory. At some point while writing the play, however, Wilson had other plans. He explains, "Originally I thought the rally was going to be a more important part of the play than it is—this Malcolm X rally that was looming over the play. Somehow it stayed in the background as other stories of the characters moved" (interview). What comes to the forefront of Wilson's consciousness, then, is the celebration not as pro-Malcolm demonstration but as exposé of what has come of his legacy.

The third alternative offered to the play's characters for changing their lives is Aunt Ester, an off-stage clairvoyant supposedly 322-years-old. She is Wilson's living metaphor of past black experience: her age is equivalent to the number of years African Americans have been in America. Aunt Ester also embodies decades of cultural memory. Existing on the fringes of the play's reality, she demonstrates mystical powers by "laying on the hands" and offering sound advice. Although her methods play upon the superstitions and gullibility of her clients, they are softened by her maternal air and effective guidance. Aunt Ester fills a spiritual void in the lives of Memphis's weary group. Instead of resorting to Christianity (which they claim to be the white man's religion) for their sustenance, they find their way to the red door on 1839 Wylie Street, behind which Aunt Ester works her soothing healing powers. Her chief publicist and doting fan, Holloway, does not miss an opportunity to recommend her to anyone in need of counsel.

This elusive entity is a god of the folk. They see her as a personal ally and someone who can indulge their faith in get-rich-quick schemes or other means of gaining easier access to money. Her clients pray to her for luck that they might beat the seemingly insurmountable odds they face in a society where—unless they resort to illegal activities—they are doomed to economic misery. Thus in supporting their efforts to improve their circumstances, she addresses their spiritual needs. Aunt Ester exerts her powers as a god of the folk in noneconomic ways as well. Several years earlier she had granted Holloway's wish by supposedly playing an indirect role in eliminating a grandfather whom he despised. For a $20 fee, she fixes things so Memphis gets more than what he asks city officials for his restaurant. For a similar fee, she gets rid

of West's rival and launches his successful career as undertaker. She also
confirms Sterling's hopes for a relationship with Risa.

The related themes of economic disparity and going back to pick
up the ball converge in the character Aunt Ester. Contained in the
advice she gives Memphis is a directive to be heeded by all who wish to
emerge into the future but who carry the weight of their past upon
them. Memphis recalls the words that so lifted his burden:

> She say, "If you drop the ball you got to go back and pick it up.
> Ain't no need in keeping running, cause if you get to the
> endzone it ain't gonna be a touchdown." She didn't say it in
> them words but that's what she meant. . . . That's what I'm
> gonna do. I'm going back to Jackson and see Stovall. (109)

Aunt Ester's wise counsel not only helps Memphis win an economic
victory but it also convinces him to face the demons of his past. His
realization that he cannot go into the future unless he confronts his past
has far-reaching implications, for his circumstances parallel those of an
entire race of people similarly immobilized because they suspect that
embarrassment or heavy emotional setbacks may follow if they embrace
their cultural heritage.

Two Trains Running ends on a note of both economic and cultural
redemption. Just as in *The Piano Lesson* or *Joe Turner's Come and Gone*,
Wilson advances his theme in a climactic epiphany during which one
character suddenly understands what he or she must do to move forward unencumbered by tragedies of past generations. Playing a sacred
piano, grappling with a haunting vision of the Middle Passage, and
returning to Jackson are all means of retrieving the symbolic dropped
ball. However, the point of going back to pick up the ball is not simply
to stand with it in hand. Wilson believes that, for African Americans,
the psychological journey back is a therapeutic mission, completed only
when they are pointing toward the future equipped with knowledge of
all that is good, bad, or ugly about their rich cultural heritage.

To date, Wilson's dramatic vision has not extended beyond the early
1970s. As of this writing, his most recent play, *Seven Guitars*, has begun
the now familiar route taken by the majority of his previous black
history chronicles—working its way through various regional theatres
and, ultimately, toward Broadway. The play, directed by Walter Dallas, opened at Chicago's Goodman Theater on January 13, 1995.

Although it immediately follows *Two Trains Running*, *Guitars* does not direct the attention of Wilson's audiences to the '80s or '90s; instead the play, set in Pittsburgh, hearkens back to 1948, an era he explored before in the little known *Fullerton Street*. *Two Trains Running* and *Jitney!* (set in 1971) represent the nearest limit of his journey back in time to relive select moments of the black experience.

When questioned about the future direction of his project, Wilson seems to shy away from the idea of writing about the 1980s or 1990s, preferring instead the comfortable buffer afforded by earlier decades. Such an approach also reveals that Wilson's dramatic vision of history is much more sharply focused when he feels freer to embellish certain aspects of the past. He explains, "Since I was not a historian but a writer of fiction, I saw as my task the invention of characters. These personal histories would not only represent the culture but illuminate the historical context both of the period in which the play is set and the continuum of black life in America that stretches back to the early 17th century" ("Characters" H5). Apparently he is most creative and most dramatically inspired in exercising his imagination, rather than his memory. Nevertheless, in *Two Trains Running*, the historical realities of 1969 come to life as Wilson's characters all struggle to release the internalized pain and suffering of an explosive decade that has essentially passed them by.

CONCLUSION

August Wilson's Staying Power

Success in the theatre business—especially on Broadway—hinges upon immediately visible and tangible results; that means large audiences, cash profits, and a production's overall staying power. This being the case, Wilson is undoubtedly a ringing success story. Yet evaluating the product of his dramatic vision is not nearly as simple as counting dollars and cents; something else is needed to describe the full ramifications of Wilson's decade-long efforts in the theatre. Since his project attempts to alter attitudes among black Americans, measuring success in his own terms becomes virtually impossible. One can only observe an audience's reactions or gather individual testimony to assess the impact of his plays.

Having avoided the label of the "one-play playwright" that stigmatized fellow black dramatists such as Ntozake Shange, Charles Fuller, and Joseph Walker, Wilson has set for himself the more long-term goal of putting the importance of culture back onto black America's agenda. In an afterword to *August Wilson: Three Plays*, Paul Carter Harrison observes, "Wilson's plays arguably represent the culmination of political, social, and aesthetic objectives presaged by the Harlem Renaissance in the twenties and the Black Arts Movement of the sixties" (316). Working through the medium of his writing, Wilson advocates cultural pride, responsible action, and self-determination: "I think there are some questions of aesthetics and questions of exactly how writers can contribute to the development of the culture, not contribute to anyone's polemic, not contribute to anyone's idea about what we should not be doing, but to the thing that remains the basis of our culture. This is our culture. How can we contribute? How can we develop it?" (interviewed by the author). In the tradition of collagist Romare Bearden, cultural nationalist Amiri Baraka, novelist Toni Morrison, blues singer Ma Rainey, and poet Sterling Brown, Wilson's history chronicles teem with black cultural referents. Indeed, taken together the seven plays from *Jitney!* to *Seven Guitars* can provide a course in black culture, demonstrating the history of black achievements and setbacks.

The teacher/critic in Wilson is particularly concerned that his work reach a black audience, although his dramatic texts are open to any reader. He attempts to communicate blackness as a positive force whose continued health is linked to blacks reestablishing emotional links with the past, particularly with Africa. He is bothered that Africa and slavery have become sources of pain for some and embarrassment for others. Thus he attempts to represent Africa in his plays as an emotional balm—usually the wiser choice between the frenzy of modern life and the symbolic refuge of the motherland. Wilson is uneasy about widespread cultural apathy among modern blacks. He sees the need for blacks to celebrate Juneteenth, for example, with as much resolve as is shown in commemorating the atrocities of slavery.

As a staunch advocate of sustaining one's cultural ties, Wilson is apprehensive about blacks who cast culture to the wind in favor of assimilation. He argues that political and economic equality in America does not have to mean giving up one's distinct attributes: "Blacks have been all too willing and anxious to say that we are the same as whites, meaning that we should be treated the same, that we should enjoy the same opportunities in society as whites. That part is fine . . . but blacks are different, and they should be aware of their differences" (Rothstein, "Round Five" 8).

Wilson hails cultural differences as sources of pride rather than as evidence of inferiority. He is well aware that black people do things differently from whites and demonstrates in his plays in both subtle and more obvious ways a host of cultural distinctions. Even in the least conspicuous of the daily rituals of blacks, Wilson finds their cultural signature: in the way they decorate their houses, in the way they bury their dead, in they way they talk, in the way they worship, and so on. In each play, he constructs a black world, drawing from as many aspects of the culture as possible: folk customs and beliefs, music, religion, work, language, food, clothing, and so on. Black Ensemble director Jackie Taylor notes, "The African-American community has always struggled to preserve its stories, to reach into history's bag and bring out something accurate and honest. Wilson intensifies that search and brings it to a much larger market" (Bommer 17).

Wilson's typical play represents an infusion of a number of recognizable signs of blackness peculiar to a particular decade; some are immediately obvious, while others operate on the level of the collective unconscious. For example, in *Joe Turner's Come and Gone*—set some fifty years after slavery—Herald Loomis's frightening vision of bones rising to the water's surface is a not-so-subtle reference to the thousands of slaves captured or bought in Africa who perished during the Middle Passage to America. Similarly the ghost of Robert Sutter in *The Piano Lesson* suggests more than what meets the eye: on one level the white man's ghost demonstrates a long-standing belief among blacks in the supernatural; on another his ghost exemplifies the looming threat of the white power structure. Collectively Wilson's plays provide a veritable museum of black cultural artifacts ranging from the ever-present narrative tradition to the prevalence of the blues aesthetic and the signifying trickster.

By highlighting the black experience, August Wilson's on-going ten-play chronicle challenges the exclusionary tradition of white America's history. Like re-creations of history envisioned by Shakespeare, O'Neill, and Fuller, Wilson's project transcends the limitations imposed by past events and sets the black experience within a more positive context. He explains:

> Seldom, if ever, was the black experience and presence in America given any historical weight, seldom were they admitted to the larger playing field of cause and effect. I sought then to simply restore that experience to a primary role, thereby giving the facts of history a different perspective, and creating, in essence, a world in which the black American was the spiritual center. ("Characters" H5)

In order to transform select images from his emotional landscape into written and staged performances, Wilson must draw on his imagination and memory. In the process he consciously avoids historical research and turns instead to the blues and past episodes of his life as inspiration for his characters as well as for the plays' dialogue and action. Encoded in the lyrics and musical notes of Wilson's favorite blues pieces are voices from the past—what he calls "an emotional reference" (Moyers 168). These songs and musical pieces, together with Romare Bearden's visual equivalents that also represent black life, move him to summon the experiences of the people to whom he gives voice in his work. Thus, his own memory, combined with an active artistic imagination inspired by the blues, are the key ingredients in his dramatic vision.

To suit his dramatic vision, August Wilson alters the motions of history. The mission of this modern-day mythmaker is not so much to assail the wrongs of the past but to bring them into focus to show how African Americans addressed them and emerged from them. So far, in plays set in 1911, 1927, 1936, 1948, 1957, 1969, and 1971, he challenges today's African Americans to see themselves on stage participating in an historical dialectic intended to teach them to avoid the mistakes of previous generations. His plays are to be used as means of communicating and empowering. Despite the seemingly insurmountable odds against characters such as Troy Maxson, Ma Rainey, or Memphis Lee, they endure oppression with relative grace and heroism. The decisions that they make in terms of their private lives may seem controversial, but these choices merely confirm that they are human. Looking past these details and considering the context of their times, one can admire how each stands up to his or her persecutors while continuing to work under near unbearable circumstances. Some, like Troy, die having never realized their life's dream; others, like Memphis and Ma Rainey, thrive financially and gain the respect of their peers for their willingness to confront their oppressors.

However, Wilson's plays do not portray blacks exclusively as victims of racism. Like the Revolutionary Theatre of the 1960s, Wilson's theatre holds racism accountable for lowering the quality of life for black Americans. He de-emphasizes racism, however, as a primary cause for oppression and gives it a less pronounced presence in his work. While Revolutionary Theatre typically featured black men whose warrior spirit manifested itself as the ever-present urge to eradicate white oppression (as well as the oppressor), Wilson peoples his plays with black men and women who grapple with *themselves* within the racist scheme of things. They spend a good deal of their rhetoric and energy reacting to their own unfulfilled lives, their own wrong decisions, their own missed opportunities.

While the plays largely internalize conflict within the characters, Wilson structures them with an unmistakable awareness of the role that racism plays in the black man or black woman's condition. For example, Troy Maxson simmers with discontent about his unfulfilled life. He recognizes how racism has destroyed his dreams of playing professional baseball and how it continues to plague him on his job as a garbage collector. Yet Troy does not address his discontent as, say, a typical LeRoi Jones–style revolutionary hero would. Instead of hurling curses and other threats of bodily harm against whites, Troy handles his frustration on a more personal level and thereby allows a more intimate look at the indirect human costs of racism. To be sure, he confronts his white oppressors without fear, but the resulting promotion from garbage hauler to dump truck driver is hardly a cure-all for other injustices he experiences daily both on and off his job. His despair over the band-aid treatment of his complaints finds its way to the surface in the form of numerous eloquent speeches, a brief wrestling match with his younger son, and an affair with "one of them Florida gals" (*F* 4). Likewise, Ma Rainey realizes that she is no better than a prostitute to the white men who essentially steal her singing talent. However, with every fiber of her being she rejects the label "victim." Like Troy she confronts her oppressors at every turn. As a result, she commands and gets respect from them and enjoys a relatively heroic stature. Wilson allows his characters to confront their persecutors, not with intent of bodily harm or annihilation but with an honor that comes with simply knowing the rules of their games.

Wilson's decision to take his theatre in a direction different from the angry hype that fueled earlier black theatre has much to do with his work's appeal to today's heterogeneous theatre audiences and readers alike. Not only are whites once again attentive to the black experience but, much to Wilson's delight, blacks are also, once again, experiencing the theatre. During the '60s and early '70s, many had lost interest in black theatre as a result of being inundated by negative images of gangsters, pimps, prostitutes, and whores as protagonists. And, to the surprise of nationalist playwrights, they were also repelled by bitter recurring antiwhite propaganda. One exasperated playwright and university professor explains the earlier disinterest by pointing to "the absence of a legitimate theatre-going tradition": "The Black middle class has never been devoted to the theatre. Black community theatres are few and far between, and poorly supported" (Pawley 314).

To give Wilson sole credit for a renaissance in black theatre would be an overstatement. Nevertheless, his good fortune has benefited black theatre appreciably. In addition to sparking renewed interest among black audiences in frequenting the theatre and laying to rest the myth that black theatre is exclusively a vehicle of antiwhite propaganda, Wilson's work, on a less grand but also important level, has given a number of otherwise unemployed, unknown black actors, actresses, and theatre technicians a means of both displaying their talents and supporting themselves financially. As Mark Rocha observes, "For Wilson, capitalism implies a special communal responsibility among blacks. As one who has achieved a popular success in the theater no other black playwright has enjoyed, Wilson takes his own responsibility quite seriously" (39).

Evidence of Wilson's staying power is demonstrated in the continued support from fans, financial backers, his mentor and collaborator, the director Lloyd Richards, and in an ever-increasing repertoire of plays. One can only surmise that Wilson will continue the pace he established by writing six plays in the span of eleven years. Also, whether his completed undertaking receives as much serious critical attention as did his plays *Fences* and *The Piano Lesson* depends upon how successful he is at avoiding what Robert Brustein calls "McTheater"—that is, theatre whose artistic integrity has been sacrificed in favor of sheer numbers of productions. So far Wilson has not been adversely affected by such criticism, although the critical accolades his work regularly receives are sometimes accompanied by ruthless attacks on the artistic soundness of a particular play or the wisdom of his overall project. He also continues to deflect criticism from those who charge, for example, that his characters talk too much, that the supernatural additions to his plays simply do not work, or that characters are often too enigmatic and sometimes downright unnecessary.

The dramatic vision of August Wilson grew out of his overall appreciation of language, his fascination with the sounds that different words produce, and his fondness for metaphor. Early on, he tried to fashion poetry out of the limited experience Pittsburgh had offered him but found that his voice lacked the authority that comes with age and life's experiences. The overheard conversations of old men in the city's bars and restaurants, his brief stint as a short-order cook, and his involvement with Pittsburgh's Black Horizons Theater were not enough to inspire the high quality poetry he so desperately tried to produce.

Although he may not have known it at the time, Wilson's lackluster career as a poet was a training period for the future two-time Pulitzer Prize–winning dramatist. The years between his experimentation with the poem and his reluctant conversion to the play were periods of struggle for a young man coming into adulthood as well as for an artist searching for his voice. His dramatic vision is now in sharp focus as he makes his way through the remaining years of the twentieth century.

Wilson has also mastered the art of writing for the stage and, by so doing has found new ways of capitalizing upon the excellent educational medium it offers. Having witnessed first-hand the electricity created among black audiences of the 1960s Black Theatre movement as well as the political theatre of Athol Fugard, he knows well the power of the stage to effect change as well as to empower. Thus the stage provides a most fitting arena for his agenda of reexamining past moments of the black experience in America.

The huge critical acceptance Wilson now enjoys continues to pro-vide ready audiences for his work and extensive exposure for his on-going chronicle of the black experience. Having passed years of initiation, he now enjoys the stature of a cultural architect, a cultural critic, and, most important, a major American playwright.

APPENDIX

August Wilson Explains His Dramatic Vision: *An Interview*

August Wilson granted me the following interview while he was in Washington, D.C. for the November 1991 premiere of *Two Trains Running* at the Kennedy Center. Extremely personable and undeniably committed to his art, Wilson carefully outlined his answers to my questions about his growth from poet to playwright, about the cultural and political agendas underlying his plays, and about his role as a black writer.

The conversation that follows represents the uncut version of the same interview published in the Winter 1993 issue of *African American Review*, 27 (539–59) as "Blues, History, and Dramaturgy: An Interview with August Wilson."

~

SHANNON: The following lines come from your poem "For Malcolm X and Others," which was published in the September 1969 issue of *Negro Digest*:

> The hour rocks a clog,
> The midnight term,
> In bones no shape before
> has warmed in such
> That loves these cold as dead,
> As stone; a flock of saints
> Run ground as thieves.

In another poem entitled "Muhammad Ali," you write:

> Muhammad Ali is a lion.
> He is lion that breaks the back of wind,
> Who climbs to the end of the rainbow with three steps

and devours the gold,
Muhammad Ali with a stomach of gold.
Whose head is iron.

What do these two poems suggest about your early years as a poet?

WILSON: One idea was that I was writing obscure poetry certainly first. It actually took me from '65 to '73 before I could actually write a poem that I felt was written in my own voice. The Muhammad Ali poem, however, is modeled after an African praise song in which you give praises of any kind: "Muhammad is a lion. He's a lion that bounces into the rainbow with three steps and devours the gold. Muhammad Ali with fists of diamonds. His fists are bullets. Muhammad Ali . . ." You can say virtually anything you care to say. It's just one praise after another. The Malcolm X poem—I have no idea what it means.

SHANNON: Early in your career you made a gradual shift from writing poetry to writing plays. How has being a poet affected your success as a playwright?

WILSON: Well, I think that it has been important to my writing. It's the bedrock of my playwriting. Primarily not so much in the language as it is in the approach and the thinking—thinking as a poet, one thinks differently than one thinks as a playwright. The idea of metaphor, which is a very large idea in my plays and something that I find lacking in most other contemporary plays. So it's been very helpful. I think I write the kinds of plays that I do because I have twenty-six years of writing poetry underneath all of that.

SHANNON: I'm fascinated by the combination of memory, history, and mythmaking and the blues in your work. Do you perceive your role as an historian, as a prophet or healer, or perhaps something else?

WILSON: Well, I just say playwright. Of course, I use history. I use the historical perspective. My work benefits from looking back because we can look and see—for instance, in *The Piano Lesson*, you can see the actor, the character going down a road that, given the benefit of a fifty-year historical perspective, we can see whether that is the correct road or not because we've learned. We know how all this turned out. So, history is certainly an important part of my work, and I try to actually keep all of the elements of the culture alive in the work, and myth is certainly a part of it. Mythology, history, social organizations—all of these kinds of things—economics—all of these things that are part of the culture, I make sure—I purposefully go through and make sure each element of that is in some way represented—some more so than others in the plays, which I think gives them a fullness and a complete-ness—that this is an entire world.

SHANNON: What is your reasoning behind writing a four-hundred-year-old autobiography in ten plays? At what point did you decide upon this strategy?

WILSON: Well, actually, I didn't start out with a grand idea. I wrote a play called *Jitney!* set in '71 and a play called *Fullerton Street* that I set in '41. Then I wrote *Ma Rainey's Black Bottom*, which I set in '27, and it was after I did that I said, "I've written three plays in three different decades, so why don't I just continue to do that?" Also, the assumption everyone makes is that any writer's work—it's not just my work—they assume it's autobiographical, that you're writing about yourself. None of the characters, none of the events in the play are events in my life. None of the characters are modeled after me. Because I feel if you write your autobiography, you don't have anything else to tell. So I thought when people would ask me that, and I'd say, "Well, you know I got a four-hundred-year-autobiography." That's what I'm writing from. There's a whole bunch of material. You never run out of stories. I think—

SHANNON: But you're part of the story?

WILSON: Oh, absolutely. I'm definitely a part of the story. It's my story. I claim it—all four hundred years of it. I claim the right to tell it in any way I choose because it's, in essence, my autobiography; only it's my autobiography of myself and my ancestors.

SHANNON: Mr. Wilson, as you know, I am in the midst of writing a biocritical study of your work. During my research I have come across quite a few titles and have acquired the scripts of several never-before-published works. For example, you wrote several brief scripts for the Science Museum of Minnesota. The plays that I have read include *An Evening with Margaret Mead, How Coyote Got His Special Power*, and *Eskimo Song Duel*. Could you talk briefly about that experience?

WILSON: Well, it was a good experience. If nothing else, it was the first time that I was getting paid for writing. Someone was actually paying me—it was good money as I recall—to sit down and write these things. There wasn't, though, a whole lot of creativity necessary to document a northwest Indian tale for this group of actors to act out on the anthropology floor. I never could understand why they were willing to pay me so much money to do that. There weren't very many projects assigned to do because you would do a project that cost money to get the costumes and to actually rehearse the actors to actually put them on the floor. So once they had two or three things on the floor, they didn't want to have anything else. They could have fired everybody and said, "Okay, that's it." To try to make it interesting, I came up with this idea called "Profiles in Science," and I was going to write a one-woman or one-man show about various scientific characters, which I did—one on Margaret Mead, William Harvey, Charles Darwin. They never did any of them. They never performed them.

SHANNON: They had them on file at the library?

WILSON: They had them on file as part of my work, but, here again, to actually do that, they would have actually had to hire a director, and he would have to rehearse it, and they would have had to do whatever—at that time the person was just satisfied to have the three skits, more or less, and these actor cameos. One woman, for instance, was a Guamayan weaver, and we had to write a little spiel for her. She would sit there and explain about the holy weavers of the Guamayan culture. It was a very wonderful idea actually to make that come alive.

SHANNON: Mr. Wilson, you discovered the blues in 1965 with Bessie Smith's "Nobody Can Bake a Sweet Jelly Roll Like Mine." In *Ma Rainey's Black Bottom*, you take up the cause of the blues singer. This also seems to be the case in an earlier play called *The Homecoming*. Could you explain your compassion for the plight of the blues singer?

WILSON: Well, you see, it's the singer, but it's also the music. I think that the music has a cultural response of black Americans to the world they find themselves in. Blues is the best literature we have. If you look at the singers, they actually follow a long line all the way back to Africa and various other parts of the world. They are people who are carriers of the culture, carriers of the ideas—the troubadours in Europe, etc. Except in black America—in this society—they were not valued except among the black folks who understood. I've always thought of them as sacred because of the sacred tasks that they had taken upon themselves to disseminate this information and carry these cultural values of the people. And I found that white America would very often abuse them. I don't think that it was without purpose in the sense that the blues and music have always been at the forefront in the development of character and consciousness of black America, and people have senselessly destroyed that or stopped that. Then you're taking away from the people their self-definition—in essence, their self-determination. These guys were arrested as vagrants and drunkards and whatever. They were never seen as valuable members of a society by whites. In fact, I'm writing a play which deals specifically with that.

SHANNON: Your 1977 play called *The Coldest Day of the Year* seems to be about reconciling relationships between African American men and women. What inspired the play? Can you explain the circumstances surrounding its composition?

WILSON: Well, that was undoubtedly inspired by the breakup of my relationship with my girlfriend. I thought I'd write this play. It certainly was not written in the language that I write plays now.

SHANNON: Very poetic with lots of figures and metaphors.

WILSON: Yes. Primarily I thought that in order to create art out of black life—because I didn't value the way that blacks spoke—I thought in order to create art out of it, you had to change it. So you had lines like "our lives frozen in deepest heats of spiritual turbulence."

SHANNON: Which means?

WILSON: (chuckle) Well, it has meaning to it. It has a meaning to it. Now, if I was going to write it, I guess the guy would just walk up to her and say, "How you doing, mama? We're out here in the cold."

SHANNON: You wrote a similar play in 1973 called *Recycle*, which, as you explained, exorcised "man-woman stuff." What inspired this work?

WILSON: The breakup of my first marriage. Actually, this is the first play I ever wrote, so it has specialness to me. I was examining the cycle aspect of nature, I guess. There's a cyclical kind of thing that goes on in *The Coldest Day of the Year*. But I actually started writing the play one night as I saw this man get his brains blown out. As I was walking down the street and approaching this corner, this guy came out of the bar and was standing looking up and down the street as though he was trying to decide which way he wants to go, and a hand came out of the bar—it was the bartender I found out later—with a gun. And there was a woman, and he fell on the sidewalk near his car. The woman went over—she was a nurse in the hospital—and she began to beat on this man's chest. She just kept beating him very hard in the chest. And one guy standing there says, "Baby, that man dead. Ain't no need you doin' that. That man dead." Then she just got up and turned and walked away, and I followed her. She went into this bar. She walked in and she said to the bartender, "The niggers are killing one another these days." And he said, "I heard. Is he dead?" She said, "Yeah, he's dead. I beat on his chest." I started out the play with this line. Something happened.

Something happened, and I was curious about this woman who beat on his chest almost as if she could have been the murderer—"Yeah, he's dead. I beat on his chest." She didn't say, "I beat on his chest to try to get his heart beating" or anything. She just said, "I beat on his chest." So she got a drink, and I got a drink. I began to write this play. I didn't know what I was going to write about until a guy came by and said to the woman, in essence, "Remember me," and that started the man-woman aspect of the play as though she had murdered him and he is coming back. She looks up and says, "Where did you come from?" He says, "Down the street, lady, or did you forget?"

SHANNON: That reminds me of the aspects of reincarnation that comes across in *The Piano Lesson* with Sutter's ghost coming back. Is that an attempt to draw parallels?

WILSON: No, not at all. I would place them in two entirely different categories. The idea of ghosts and the idea of supernatural phenomena in black American life is a very real phenomena that is quite different from someone or what, in essence, may be an accusatory play in which you simply come back to accuse someone for murdering you.

Another little addendum in my mind is who owned the bar. This is a guy named Pope. I use Pope's name in *Fences*. Troy talks about Pope opening up that restaurant down there and fixed it up real nice and didn't want anybody to come in it. There's this guy named Pope, and, in essence, he has this restaurant. I used to go in there all the time, and he used to hate for me to come in there. And as I got a little older, I understood. I come in there and spend ten cents on a cup of coffee. He had this big empty restaurant, and he's waiting for somebody to come in and spend ten cents and want ten cups of coffee for it. So, as a result of that—and I went anyway, even though he didn't like for me to come in there, I still went. But we never talked anyway or anything. Then he bought this bar, and this bar was the most popular bar—I mean Friday and Saturday night, you couldn't even get in the door. I mean there were five hundred people piled up in this store's space when a white guy owned it, and as soon as Pope got the bar, nobody went in there. And so I was almost his only customer at the bar—

SHANNON: And he didn't want you to come in.

WILSON: Well, the bar was built different. By this time it was four or five years later, and I guess we both had changed. And I used to go in there, and he remembered me from the restaurant. So now I am his favorite customer—his only customer almost. Of course, there were other people. One night he started talking to me, and it shocked me that Pope would even say anything to me. We started talking about Bessie Smith and Ma Rainey, and he said, "Oh yeah, I remember Ma Rainey coming down to the Star Theater down there on such-and-such street." So he gave me a lot of the history of the neighborhood. And I had gotten to know this guy. We could have been doing this for five years. That was really important to me when Pope started talking to me.

SHANNON: Was that the time when you were referred to as "Young-blood"?

WILSON: It was the same era, same time.

SHANNON: I think you may have answered this, but which play do you consider to be the beginning of your history cycle—*Fullerton Street* or *Jitney!*? As I have not read *Fullerton Street*, could you give me a synopsis of its plot?

WILSON: *Jitney!* was the first one I wrote in terms of order of writing. *Fullerton Street* was a play centered in the '40s in which I try to examine the urban northerner. What I wanted to do was to show some people who had come North and encountered the cities and had lost whatever kinds of values they had in the South—almost as if the environment determined that you had to adopt different values in order to survive up here. Domestically a husband and wife whose—the parents of the husband are living in the household with them. It's been six or seven years since they've been up North, and they have become alcoholics living on and waiting for welfare checks. In the South they would not have been living like that.

The important action of the play takes place on the night of the Joe Louis–Billy Khan fight, which they listen to around the radio with a group of male characters who are friends of the husband—the young man Moses, who is like twenty-five or twenty-six years old. After the fight they sit around talking, and they start telling jokes. In this night of telling jokes, what starts off as a joke degenerates into a very vivid description of a lynching they had witnessed when one of Moses' friends was lynched. And I think it was for something for which Moses was the culprit as opposed to his friend, since white folks can't tell one from the other. So he had a special burden of guilt to carry there. It was a very vivid memory, which, from that point in the play, changes his character, and he begins to move closer to at least adopting some new guidelines. So that was supposed to be cowardice. His mother dies—that was the first person I killed off in any of my plays. I remember her name was Mozelle, and I remember when I wrote the scene of Mozelle dying, I was crying, and the tears were falling on the page, and I was trying to write, and the ink was getting all screwed up—

SHANNON: You were crying?

WILSON: Oh, yeah! It was like "Mozelle is dead." And I had lived with her for so long.

SHANNON: There's a lot of death in *Two Trains*. You seem to have gotten good at that.

WILSON: Absolutely. It surprised me. There's death in all of the plays. When I wrote *Joe Turner*, I said, "Hey, good. Nobody died. No death!" Then I started looking back, and there was Mr. Seth's mother, and there's a ghost in *Joe Turner*. Miss Mabel comes back, and there were constant references to death. I didn't realize it—the two babies. And I thought I had gotten away and wrote a play in which it wasn't—but death is such an integral part of life. You can't have one without the other. So I was very conscious. I mean I wanted to move closer and closer to—I thought this time I wanted to bring the specter of death in the persona of West, the undertaker with his black gloves. I didn't get any menace, any threat in him as he developed into a different character. But I think when I started out, I wanted to have him just as a more menacing kind of presence within the play—sort of like lording over and waiting for each and every one of them, and it turns out he didn't become that menacing character that I originally started to write.

SHANNON: Hambone dies, and, of course, Aunt Ester never dies.

WILSON: Aunt Ester never dies. Hambone dies—the first line in the play is when he talks about the second time that 651 came out. He said, "That was LD's number. If he was still living, he'd be in big money." So it starts with LD and reference to the people and Memphis's mother—in a big speech at the end of act 1, he tells about when his mother died. Holloway's grandmother. Bubba Boy's woman dies in the play. West's wife died.

SHANNON: The mule dies.

WILSON: The mule dies. That's kind of appropriate. He's [Memphis] the only one in the community that's making it—he's a rich man.

SHANNON: I like that. The play ends on a good note with him getting more than what he expected for the restaurant.

What do you think you accomplished in *Jitney!*?

WILSON: I simply wanted to show how the station worked, how these guys created jobs for themselves and how it was organized. There was a head of the station. All of these guys pay their dues; they pay $15 a month. That gives you the right to use that phone. People know that number, and they call up and order a cab. There were certain rules and things. One of the rules is that you can't drink. Otherwise they won't call your number. They'll call somebody else. There was a lot of competition in jitney numbers. There must be a thousand of them. There's a certain one—COURT-1-9802—which has been a jitney number for about forty-five years. If you go to Pittsburgh now and call "COURT-1-9802," you'll get a jitney. Certain stations have different reputations about whether they come on time or whether the drivers are honest or whatever. But I just want to show these guys could be responsible. They make jobs out of nothing. I think it is very ingenious. Then, of course, in that you had to get into the lives of the characters. It was an attempt to show what the community was like at the time. The important thing was for me to show these five guys working and creating something out of nothing.

SHANNON: I found that the Vietnam War is looming, and it has a lot to do with the tone of the play. I went back to some lyrics by Marvin Gaye, "What's Going On?" and I find that what he is saying captures the essence of *Jitney!*.

WILSON: That's interesting. That was the only song in the '60s—I used to get so mad at popular rhythm and blues of the day. With all the stuff that was going on, Stevie Wonder was singing "My Cheri Amore," and the music isn't responding to what's happening except Marvin Gaye. I remember when me and Claude were together, I challenged him to go to the jukebox and find just one song, just one song that had any meaning and wasn't about "I love you. You love me. You done left me." And he went over there—he considered himself lucky to have found "What's Going On?" And I said, "You're right." I can see that that was the only one that I could recall. I think James Brown's "Say It Loud. I'm Black and I'm Proud" was also a very important song which we used in *Two Trains*.

I didn't make the Vietnam War as large a part of *Jitney!* as I could have. And I think it is personal because even though there was a tremendous number of blacks who were killed, that never, for me—there was only one person I had known through a friend of his up in the projects. Their son had gotten killed in the war, and they had a little wake on the lawn. There was the flag, and you went up and paid your respects. Those were the only marks of the war that ever actually touched me or my observation of that community. So it was not a large part. If it had been, then I think it would have become a larger part of my work.

SHANNON: Like many other nationalists during the 1960s and early '70s, you seem to have been affected by Malcolm X and his unfortunate death. I note that Malcolm X's death looms in the background of *Two Trains Running*. How does his symbolic presence shape the play?

WILSON: Well, it offers an alternative in the sense that in *Two Trains Running* there are three ways in which you can change your life. You have Prophet Samuel, Malcolm X, and Aunt Ester. Originally I was going to have someone who was representative of the idea of assimilation—cultural assimilation to American society and adopting the dominant values of the culture. But I couldn't find any of those characters who were willing to take that view. There were people in the community, of course, but not in my play. I couldn't make any of those characters. So that idea became lost. Originally I thought the rally was going to be a more important part of the play than it is—this Malcolm X rally that was looming over the play. Somehow it stayed in the background as other stories of the characters moved. So actually Aunt Ester has more impact on the play. Two of the characters do go up to see Aunt Ester. So she has more of an impact than Malcolm.

SHANNON: At one point in your life, you seemed quite interested in the Muslim religion. What caused this interest, and how did the religion affect your view of the world?

WILSON: Well, I was always—as I think most black Americans—supportive of the Honorable Elijah Muhammad and the ideas. Most people who were sympathetic or simply supportive of his ideas would not join because of the discipline required of the organization. If I look at the Honorable Elijah Muhammad's program, there is the idea of self-sufficiency. The idea of doing for self is the idea that drew me even sympathetically toward him. My first marriage was over religious discrepancies, over the fact that I did not want to join, even though I was sympathetic. But I always had a tremendous amount of respect for him. There was a time after the breakup of my marriage when I went and joined the Nation of Islam in an attempt to save my marriage, which didn't work. So my relationship was such that I still respect all of the teachings, even though I can look at some of them—their attitudes and their feudalistic ideas about their relations with women always can be traced to Islam itself. But I think Elijah Muhammad is one of the most important black men that ever lived in America. I'd put him right up there with Du Bois because he was the one who had an idea. For instance, if you look at the criteria of culture using Maulana Ron Karenga's criteria of mythology, history, religion—we had all those things. But the one thing which we did not have as black Americans—we didn't have a mythology. We had no origin myths. Certainly Elijah Muhammad supplied that. So you could say that he contributed a lot to black American culture—the myth of Yacub, etc. These are things the culture was lacking, and they are forever a part of us. Now whether you agree or disagree, you could always say, "This is how the world started." So I think it's important, if for nothing else than that. I think the ideas that he propagated in the '60s are ideas that we're debating, and we still may emerge following those ideas.

SHANNON: The short piece *The Janitor*, which I read in a recent issue of *Antaeus*, is brief but carries a profound message. Can you recall what inspired this work?

WILSON: First of all, I was a member of New Dramatists. They were having a fund-raiser, and they asked all the playwrights to write a four-minute play—not five minutes but a four-minute play. This was kind of difficult. How do you write a four-minute play? So I came up with the idea of the janitor who is someone whom this society ignores and someone who may have some very valuable information, someone who has a vital contribution to make, and yet you have relegated him to a position where they sweep the floor. They do it for some years, and never once do we think to say, "Hey, do you have anything to say about anything? Do you have any contribution to make other than being a janitor or running an elevator or whatever?" So in that sense we really do not take advantage of all of our human potential. And I look at how the Israelis are just absolutely delighted in the fact that they have close to a million Soviet Jews that are coming into the country, and they are looking forward to what those Soviet Jews have to contribute. This is a lot of intellectual power and intellectual potential that is coming in their country, and they're going to use that. And we're sitting over here with thirty-five million blacks who have a lot of untapped potential—thirty-five million. So there's the idea of not taking advantage of your potential. So I thought I'd show this guy here who is sweeping up the floor, and there's this microphone, and he just goes up and starts talking into the microphone.

SHANNON: It seems to show that we're caught up in status also—

that if you're not of a certain status, then you don't matter. This is dangerous.

WILSON: Absolutely. They're going to get all of these people at this conference to talk about youth—a conference on youth. And all of these people with academic backgrounds and status are not going to say as much in all of their days of seminars and conferences as this man has said there in five minutes. And that was my idea in the play.

SHANNON: Can you talk about *Black Bart and the Sacred Hills*? What were you trying to achieve? I'm familiar with the story of Black Bart, the cowboy.

WILSON: This is what I call one of my zany characters. First of all, it is a musical, and it's kind of zany. It's a satire on American society. I have a character, Black Bart, who is a magician. He used to be a cattle rustler. He broke out of jail, and he carved this retreat called the Sacred Hills. And he's making gold out of water. He had the idea he's going to flood the world with so much gold that it was going to be despised as "cockroaches in a sweet woman's kitchen." Gold is going to be utterly valueless.

SHANNON: How do you put together a plot like that? Where do your ideas come from?

WILSON: I'm not sure. I did this from one Sunday to the next. And I think it was the idea of satire, and the most brilliant satirist I knew was Ishmael Reed.

SHANNON: What was it about Black Bart that made you choose him as a character to build the play around?

WILSON: Well, I think Bart actually has his roots in Bynum and Holloway and all of these kinds of characters—many of their roots are in Bart. *Bart* started first as a series of poems in which this character named Black Bart was a magician, but he was also very philosophical—sort of like Holloway and Bynum.

Claude Purdy heard these series of poems and told me, "You should write a play with that character." Then I just started thinking, and the more I thought I came up with the idea of a multicultural satire on American society.

SHANNON: Is that fairly long? Is that a fairly long script?

WILSON: It's about three-hundred-something—a lot of pages.

SHANNON: I'd like to read that. I'm curious about the title of *Two Trains Running*. Does the title suggest that black people still have choices?

WILSON: I think so. That's very interesting. I've never thought of that. There's only two choices that I see. The question we've been wrestling with since the Emancipation Proclamation is "What are we going to do? Do we assimilate into American society and thereby lose our culture, or do we maintain our culture separate from the dominant cultural values and participate in the American society as Africans rather than as blacks who have adopted European values?" And I think that this is a question that, for the past hundred years, black America has been trying to figure out and debating which way should we go. On the surface it seems as if we have adopted the idea that we should assimilate, and that's simply because one has received more publicity than the other. But if you look at it, you'll find that the majority of black Americans have rejected the idea of giving up who they are—in essence, becoming someone else—in order to advance in American society, which may mean why we haven't moved anywhere. Because that's something—what I see is the majority of the people saying, "Naw, I don't want to do that. I'm me." And because they haven't adopted the values—these are the people in the ghetto; these are the people who suffer; these are the people with—. I think white America needs to put some more pressure on in an effort to force them to the idea of assimilating and adopting cultural values and say, "Okay, if you don't do that, then you are going to suffer. And you can look at these people who are here and see that they're doing good. That could be you. They still say, "I don't care. I don't want to do that." They still say "No" even though they are suffering for it. If you go into the black community, you have the culture of black America still very much alive. They still practice the values that their grandparents had, with some exceptions, of course. For instance, black people—we decorate our houses differently. I've always said that I was going to get together some kind of multimedia presentation that will illustrate all these things. Because you can take black gospel and white gospel and put them side by side, and you cannot tell me that these are not different people. And then you take a black person's house and a white person's house—just the way that they are decorated. They have the same things now. They have tables, chairs, and a couch, but our couches got little mirrors on the side. This is what I have studied. I'm working on business cards. I'm collecting business cards, and I am amazed—not amazed. This just proves my point. Black folks will generally give you this business card that is very colorful and highly designed and, according to some white folks, would look amateurish. White folks always have these kinds of cards. I met a guy last night—Bernie Slain. You may know him.

SHANNON: Bernie Slain?

WILSON: Yeah, he's got a radio show or a TV show. Bernie Slain. Anyway this guy has got a white card with a big yellow star in the center. And he had another one—this black one with big red letters, and it's got its own special symbols up here. This guy Bernie Slain obviously has a TV show somewhere, so he's doing all right. But still he hands out a card that looks like that.

SHANNON: You say that there are differences and that black people ought to acknowledge them. It's not suggesting that one person is better than the other.

WILSON: Oh, absolutely not! It's white America who says, "Our way is better than your way. You're not acting right. You're not doing this right. You're not suppose to act like that." I had a line in *Two Trains* that I took out because it was in the wrong place, and I couldn't make it work there in the speech. He [Holloway] was saying, "It's not how you look; it's how you do. You do ugly. If you change the way you do, we'll let you in the game. Otherwise, you stay over there and suffer."

SHANNON: Have you followed the Amiri Baraka versus Spike Lee controversy over the making of a movie on the life of Malcolm X? What are your thoughts about this issue?

WILSON: I think the whole idea of—it's only a movie. We're not talking about something that is going to affect the lives of thirty-five million black people in America. We're talking about a movie about Malcolm X. I think the real issue should have been made fifteen years ago when the guy bought the rights to do Malcolm X and how he sat on the rights to do Malcolm X for twenty years. He's had five, six different people write scripts for him. The guy, Marvin Worth, was simply afraid to make the movie. He told me, "You only get one chance." I said, "Yeah, but you got to take that one chance." My point is why did not Quincy Jones and Bill Cosby and all these people who now say "Malcolm"—why didn't somebody black go and buy the movie rights and say, "Hey, this is one of our icons. We don't want you to have nothing to do with this movie." It should have been in black hands from the beginning. That's what ruined his image. Ain't nobody talking about that. Norman Jewison was going to direct the film. I didn't hear one peep from anybody. I didn't hear Baraka then say, "Hey, a white man is directing a film of Malcolm." The only one that I know that said anything was myself and Spike.

SHANNON: Well, it is kind of suspicious now with all of this media frenzy.

WILSON: I think Spike has the right to make whatever kind of movie he wants to make. The people are going to ultimately decide. It's the people who will go in there and say, "Yeah, that's Malcolm" or "Naw, that ain't Malcolm." Mao said, "Let a thousand thoughts contend. . . . The strongest idea will always dominate." So, if you don't like the movie, go make your own. That's what Ralph Ellison said. He said, " The best way to fight a novel is to write another one."

SHANNON: You have some very definite ideas on the director's sensibilities in interpreting your work. If you care to elaborate, what is the status of your request that a black director be secured to direct the Paramount release of *Fences*?

WILSON: I said that I wanted a black director—which was from the beginning—I told Eddie Murphy that. Eddie Murphy said, "I don't want to hire anybody just because they are black." Well, neither did I, meaning that I wanted somebody who was black and talented. But I have since learned to look behind that phrase "I don't want to hire anybody just because they are black." And what, in essence, you are saying is that the only qualification that a black person could have is that they are black. "I don't want to hire anybody just because they are black." That means that's the only reason you would have to hire anybody is for their skin color. So when they say that, they just speak ill of everyone. All of those black directors in Hollywood and you say, "I want a black director," and they go, "I don't want to hire nobody just because they are black." I say, "Naw, hire them because they are talented."

SHANNON: It suggests that there are no talented black directors.

WILSON: Yes, and the only reason he was going to hire them was that they were black. But they don't know what they're doing, but they are black. So I said when they had lined up Barry Levinson, who's a very nice man. I met with Barry. Barry wanted to do the film. And I went over to Paramount's office and I said, "I don't want Barry to do the film. He doesn't qualify." The qualifications were that he be black, that he had some sensibilities to the culture. This is a drama about the culture. It comes straight out of the culture. And in those instances, I think you should hire—If this were a film about Italian culture, you should hire an Italian director. This is common sense. Now if you have an adventure movie that's not specific to a particular culture, you can hire anybody to direct that.

When I was out there in Hollywood, a black director gave me a lesson. He said, "Man, let me explain something to you. I appreciate what you're doing by wanting a black director, but we've been out here for fifteen years telling these people it don't matter if we're black or not. We're trying to get a job directing *LA Law*, and we've been telling them it don't matter. A black person could direct *LA Law*. A black person could direct these sitcoms. We're trying to get some work. And finally they say 'Yeah, that's true. Okay.' And they started letting black directors direct episodes of stuff that was noncultural specific like *LA Law*. Here you come along wanting us to say that it does matter. We can't say that." I was saying, "How come I can't get any help from the black directors? How come no black directors are stepping forth and saying, 'Yeah, the boy is right.' " And he said, "We can't say that because as soon as somebody says that, they ain't working no more. So I really appreciate what you're doing, but don't do us no favors."

SHANNON: How have you most benefited from your collaboration with Lloyd Richards? What is the current and future status of your working relationship with him?

WILSON: Well, I will continue to work with Lloyd even though he is not at the Yale School of Drama. I've learned a lot about theatre just in the process of working with Lloyd. When I started, of course, I knew very little. I think one of the important things was when I got off the train in New Haven to go to the rehearsal of *Ma Rainey's Black Bottom*, I didn't know Lloyd as a director, and I didn't know how these things were going to turn out. And we went into rehearsal, and we read through the script, and the actors started asking questions. I'm all prepared to answer all these questions, and they ask a question about Toledo, and Lloyd spoke up, and Lloyd answered the question. Not only was it correct, but it gave me some insight. I said, "I didn't know that about Toledo." This went on, but from that moment I visibly relaxed. I said, "Everything's going to be all right. Pop knows what he's doing." It's been that way ever since.

SHANNON: I know you said "Pop" jokingly, but do you have a paternal relationship with him?

WILSON: Oh, without question, without question. I think so. Yeah. I have certainly grown up without a father, and he is about twenty-five years older than me. So, yeah, I defer to him in that regard. And another way I look at it since I love boxing is that I am the boxer, and he is the trainer. He's my trainer—"My boy August will get them." So we have had this relationship recently. He'll say, "You've got to throw that left hook a little more." So obviously there is this mentor kind of trainer-boxer relationship. I look at it like that sometimes.

SHANNON: Do you ever just marvel sometimes at just how coincidental it was that you and he got together? I mean out of the scripts that he could have chosen, he chose *Ma Rainey's Black Bottom*.

WILSON: Well, I think it's kind of luck that you make happen. He chose *Ma Rainey's Black Bottom* because it was a good script. So that was important. If he hadn't been able to recognize it was a good script—the actual first reader of that script was Michael Feingold, who then passed it on. But then Lloyd recognized it. So that's the first thing. You sort of make luck happen. It almost didn't happen. These producers wanted to do the show on Broadway, and the Dramatist Guild's minimum for an option is $2,500 for a play, but they were offering me $25,000. At that time I was still making $88 a week cooking for Little Brothers. So I called Lloyd up and said, "Hey, I'm going to talk to these people over here." And Lloyd said, "Well, I can understand that." So we went on, and my agent started negotiating this contract with them only to find out six months later that they're talking about making a musical out of *Ma Rainey*. They want me to turn it into a musical. They sent me a contract—just a terrible contract. They had rights to bring in other writers, and I thought, "What's going on here?" And I'll never forget I called one of the guys up on the phone and I said, "Hey, I'm not signing this contract." He said, "Listen. It doesn't matter what the contract says. The important thing is for you to sign it and get to work. A lot of things in this business are done on faith." So I said, "Okay"—

SHANNON: But that's hard to take though.

WILSON: —"If it doesn't matter what the contract says, let's make it say what I want it to say." Whereupon I was met with silence. So I called Lloyd and said, "Lloyd." He said, "August, how are you doing?" I said, "Fine. Are you still interested in doing *Ma Rainey*?" Lloyd said, "Well, yeah, but I just want to make sure that these other people—I don't want to step into any muddy water. I just want to make sure that you are through." I said, "I am definitely, absolutely through talking to them." He said, "Well, come up and see me," so I went up and saw him, and we agreed that he'd do it—to put it on that season—and he did it. Now, I guess that my point in all of this is that it almost didn't happen. I'm trying to say it's a happy coincidence, but it's also a coincidence that you make happen yourself at the same time because I could have gone with some other people, and I don't know what kind of crew I would have had. They could have ruined my script, turned it into a musical, and I would have been a one-shot playwright. Something told me—and I think it was the force of Lloyd's personality, his presence and who he was—that I would much rather be associated with this man than be associated with these other people. So I almost made a misstep, but I trusted my heart, and I went with Lloyd.

SHANNON: That's interesting because it seems to be the history of African American playwrights to be "one-shot playwrights." And you came so close to that. What advice—what could one do to prevent that? And it doesn't suggest that they are not talented. It boils down to business sense it seems.

WILSON: It doesn't suggest that they are not talented. Of course, I was aware of this when I started writing plays. I looked at all of the highlights and everything, and I was determined that that was never going to happen to me. I said, "I'm not going to follow that road." So I asked around: "What happened to Lonne Elder?"

"Oh, he went to Hollywood."

"What happened to Joseph Walker?"

"Oh, he went to Hollywood."

SHANNON: Charles Fuller.

WILSON: Well, Fuller is an example which comes later, but at that time I knew to stay away from that and because I was determined not to be a one-play playwright, I wrote *Ma Rainey*. Then I sat down and wrote *Fences* right behind that, so at the time that I am talking to these people about this thing, by the time Lloyd and I had agreed that we were goint to do *Ma Rainey*, I was already on my way up to the O'Neill to do *Fences*. And so after thirty days—you had to wait thirty days after the conference—Lloyd said, "I want to do that one too." So I had a second one. If I didn't have a second play, I'd be still sitting around resting on my laurels, so to speak. But I was already working before we did the first production of *Ma Rainey* at Yale; we knew we were going to do *Fences* the next year. Then no matter what happened, no matter how that went, we were going to do *Fences*.

SHANNON: Let me ask you this. How did it feel to have a play on Broadway? What were your emotions?

WILSON: It felt good (pause).

SHANNON: But you always kept it in perspective.

WILSON: It felt good, but the theatre we were in—we were in a theatre that was on 48th Street on the left side of Broadway. So you have to go out of your way to get to that theatre. Now they have 44th and 45th Streets, two streets on which there are theatres on both sides. They will not put black plays in some of those theatres. I mean black audiences—all of the people have to rub elbows during intermission when they come out and stand on the sidewalk. And at the end of a black play, there's a whole bunch of black folks standing there rubbing elbows. Go up 48th Street, go up 47th Street, or 46th Street, but you don't get no 44th and 45th. So at the time—I mean it was tremendously exciting. It wasn't like my second play that I had ever gotten produced. It was nice to walk down there. It didn't have my name on the marquee. They don't put—they didn't have Lee Vincent's name on there when he did A *Walk in the Woods*. And I constantly recognized this because—they say, "Well, you've got to wait. It's your first time and all that." That's what they tell playwrights. But I think any playwright—first play, last play, or whatever—should have their name on the marquee identifying him as the person who wrote this play. If your name has no name value, they don't put it up on the marquee; they put the actors' names up there in big letters because it's a business, and that's what it's about. It doesn't matter who wrote the play. It doesn't matter whether the play is any good or not. If you can get a star in there to do the role, you're going to have people come see it. Geraldine Page is in this play. Jason Robards is doing a play that right now has gotten terrible reviews. Here's one of America's premiere actors—can't find anything for him to do, nothing worth his talent. So he's in this—I mean the play got some really bad reviews. But people don't care. It's Jason Robards. They go to the theatre to see Jason Robards. They don't care if it's a bad play. So I had a lot of problems with it. They didn't put my name on the marquee; we're on the wrong street—

SHANNON: But see I got no inkling of that. I just saw "Wilson on Broadway." That's what trickled down.

WILSON: Yes, but it was tremendously exciting to be there. When we were in Philadelphia prior to that, the cast was in a hotel right across from the theatre. I chose to stay in another one just because it was picked off a sheet. The point that I'm trying to make is that Theresa Merritt (who starred as Ma Rainey in the Broadway production of *Ma*

Rainey's Black Bottom) gets locked out of her hotel room. They locked her out because she didn't pay her bill. She was staying in the hotel and had told them, "I'll pay you at the end of the week." They wanted her to pay night by night. And she said, "No, no, no. I paid you last week, didn't I? I've got to wait until I get my money from the company. I'm in this play, and I'm not going to come down here every night and give you $59 day by day by day." So one time she went up to her room, and it was locked. They had locked her out of her room. So they had to call in the middle of the night—it was about one o'clock in the morning— the general manager had to come down there and straighten it out. This is straight out of the play. We went up to her and asked, "Theresa, what did you do?"—which is the exact line that they say to Ma: "Ma, what did you do?" Theresa was livid. "What do you mean what did I do?" Anyway they got her out of there, and she went over to the Hilton, where they had put flowers in her room. The manager said, "Oh, here's Theresa Merritt! Here's flowers. Here's some fruit." He treated her like she should have been treated.

The company in New York was good, but I've got to tell you about when we made the recording of *Ma Rainey's Black Bottom* at Manhattan Records right there in New York in January 1985. The guy that's making—the producer of this recording. We arrived at his studio. He greets us with the words—and I swear to God this is exactly what he said: "You boys come on in. I've got some sandwiches for you." And we looked at one another and said, "This is a line from the play!" He doesn't even know it. He's really trying to be a nice guy. And sure enough he had some sandwiches there. And it's cold in the studio, and Theresa was late. And Theresa walks in and says, "Y'all want to make a record, you better put some heat on around here."

SHANNON: She said that jokingly, right?

WILSON: Well, she said that knowing that it was a line from the play, but she was absolutely serious because the studio was cold. And the response was "We're working on it, Ma."

SHANNON: Life and art. Of course, Ma Rainey was treated the same way in terms of hotel accommodations, hospitals, and things like that also.

WILSON: This is what I'm trying to point out. The heat never came on. They did bring an engineer up there who looked at the pipes or something and went back in the basement, but the heat in the studio—

they recorded the whole thing in their coats, not only in their coats, but they were in their coats and still shivering.

SHANNON: That's all so uncanny.

WILSON: The recording booth was nice and warm. I'm in the recording booth. Lloyd is directing the recording. These guys were out there freezing to death. And there's this guy standing around with a few other people. I didn't know who they were. There was this strange guy with this beard standing around. So I get ready to leave—I'm doing the liner notes. We agreed in my lawyer's office with the president of the company. That was one of my conditions. So I'm ready to leave, and I was with Claude, and I said, "Let me see when he wants these liner notes." So I went back and said, "Mike, when will you need the liner notes?" And he said, "Oh, Mort's doing them." And he points to this guy named Mort Good. And I said, "I don't believe this. Now I'm Levee—Mr. Sturdyvant, you said you'd let me record them songs." And he says, "Well, no. Mort's going to do it." And then he says, "Mort's going to say some nice things about you." I looked at him like he was crazy. And I decided there is no point in me going off on this man and punch him in his mouth, hollering and screaming at him. So I went and called my lawyer and I said—I hadn't signed the contract at that time. And I said, "It's costing them $35,000 to record. It's a waste of $35,000, and I am not signing a contract." So I get a call from the president of the company. "You can do the liner notes. Of course. You know we agreed to that, and there's no problem. You can do the liner notes. And Mort is going to write a little thing on—" I said, "Mort ain't going to write nothing on there." I was adamant by this time that this man's name was going to be nowhere on that album. And see this comes from every blues album that I ever picked up has got liner notes that's done by some white guy. So here was my record, and I was ready to die before I let him. And nobody could see that this was the play being acted out in 1982.

SHANNON: Did you have them to pay you in cash?

WILSON: (laughs) One of these days I'm going to write a story about that. It's just totally unbelievable that this stuff is going on in 1982.

SHANNON: That means that you are right on target with the subject matter of the play.

WILSON: And they did this stuff so innocently like "Oh, are we doing something wrong? We thought it would just be nice if Mort just . . ."

SHANNON: To date all of your plays feature men occupying center stage. How do you perceive women's roles in your work? Are you concerned that, so far, women have not been the focus of your plays?

WILSON: No, I am not concerned, and I doubt seriously if I would make a woman the focus of my work simply because of the fact that I am a man, and I guess because of the ground on which I stand and the viewpoint from which I perceive the world. I can't do that although I try to be honest in the instances in which I do have women. I try to portray them from their own viewpoint as opposed to my viewpoint. I try to, to the extent that I am able to step around on the other side of the table, if you will, and try to look at things from their viewpoint and have been satisfied that I have been able to do that to some extent.

SHANNON: I see that. That's the basis of the essay that I gave you—that the women are strong and that if somebody else perceives them as victims, I think that person doesn't read the plays carefully enough because these women choose their routes rather than become victims of men.

WILSON: Yeah, I would agree with that. I try not to portray any of my characters as victims. There was a line in *Two Trains Running* when they are tearing down the building and Memphis is talking about what his business used to be and how he used to sell four cases of chicken a week, but now he's down to one case. "But that's alright," he said. "I ain't greedy. I'll take that. Only they don't want me to have that." I took that line, "They don't want me to have that," out of the script because that makes him a victim of someone else who's doing something to him. They are not doing anything to him personally. It's not like they don't want him to have it. They're tearing down the building. So there was a little suggestion that he would be a victim. And I heard that, and I said, "No, no. I'm going to have to take that out."

SHANNON: That reminds me of a conversation between two of the jitney drivers in the play *Jitney!*. I think Youngblood is talking, and he's talking about them sending him over to Vietnam. He says, "The white man did it to me." And I think it's Turnbo, who says, "No, the white man didn't do that to you."

WILSON: Well, I try not to—

SHANNON: He said, "They didn't know you were black when they sent you over there." And I think Youngblood comes back with the line "They knew I was over there when they were shooting at my ass. They knew that."

WILSON: It didn't make any difference if he was white or black when he was over there.

223
•
Appendix

SHANNON: Can you talk for a moment about the restaurant waitress Risa in *Two Trains Running*? What is the meaning of her self-inflicted scars? What inspired you to depict such self-destruction in an African American woman of this decade? What is the larger meaning of her wounds?

WILSON: Well, I wish that I could talk more about her than I can. For me the scarring of her legs was an attempt to define herself in her own terms rather than being defined by men. The closest that I could come up to what kind of psychological motivation that may have been was I think in Holloway's speech: "She makes her legs ugly. That forces you to look at her and see what kind of personality she has." That may be, but basically for me it was her standing up and refusing to accept those definitions and making her self-definition.

I think in almost every play most of my male characters have scars. Levee has a thick scar. Troy has a scar where he was shot. Loomis inflicts scars upon himself.

SHANNON: Physical scars?

WILSON: Physical scars. Lyman has it in *The Piano Lesson*. Lyman lost half of his stomach.

SHANNON: And Gabriel losing part of his head.

WILSON: Gabriel losing part of his head. The only scarification in *Two Trains* is Risa. Normally it would have been Sterling, but for some reason—. People would ask me, "Man, have you got a scar on your chest or something?" It's just unconscious.

SHANNON: I know I'm tempted to see some sort of religious parallel in it. I don't know with the nailing to the cross. I don't know. I may be reading too much into that.

WILSON: I'm not sure. It's unconscious whatever it is. But it's no longer unconscious because I recognize it although I didn't purposefully decide. It just emerges. For instance, I didn't decide that death was going to be part of the play. Once you get in there and you're working, you're not even thinking. You're working from another place. It's sort of like this stuff is given to you if you open yourself up for it, and half the time I just accept what I hear. When Boy Willie says, "Sutter fell in the well," I wrote it down. I don't know who Sutter is. But Boy Willie has said, "Sutter fell in the well." Now I've got to go back after I've started typing this and say, "Who is that guy that fell in the well? Who is he?"

Then I go back and put it in or find something, but I don't question it when the character says it. Likewise, when Loomis cut his chest, I didn't question it. I just wrote, "Loomis slashes his chest." I didn't say, "Well, I know what I am going to do. I'll have him cut his chest and—." I'm writing a scene—in fact, the last scene of that play I had not written, and it's December 1, and I had to have this thing postmarked by midnight, and it's about three o'clock in the afternoon, and I still have this last part of the play that's still not written. So I took my tablet, and I went to a bar, and I sat down. It took me about a half hour from the time I got there and a half hour later I wrote the scene. I will always recall this scene because I was sweating so. Sweat was just pouring off me. When I came out of that scene, I was drenched. I was soaked with sweat. I said, "I got it!" And I went home, and I typed it up, and at seven o'clock or eight o'clock I'm up there getting it copied so I can get it in the mail by midnight.

SHANNON: I'm interested in the idea of being led by the characters and listening to the characters as opposed to manipulating and creating them. How does that work? How do you allow that to happen?

WILSON: Well, I think the key word is what you just said—"allow." You have to allow it to happen. In other words, I trust the characters. I've learned that if I just write down what I hear that the characters say. I have a premise; everything that they say is true. I don't have to use everything that they say, however, to tell the story. But the more I know, the more I know about the characters. The more they talk, the more I learn about the characters. Then I have the right to censor that and take parts. I know it's true, but I don't want to use that part. I'm going to use this part. So I just write down whatever they say without thinking. I started *Two Trains* with the line, "When I left out of Jackson, I said I'm gonna buy me a V-8 Ford and drive by Mr. Henry Ford's house and honk the horn. If anybody'd come to the window I was gonna wave. Then I was going out and get me a thirty-aught six and come on back to Jackson and drive up to Mr. Stovall's house and honk the horn. Only this time I ain't waving." Now when I wrote this I had no idea, and the character did not have a name. I had no idea who he was. But I started, and then it's like "Who is Stovall?" Why does this guy want to get this car and go by Stovall's, etc., etc.? So I more or less ask the character, "Who is Stovall?" And he says, "Well, I had this old farm down there, etc., etc.," and he started to explain the whole story about Stovall. Then, he started talking about Stovall, and then somehow he ended up talking about this woman who left him after nine years, and she wouldn't even shake his hand. And now I have a woman character, and I have to decide whether I am going to go to her and get some dialogue or whether I want her to be a character. Then I decided that I didn't want her to be a character and that I would just use Risa as a character, and you could see through his relationship with Risa some possibility as to why his wife may have left. And I thought Risa has to carry all of the women's stories in the play. Risa is the only woman who has to carry all of them and somehow make sense of certain things you know. But I just wrote down whatever—at some point I named him Memphis. I have a couple of short stories with a character named Memphis, who was a farmer—a sharecropper, down in Alabama—that I'd used. And I liked that name. It's the name of an Egyptian god, Memphis. Sterling because he's a sterling man. I knew what his name was before I ever wrote a line of dialogue for him, which is unusual. Most of the time I don't know who they are. If I'm writing and I don't know the name, I just put a little dash and keep on going. And so Memphis, and there's this guy who's talking back to Memphis. I don't know who he is. I put a dash.

Holloway's name was originally Brownie, but I had used a Brownie in *Fences*. Troy talks about Brownie. Brownie's kind of an Uncle Tom character, so I didn't want people to think that this was the same Brownie. So I changed his name. I got his name from a blues song.

SHANNON: Now Hambone and Gabriel—do they have any relationship? They seem to be similar.

WILSON: I think so. In one instance, there is something that I call a "spectacle character." It's part of that. They are both mentally deficient. One has a war wound, which I think is most important. They make me mad when I read the reviews and they would refer to Gabriel as an idiot or some other kind of description without making reference to the fact that this man had suffered this wound fighting for a country in which his brother could not play baseball. That was the important thing about Gabriel. Gabriel is one of those self-sufficient characters. He gets up and goes to work every day. He goes out and collects those discarded fruit and vegetables, but he's taking care of himself. He doesn't want Troy to take care of him. He moves out of Troy's house and lives down there and pays his rent to the extent that he is able. Yeah, there is some correlation between them [Gabriel and Hambone]. But they are very different in the sense that, one—Hambone has a much more important part in *Two Trains*. He has an effect on everybody's life in the play. He starts off as this guy who says, "I want my ham!" But he emerges as most important because of his life and his death. Risa has this relationship with him. Sterling gives him help. Memphis is throwing him out. Memphis can see himself. "I'm going back to Jackson one of these days." Well, that's Hambone. "Man been 'round here saying the same thing for ten years." Well he's [Memphis] been around for ten years too. He has to come to see that. So Hambone's presence, first of all, and his death affect the whole play, and then Sterling can resurrect and redeem Hambone's life by taking the ham. This produces the man of action. Without Hambone, you don't have a Sterling. And also it's the demonstration of his willingness to shed blood in order to get the ham. So when he comes back inside, it's very important that there is blood on his face where he cut his face, where he cut his hands. So it's the willingness to bleed, Loomis's willingness to bleed, the willingness to shed blood.

SHANNON: "I don't need anybody"—what was it?

WILSON: "I don't need anybody to bleed for me. I can bleed for myself." There's also Boy Willie's willingness to engage Sutter in battle. He doesn't like say, "Oh there's a ghost," and run the other way. He went after the ghost whose presence is made known to him through this force field. Only he goes toward it as opposed to run from it.

SHANNON: Absolutely. Troy's personification of Death through wrestling—

WILSON: He's wrestling with Death. In fact, when Troy got shot when he was trying to rob this guy, he fell forward. He said, "When the guy shot me, I jumped at him with my knife." So here's a man who has pulled a knife on somebody who could pull a gun and shoot him. He takes that, but then he comes forward and ends up killing him. So there's always that willingness to shed blood.

SHANNON: Are you moved to write plays in the future giving women more voice?

WILSON: I always say whatever the material dictates, that's what I will follow. However, in the play that I am working on now, which was originally an all-male play. I looked up one day, and this woman had come on stage and sat down in a chair. The guys in the play said, "What the hell is she doing here? I thought you told us that this was an all-male play. What's she doing?" Then they started shouting, "Get out of here!"

SHANNON: This actually happened?

WILSON: No, this was in my head. They said, "Get on away from here. Man, what she doing?" I said, "Hold up a minute. Let's go find out." So I went over and I asked this woman what she was doing, and she said, "I want my own scene." She just sat there, and they're shouting at her. These are crude men who were working. At first when she came in, she said, "Mr. Wilson said that I could come in." That's when they came and got me. And I said, "You want your own scene?" She said, "Yes, I want my own scene." Okay, I close my tablet up, and I'm thinking about this. In the process of writing this all-male play, this woman emerges into the play. Now I've got to figure out what to do with her—not only that, but she wants her own scene.

SHANNON: Could that perhaps be the voice of a critic or two suggesting—

WILSON: No, it was the voice of this woman saying, "How are you going to write this play about these guys and not include me in it? I'm a part of it. They didn't get to be who they are without me, etc., etc. You can't ignore me."

SHANNON: So that is part of listening to the characters?

WILSON: Yeah. That was unconscious. How could I write a play without a woman in there? That's what I was trying to do. She said, "I got a part in this story. You gonna write a play about blacks in America in the 1940s and ain't going to have no women in it? How ridiculous can you get!" I said, "Well, you are right." So then I opened up my pad and said, "Okay, you got your own scene." This guy knocks on the door. He had a radio under one arm and a chicken under the other. She knew his name and invited him in, and I closed up my tablet. Now I've got to figure out how I'm going to use that. What's happening is that it is emerging as my man-woman play, which is something that I have, at some point, included in all of the plays, but I never really focused on black man–black woman relationships. It was a big thing, but that's just not something that I chose. Maybe it's just something that I had been wanting to write for a long time. But it's not that I am crazy; it's just me telling myself, "Okay, you're ready to do this now." I think that I have acquired a certain maturity. So I think that all of that is possible.

SHANNON: I've noticed that Pittsburgh locales in two of your plays in particular—*Two Trains Running* and *Jitney!*—are about to be demolished. What does the imminent wrecking ball suggest in these two works? What does the city mean to your play?

WILSON: I set them in Pittsburgh I guess because that is what I know best. I think that a lot of what was going on in Pittsburgh was going on in Detroit, Cleveland, or anywhere black Americans were. So they actually could be set anywhere there is a black community in various cities. There's some peculiar kinds of things in relation to Pittsburgh. And that's what I know best. I couldn't set them in Cleveland because I don't know Cleveland, but you could transfer them to Cleveland and they would play just as well.

SHANNON: In previous interviews, you've noted the influence of the blues, Romare Bearden, Amiri Baraka, and Jorge Borges. What or who influences you most now?

WILSON: I think that they are the same. The blues I would count as my primary influence. I've been more and more influenced by art, whether it is Bearden or any artist. It's the idea of the artist. It's the visual artist and how they think and how they approach a particular subject—what they want to paint about. I'm not sure that a writer can use the same approach as a painter, for instance. Even though the painter's tools are different—he's working with form and shadow and mass and color and lines, I think that there are some corresponding things in the tools of the playwright. In some of my characterizations, I use color. So I became more and more fascinated with painters. So Bearden has become more of an influence from art.

Baraka less so. Mainly the ideas that Baraka espoused in the '60s as a black nationalist—ideas that I found value in then and still find value in. Baraka's influence is not so much upon the way that he writes or his writing style other than the ideas of the '60s that I came through and improved a lot using that influence. Jorge Luis Borges, the Argentine short story writer—I was just fascinated with the way he tells a story. I've been trying to write a play the way he writes a story. One of his techniques is that he tells you exactly what is going to happen. He'll say the gaucho so-and-so would end up with a bullet in his head on night of such and such. At the outset the leader of an outlaw gang with a bullet in his head would seem improbable. When you meet the guy, he's washing dishes, and you go, "This guy is going to be the leader of an outlaw gang?" You know that he's going to get killed, but how is this going to happen? And he proceeds to tell the story, and it seems like it's never going to happen. And you look up, without even knowing it, there he is. He's the leader of an outlaw gang.

SHANNON: So he doesn't spoil the plot by telling it. He sort of initiates suspense.

WILSON: Yes. The suspense is how is this going to happen? You know that this guy is going to get shot in the head, and it's so masterfully done that you don't see it coming. Even if you stop and say, "Okay, how is he going to get shot?" Then, there it is. It just unfolds itself. It is the idea of the discovery as to how it happens. See if you write a play like that, the audience will be just intrigued with trying to—. So it's more or less in the play that I'm doing now, which is a murder mystery in which somebody named Floyd Bannister gets killed. There are all kinds of possibilities. Any number of people may have killed Floyd Bannister in the play. And then if you have a scene with Floyd Bannister in it, you go, "Hey, Floyd, you're going to get killed!" You know that about him, so you then have to look at Floyd in whatever relations he is having with anybody in the play. He gets into an argument with someone and you say, "Could that be the guy who killed Floyd?" because you know this. So then it becomes intriguing just sitting there trying to figure it out. But what most intrigues the audience is that you know he is going to be killed and he doesn't.

SHANNON: It sounds challenging to translate that to the stage.

WILSON: Oh, it is. I'm just not sure how to do it. I haven't been sure of how to do anything other than when I started *Joe Turner*. I started *Joe Turner* as a short story. On page twelve of the story, I said, "You've got to write another play. Maybe this is the play." I said, "I can't make this story into a play. How am I going to do that?" So I wasn't quite sure how to do it. But the fact that I don't know how to do it is what makes it challenging. I say to myself, "If I can do that it would be quite interesting." I'll try anything. If it doesn't work, tear it up and start on something else. Writing is free; it doesn't cost you anything. There is nowhere where it says that five hundred words cost twenty-five cent or a dollar. They're free.

SHANNON: Do you have a lot of incomplete projects lying around?

WILSON: Oh yeah. I've got all kinds of stuff—a bunch of stories, some plays that I started and abandoned. But all of that is important. *Ma Rainey* I started writing in 1976. I actually wrote it in 1981, but I started a play called *Ma Rainey's Black Bottom* in 1976 and abandoned it because I didn't know what I was doing. So I've got parts of plays and stuff that I'd written, and all of this stuff proves useful. I may go back to it. I may ultimately go back to *Fullerton Street* and say, "Okay, how can I approach this differently—the same story in a different way now with what I have learned about playwriting?" So I don't consider anything a waste of time.

SHANNON: That was your 1940s play—*Fullerton Street*? You've since decided to write another '40s play, *Moon Going Down*. How is that going?

WILSON: Well, that turned into this play with this woman. Instead of being about all of these guys in a turpentine camp, this woman—and I always say if your idea doesn't change, then you're not writing deep enough because you start off with an idea that turns out to be something entirely different once you get into the actual writing process. Your writing more or less dictates itself. It has its own requirements. And this woman suddenly appears. Now I'm going to have to deal with her. If she's in her scene in her apartment, then maybe this play doesn't take place in a turpentine camp.

SHANNON: Would it be kind of awkward to put a woman in a turpentine camp?

WILSON: Well, it might be possible. I don't know if that is the correct setting though for what I want to say at the moment, so I may end up having to abandon the turpentine camp idea. Only it may not be a turpentine camp in the '40s. It may be a penitentiary in the '90s in which there is the same kind of situation. So the idea can change as it grows and develops, and it very often does change.

SHANNON: You've made several geographic relocations since Pittsburgh. What motivated your most recent move to Seattle? How has the move affected your writing?

WILSON: Well, I haven't really written anything since I've been in Seattle, although I can write anywhere. I don't think that will affect my writing. I moved to Seattle because I got divorced. Seattle is a nice town. I had been there a couple of times, and it was as far west as I could get and as far away from New York as I could get. And I didn't know anyone in Seattle. I still don't know anyone in Seattle. That's fine with me.

SHANNON: So it wasn't an aesthetic move?

WILSON: No.

SHANNON: How have two Pulitzer Prizes affected you?

WILSON: Neither one has affected me. What it does is change the way people look at you, but it doesn't change the way I look at myself. What did I do? I wrote some plays. I wrote a couple of plays. I've been writing twenty-six years, and I've got a whole bulk of writing.

SHANNON: I think that also has a lot to do with the fact that you are not a one-shot playwright. Sometimes you may rest on your laurels and not push yourself to go beyond that.

WILSON: Yeah, here again I've been a writer for twenty-six years, and it is what I have chosen to do with my life. Even behind *Ma Rainey*, I didn't just suddenly become a writer and pick up a pen and say, "Oh, I'm going to write a play." I had been wrestling with ideas and forms of writing and trying to say all kinds of things many years before. It's just part of being a writer.

SHANNON: Have you seen the sitcom *Roc*? As you know the whole cast of the Broadway production of *The Piano Lesson* may now be seen every Sunday evening prime time. What are your thoughts on this transplanted cast and about the show?

WILSON: I like the show. Here again, it's a sitcom, and I think you have to approach it as that, which is the lowest common denominator. This is, after all, TV, and it's a comedy. They're concerned about advertisers. That's where they make their money. They're concerned about the ratings. So we're not going to get world-class drama. I think they did a good job. The only criticism that I have—first of all, it's constructive criticism—is that there is always in the episodes I've seen a moment in the plays that I would call a "sharp moment" when the comedy is suspended for a moment.

SHANNON: When they deal with serious issues?

WILSON: Sometime the whole show can deal with serious issues, but even within that—. There's a moment where—I think one moment was when the father was talking about working on the railroad and some of the mistreatment everybody got. So the fact that you have those kinds of emphases on things is important. The criticism that I have is in regard to Joey, the character of Roc's brother Joey, who, as old as he is, is living in his brother's house. His brother has this thing about wanting him to move out anyway. The father I can see living there, but Joey I think should be trying to find a way to get out of the house. Joey, who's a musician, but we have no indication of this either. Here again, there isn't any interest in his music. We've never seen him engaged with anything. I think the first episode when he came home, they had a gig, but the band broke up or something. And I think he should constantly be trying to put the band back together, and there are all kinds of humorous things and reasons he can't and reasons why he's still there. And he and Roc argue about him being there and have these comments. Then it becomes funny that he can't get out of the house even trying. Something always goes wrong. I think at some point, some episode, something should be seen. Otherwise, he becomes lazy and shiftless like white people seem to think of Joey: "Well, as long as I live here rent free on my brother and eat his food, I'll do that."

SHANNON: That comes through loud and clear, though—that he is a parasite.

WILSON: They play this thing with the women with him. Joey is always with some woman. He walks in the bar—. You know, there is a certain responsibility that you have. In other words if there is a woman sitting at the bar and you go over and talk with her, you walk over with a certain responsibility. You can't just walk over and think, "You don't mean anything. You're just another woman. There's one over there too, so there ain't no difference in y'all." And that's what you get from that kind of portrayal. All he has to do is see a woman, and he forgets about everything else. And I think that another white attitude that they have is the way whites view black men.

SHANNON: The writers are basically white.

WILSON: No, not necessarily. That doesn't matter. If the writers are black, then they're writing what the white man wants them to write. Still there is always some white person who, having set themselves up as a custodian to your experience, will tell you how to do it. The actors go to auditions and have these people tell them, "You're not black enough. You're not buoyant. Can you do it a little more black?"

SHANNON: Sounds like *Hollywood Shuffle*.

WILSON: As long as white people maintain those positions, they can say—. Quincy Jones is not producing the show as an example; the white guy is. See, it's all filtered through his sensibilities, and they may get some things right, but I think on the whole—

SHANNON: It's troubling. It's not easy to watch sometimes. Some episodes are troubling.

WILSON: What I absolutely cannot watch is *In Living Color*. And this is done by black folks. "Here we are. We go'n clown. We go'n act up." I haven't watched any more than sixty seconds of it.

SHANNON: What are your goals beyond the ten-play cycle? What impact do you envision the cycle will have in years to come?

WILSON: Well, I don't know what impact it's going to have. I certainly hope it has one. At least you'll have a dramatic—my idea of a dramatic history of black Americans.

SHANNON: It certainly is the first time that it's been done.

WILSON: Okay, but here again I stumbled onto that, and I'm glad I did because it enables me to keep a focus. Otherwise I'd have to come up with some ideas to write the plays; only I just have to think of the decade and then go from there. I think I prefer starting like that.

SHANNON: What do you think about the current status of black theatre?

WILSON: I think, one, it's not institutionalized. The difference between white theatre and black theatre is that there are hundreds and hundreds of institutions that support white theatre. You can walk into any university, and they have a theatre program that supports white theatre. You have two-hundred-and-some-odd regional theatres in the country with budgets in excess of a million dollars. Only it isn't black. So you really have a lot of institutional support for what I call white theatre and nothing for what I call black theatre. The National Black Theater Conference, however, that they had in Winston-Salem, North Carolina—I was talking with some other people who were pleasantly surprised to find out that everybody did not know everybody that was out there. So that was the first time, in a long while anyway, that everybody became aware of everybody else. Of course, at the conference they talked about the idea of networking.

But I think after becoming aware of each other, the next question is developing an agenda that will carry you forward. I think what I really see a drastic need for is a conference of writers, some serious kind of conference at which we tackle the problems of writing. I would just like to see all writers get together and hash out some ideas more or less. I think it's time for that.

SHANNON: Black writers? All writers?

WILSON: Black writers. All writers are important, but I would never try telling anyone what you have to write. You can be a black writer and write whatever you want. I would never tell anyone what to write. You can only write what you feel to write anyway. I don't want anyone telling me what to write. And that was part of the thing in the '60s. People were talking about the black writer's responsibility. A black writer's responsibility is whatever he assumes that responsibility to be individually. So you can't say you're not doing right because you're not writing this kind of material even though you're black. You may not want to write it. You can't be forced to write it. If they assume that as a responsibility, then you have the basis to sit down and talk about what that responsibility should be—"Did you ever look at it this way?" But you can't force on anyone a responsibility for writing.

The fact is that we have not been writing long. We're relatively new to this. We don't have a large body of literature that has been developed by blacks because at one time it was a crime to teach blacks how to read and write. Europeans have been writing stuff down for hundreds and hundreds of years. Blacks, coming from an oral tradition, didn't see the necessity to write it down. We just didn't do that. So we're in America. We've been here since the early seventeenth century, and we know that there is a value to writing things down. But still it is something that is relatively new to us. I think that if writers get together, then we could—I'm not talking about coming up with any manifesto. But I think there are some questions of aesthetics and questions of exactly how writers can contribute to the development of the culture, not contribute to anyone's polemic, not contribute to anyone's idea about what we should and should not be doing, but to the thing that remains the basis of our culture. "This is our culture. How can we contribute? How can we develop it?"

SHANNON: I see that you are doing just that in your work.

WILSON: I have always consciously been chasing the musicians. You see their expression has been so highly developed, and it has been one expression of African American life. It's like culture is in the music. And the writers are way behind the musicians I see. So I'm trying to close that gap. That is one of the things I like about Bearden's art is that I think he moved art closer to where the musicians were. But they've always been in the forefront. I think writers need to consciously be aware how our expressions as writers achieve the quality of the musician's expression.

SHANNON: What are some of your current projects?

WILSON: Well, I'm writing this play. I want to put out a book of poetry, and at some point fairly soon, maybe after I write this next play, I want to write a novel, which I've got about sixty-some pages to. I want to do that except that in writing the novel there will be ideas from about ten different plays in there. Maybe I should just write the play.

SHANNON: From poet to playwright to novelist? Do you see the next genre as more of a challenge?

WILSON: It's a challenge because you see years ago I thought the novel is this vast uncharted sea, and never honestly could understand how anyone could write a novel until I discovered that you didn't have to have the whole thing in your head when you sat down and wrote. And now I can see how you write a novel. It's the same as writing a play. You discover as you go along. When you write chapter 3, you don't know what's going to go on in chapter 7, but the material dictates; it has its own requirements. And then as you write you discover all kinds of stuff, and the next thing you know, you're on chapter 12 without planning anything. It's just there as the story unfolds. A novel is simply more words. It's an entirely different medium, so you have a chance to go inside your character's head if you want. You can do description. That's probably one of the most exciting things about it—the fact that you could describe something, and in the process of describing it, you can choose the language that describes it. You can mix up that language and maybe describe a very familiar thing in a fresh way.

SHANNON: You seem to be very elaborate in your stage notes, so it seems that the novel would be your opportunity to get that kind of description into the text—make it part of the text as opposed to being aside from it.

WILSON: Also I have a very strong visual sense that I don't too often get a chance to demonstrate, except when I did the film script for *Fences*. It was fun because you're telling the story with your eye as opposed to your ear. So, yeah. I'm looking forward to it.

SHANNON: My last question is what are the chances that you will come to visit us on the campus of Howard University? I'd love to introduce you to my students and to show you the campus.

WILSON: The chances are good in the sense, as I'm sure you are aware, of the position that Howard University occupies in the history of black America. I would be delighted to come. The question is finding a suitable time, but I would be delighted.

NOTES

PREFACE

1. The script of *Fullerton Street*, originally intended to be Wilson's play for the 1940s, could not be secured for analysis in this study. During my interview, August Wilson discussed the play's focus: "What I wanted to do was to show some people who had come North and encountered the cities and had lost whatever kinds of values they had in the South—almost as if the environment determined that you had to adopt different values in order to survive up here." The play was written in 1980; to date, no productions have been mounted, and it remains unpublished.

INTRODUCTION

1. *Seven Guitars*, to date Wilson's seventh chronicle of African American history, tells the story of Floyd Barton, "a man who lives to play the blues but who dies when his dream gets too close" (*On Stage* 3).

2. *The Prevalence of Ritual* is a series of collage works called "Projections." Included in the series are *Baptism, Conjur Woman as an Angel,* and *Tidings.* See Schwartzman 213–16.

3. The Summer 1968 issue of *The Drama Review*, which emphasized black revolutionary theatre, includes works by Ben Caldwell, LeRoi Jones, Herbert Stokes, Jimmie Garrett, John O'Neal, Sonia Sanchez, Marvin X, Ed Bullins, and Ronald Milner.

4. The poem "For Malcolm X and Others" appeared in the September 1969 issue of *Negro Digest*.

CHAPTER 1

1. Wilson selected as his protagonist Charles E. Bolton (alias Black Bart), a notorious bandit who robbed twenty-seven stage coaches in California from 1874 to 1883. He would baffle and sometimes amuse authorities by leaving behind bits of doggerel poetry at a crime scene. Eventually Black Bart was arrested and his identity disclosed when a foiled robbery attempt led authorities to San Francisco, where at last they arrested the fugitive outlaw.

2. Although Wilson acknowledges the existence of three early plays whose titles also appear in various periodical references—*Recycle, Rite of Passage,* and *Black Bart and the Sacred Hills*—my attempts to secure these scripts from him for discussion in this study were not successful. Wilson's close professional associate and friend Lou Bellamy, director of Saint Paul, Minnesota's Penumbra Theater, confirmed the existence of yet another script on Malcolm X written by Wilson:

Wilson created a role especially for him in this work, which was once performed at the Penumbra. The information that follows represents details about the above plays that I was able to glean from published material as well as my interview with Wilson:

The currently unpublished play, *Recycle*, was written in 1973 and produced at a community theatre in Pittsburgh.

Wilson refers to *Rite of Passage* as his "first play."

Black Bart and the Sacred Hills is an unpublished script written in 1977 and produced in St. Paul in 1981. The sprawling musical satire features twenty-seven characters and is based upon a series of poems about a legendary rustler named Black Bart (see interview in the appendix for a detailed plot summary).

3. See Karenga's *Quotable Karenga*. See also Baraka's "Seven Principles."

4. Yacub, "the big-headed scientist," is a mythical hero among members of the Muslim faith. His well-known story involving a failed laboratory experiment that yields various shades of people is an etiological myth for the origin of the races.

5. A typical advertisement went like this:

> He could hear—and he heard the sad hearted, weary people of his homeland, Dallas—singing weird, sad melodies at their work and play, and unconsciously he began to imitate them—lamenting his fate in song. He learned to play a guitar, and for years he entertained his friends freely—moaning his weird songs as a means of forgetting his affliction. Some friends who saw great possibilities in him, suggested that he commercialize his talent—and as a result of following their advice—he is now heard exclusively on Paramount. (New York Record Laboratories 3).

6. Wilson begins his eight-page script with the following acknowledgment: "A script adapted from the taped series 'Ways of Mankind' (presented under the supervision of Walter Goldschmitt, Anthropologist at the University of California, L.A.)" (*ESD* 1).

CHAPTER 2

1. In the early '70s, the Penn Hills section of Pittsburgh was a predominately white suburban area. In order to purchase a home here, Youngblood, just as many real-life Vietnam veterans of that time, takes advantage of a loan insured by the Veterans Administration as part of the Readjustment Benefits Act of 1966. This legislation extended benefits to those who served after January 31, 1955, with educational allowances of $100–150 per month for up to thirty-six months, as well as GI Loans and other assistance.

2. The study *Afro-Americans in Pittsburgh* credits black real estate brokers with instigating the increase in home ownership among African Americans and considers them "the most powerful antidiscriminating force available to blacks in the area of owner housing in Pittsburgh" (Darden 53–54).

1. Wilson recalls in our interview (appendix) how he avoided an early career blunder by turning down a very attractive offer of $25,000 from Broadway producers to turn *Ma Rainey's Black Bottom* into a musical. Though this sum tempted the $88-per-week cook, he ultimately granted performance rights to Lloyd Richards and the Dramatist Guild for $2,500.

2. Black Theater Network—an organization "dedicated to increasing the awareness, appreciation, and production of Black Theater in the African diaspora" (*BT News* 15)—gave a sample of the problems African American playwrights faced in 1991:

> On the East Coast, the Negro Ensemble Company—producer of some of the most important works of contemporary Black drama—was evicted from its performance space at the end of last year [1990]. A 51% cut in Crossroads Theatre Company's operating budget this season forced this prominent company to eliminate one play from the season and replace it with a revival from a past season; change the performance dates of others; and move another play to next season. . . . On the West Coast, Ed Bullins' BMT Theater also has been kicked out of their space due to a 41% increase in their rent, while Bay Area's Oakland Ensemble Theatre struggles with a budget deficit of 10% of their $600,000 operating budget. (Anderson 4)

3. Gertrude Rainey, the Queen of the Blues, stumbled upon this "strange" and "weird" music (Palmer 44) by accident in 1902. This was some time before the vaudeville entertainer met and married "Pa" Rainey and, with him, started the act Rainey and Rainey, Assassinators of the Blues, and before she became a household name in the South.

CHAPTER 4

1. In addition to drawing upon her own powerful intuition to create the role of the 1950s black wife and mother, Mary Alice credits director Lloyd Richards with helping her to fully realize Rose's character. As Alice discovered, Richards's tendency is to discourage actors and actresses from struggling with a part. "Don't *manage* it. Let it happen to you" (70), he counsels. Like numerous other actors under Richards's influence, Mary Alice recognizes that the free rein he allowed in interpreting her character was a major factor in her superlative critical reviews. *New York Times* critic Frank Rich, for example, summed up her opening performance this way: "Ms. Alice's performance emphasizes strength over self-pity, open anger over festering bitterness. The actress finds the spiritual quotient in the acceptance that accompanies Rose's love for a scarred, profoundly complicated man" ("Family Ties" C3).

2. Mary Alice's comments are excerpted from a videotaped lecture given by the actress, who starred as Rose Maxson in the Broadway run of *Fences*, at the Eugene O'Neill Theater Center on April 16, 1993. Alice was the invited speaker

for students in my August Wilson seminar, who were guests-for-a-day at the center and the Monte Cristo Cottage, Eugene O'Neill's boyhood home.

3. For details concerning the controversy over changing *Fences*'s ending, see Christiansen.

CHAPTER 5

1. "Defamiliarization"—as defined by Shklovsky in his essay "Art as Technique"—is a process whereby art is made "to create a 'vision' of the object instead of serving as a means of knowing it" (18). Shklovsky asserts, "The technique of art is to make objects 'unfamiliar,' to make forms difficult, to increase the difficulty and length of perception because the process of perception is an aesthetic end in itself and must be prolonged" (12). Wilson employs this perception-based strategy in *Joe Turner's Come and Gone*.

2. Charles S. Dutton, who starred as the troubled wayfarer Herald Loomis in *Joe Turner*'s 1986 production at the Yale Repertory Theatre, was chosen by Wilson for a second time to play the lead character in his work. However, it was actor Delroy Lindo who brought the role of Loomis to life in October 1987 at the Arena Stage in Washington, D.C., as well as in March 1988 at the Ethel Barrymore Theatre on Broadway.

CHAPTER 6

1. Although Dutton has gained considerable fame as Wilson's leading man, he is conscious of the artistic paradox created when the Pulitzer Prize–winning playwright designs roles specifically geared toward his talents as an actor. While he considers Wilson's gesture "exhilarating" (Greene 39), he also realizes that the personalized role somehow loses its challenge for him. As an actor, he could not find as much space to explore the character and make of it what he envisioned. Despite Dutton's artistic reservations, he excelled as Boy Willie on Broadway, receiving a Tony nomination in 1991.

2. For a detailed discussion of the plight of Pullman porters and advancements they made in gaining equal rights as laborers under A. Philip Randolph, see Santino.

3. For an extensive treatment of various roles white slave owners played to control their slaves' activities, such as promoting widespread ghostlore, see Fry (especially chaps. 1 and 2). See also Gorn.

CHAPTER 7

1. See Backalenick, "Two Trains Running," and Johnson.

SELECTED BIBLIOGRAPHY

PUBLISHED PLAYS

August Wilson: Three Plays. Pittsburgh: University of Pittsburgh Press, 1991.

Fences. New York: New American Library, 1987.

The Janitor. In *Short Pieces from the New Dramatists.* Edited by Stan Chervin. New York: Broadway Play Publishing, 1985.

Joe Turner's Come and Gone. New York: New American Library, 1988.

Ma Rainey's Black Bottom. New York: New American Library, 1985.

The Piano Lesson. New York: Plume, 1990.

"Testimonies." *Antaeus* 66 (Spring 1991): 474–79.

Two Trains Running. New York: Plume, 1992.

UNPUBLISHED PLAYS

An Evening with Margaret Mead. Written for the Science Museum of Minnesota in 1979. Not produced.

Black Bart and the Sacred Hills. Written in 1977. Produced in 1981.

The Coldest Day of the Year. Written in 1977. Produced in 1989.

The Eskimo Song Duel. Described as "a script adapted from the taped series 'Ways of Mankind' (presented under the supervision of Walter Goldschmitt, Anthropologist at the University of California, L.A.)." Adapted by August Wilson in August 1979.

Fullerton Street. Written in 1980. Not produced.

The Homecoming. Written in 1976. Produced in 1989.

How Coyote Got His Special Power and Used It to Help the People. Written for the Science Museum of Minnesota in 1978.

Jitney! Written in 1979. Produced in 1982. Accepted by the Minneapolis Playwright's Center for performance in 1980. Also performed in 1985 at the Martin Luther King Center in St. Paul, Minnesota.

Recycle. Written in 1973. Produced at a community theatre in Pittsburgh in 1973.

Rite of Passage. According to Wilson, his "first play." Further data unavailable.

Seven Guitars. First performed at the Goodman Theater in Chicago in January 1995.

ESSAYS

"Characters Behind History Teach Wilson About Plays." *New York Times,* 12 April 1992, H5.

Foreword. *Romare Bearden: His Life and Art,* by Myron Schwartzman. New York: Harry N. Abrams, 1990.

"Hero Worship on Sunday Afternoon." 26 Super Bowl Game Program. Los Angeles: NFL Properties, 1992.

"How to Write a Play Like August Wilson." *New York Times*, 10 March 1991, H5, H17.

"I Don't Want Nobody Just 'Cause They're Black." *Spin*, October 1990, 70–71.

"I Want a Black Director." *New York Times*, 26 September 1990, A25.

"The Legacy of Malcolm X." *Life*, December 1992, 84–94.

Memory of Actor Robert Judd. In *Broadway Day and Night*, pp. 114–16. New York: Simon and Shuster, 1992.

Preface. *August Wilson: Three Plays*. Pittsburgh: University of Pittsburgh Press, 1991.

UNCOLLECTED POETRY

"Bessie." *Black Lines* 1 (Summer 1971): 68.

"For Malcolm X and Others." *Negro Digest* 18 (September 1969): 58.

"Morning Song." *Black Lines* 1 (Summer 1971): 68.

"Muhammad Ali." *Black World* 1 (September 1972): 60–61.

"Theme One: The Variations." In *The Poetry of Black America: Anthology of the Twentieth Century*. Edited by Arnold Adoff. New York: Harper and Row, 1973.

WORKS BY OTHER AUTHORS

Alice, Mary. Videotaped lecture at the Eugene O'Neill Theater Center. Waterford, Conn. 15 April 1993.

Anderson, Gary. "Black Theater: The Next Generation." *BT News* 1 (Spring 1991): 4.

Ansen, David. "Of Prophets and Profits: August Wilson's '60s." *Newsweek*, 27 April 1992, 70.

Backalenick, Irene. "A Lesson from Lloyd Richards." *Theater Week*, 16–22 April 1990, 17–19.

———. "Two Trains Running Is Unique Despite Some Imperfections." *Westport News*, 6 April 1990, A–43.

Baker, Houston. *The Journey Back*. Chicago: University of Chicago Press, 1980.

Baldwin, James. "The Discovery of What It Means to Be an American." In *Nobody Knows My Name*. New York: Dial, 1961.

———. *The Fire Next Time*. New York: Dell, 1963.

Baraka, Amiri. "Black Art." In *Black Poets*. Edited by Dudley Randall. New York: Bantam, 1971.

———. "Seven Principles of US Maulana Karenga & The Need for a Black Value System." In *Raise, Race, Rays, Raze: Essays Since 1965*. New York: Random House, 1969.

———. *See also* Jones, LeRoi.

Barbour, David. "August Wilson's Here to Stay." *Theater Week*, 18–25 April 1988, 8–14.

Barnes, Clive. "Fiery *Fences*." *New York Post*, 27 March 1987, 23.

Berry, Jane C. "Inspired in a Deli." *Tucson Citizen*, 30 December 1987, B2–B3.

Barksdale, Richard and Keneth Kinnamon. "Renaissance and Radicalism: 1915–1945." In *Black Writers of America*. Edited by Richard Barksdale and Keneth Kinnamon. New York: Macmillan, 1972, 467–79.

Bogard, Travis. *Contour in Time: Plays of Eugene O'Neill*. New York: Oxford University Press, 1972.

Bommer, Lawrence. "A Keeper of Dreams." *Chicago Tribune*, 15 January 1995, 16–21.

Brooks, Cleanth, R. W. B. Lewis, and Robert Penn Warren. *American Literature: The Makers and the Making*. Vol. 2. New York: St. Martin's, 1973.

Brown, Chip. "The Light in August." *Esquire* 111 (April 1989): 116–25.

Brown, Rob. "Ma Rainey Is Sad, Angry, Powerful." *Bristol/Valley Press*, 13 April 1984, 13.

Brown, Sterling. *The Collected Poems of Sterling A. Brown*. New York: Harper, 1980.

Brustein, Robert. "The Lesson of *The Piano Lesson*." *New Republic* 202 (21 May 1990): 28–30.

Campbell, Mary. "Theresa Merritt Takes 'Ma from Yale to Broadway." *Day* [New London, Conn.], 30 September 1984, B3.

Cassidy, 2Robert. *Margaret Mead: A Voice for the Century*. New York: Universe, 1982.0

Christiansen, Richard. "Artist of the Year: August Wilson's Plays Reveal What It Means to be Black in This Country." *Chicago Tribune*, 27 December 1987, F9–F10.

Courtemanche, Eleanor. "August Wilson Trains His Sights on the '60s." *After Hours*, 6 April 1990, 3.

Darden, Joe T. *Afro-Americans in Pittsburgh: The Residential Segregation of a People*. Lexington, Mass.: D. C. Heath, 1973.

Dean, Phillip Hayes. *The Owl Killer*. In *The Best Short Plays: 1974*. Edited by Stanley Richards. Radnor, Pa.: Chilton, 1974.

De Vries, Hillary. "A Song in Search of Itself." *American Theater*, January 1987, 22–25.

Drake, Sylvia. "*Two Trains* Now Runs Smoother." *Los Angeles Times*, 17 January 1992, F1.

Du Bois, W. E. B. *Black Reconstruction in America*. 1935 Reprint, New York: Atheneum, 1971.

———. "The Drama among Black Folks." *The Crisis*, 16 August 1916, 169–73.

Dworkin, Norine. "Blood on the Tracks." *American Theater*, May 1990, 8.

Elam, Harry J. "August Wilson's Women." In *May All Your Fences Have Gates: Essays on the Drama of August Wilson*. Edited by Alan Nadel. Iowa City: University of Iowa Press, 1994.

Elder, Lonne. Ceremonies in Dark Old Men. New York: Samuel French, 1969.

Ellison, Ralph. "Blues People." In *Shadow and Act*. New York: New American Library, 1964.

Erstein, Hap. "Trains Clicks Along on Well-Laid Drama Track." *Washington Times*, 15 November 1991, E1, E3.

Fisher, John. "Ma Rainey's Statement Needs Some Refinement." *Buck County Courier Times*, 26 September 1984, B22.

Fishman, Joan. "Romare Bearden, August Wilson, and the Traditions of African Performance." In *May All Your Fences Have Gates: Essays on the Drama of August Wilson*. Edited by Alan Nadel. Iowa City: University of Iowa Press, 1994.

Franklin, John Hope. *From Slavery to Freedom*. New York: Random House, 1969.

Freedman, Samuel. "Leaving His Imprint on Broadway." *New York Times Magazine*, 22 November 1987, 38.

———. "A Playwright Talks About the Blues." *New York Times*, 13 April 1984, C3.

———. "A Voice from the Streets." *New York Times Magazine*, 15 March 1987, 36–50.

French, Marilyn. "The Gender Principle." In *Shakespeare's Division of Experience*. New York: Summit, 1981.

Fry, Gladys-Marie. *Night Riders in Black Folk History*. Knoxville: University of Tennessee Press, 1975.

Gaye, Marwin. *What's Going On* [album and song title]. Copyright © by Jobete Music Company, 1971. Motown, MOTC 5339.

Gibson, Donald. "Richard Wright: Aspects of His Literary Relations." In *Critical Essays on Richard Wright*. Edited by Yoshinobu Hakulani. Boston: G. K. Hall, 1982.

Giovanni, Norman Thomas di, Daniel Halpern, and Frank MacShane. *Borges on Writing*. New York: Dutton, 1973.

Gorn, Elliot J. "Black Spirits: The Ghostlore of Afro-American Slaves." *American Quarterly* 36 (1984): 549–65.

Gottlieb, Peter. *Making Their Own Way: Southern Black Migration to Pittsburgh, 1916–1930*. Champaign: University of Illinois Press, 1987.

Greene, Alexis. "Charles S. Dutton: Not Ready to Accept Defeat." *Theater Week*, 18–24 June 1990, 36–39.

Gupta, Sabodh C. *Shakespeare's Historical Plays*. London: Oxford University Press, 1964.

Hansberry, Lorraine. *The Collected Last Plays*. New York: New American Library, 1983.

———. *A Raisin in the Sun*. 1966 Reprint, New York: Penguin, 1988.

Hareven, Tamara, and Stephen Thernstrom, eds. *Pittsburgh: Documentary History of American Cities*. New York: New Viewpoints, 1976.

Harrison, Paul Carter. "August Wilson's Blues Poetics." In *August Wilson: Three Plays*, by Wilson. Pittsburgh: University of Pittsburgh Press, 1991.

Hawley, David. "The Making of a Playwright." *Minnesota Pioneer Press Dispatch*, 26 March 1987, C1–C3.

Henderson, Heather. "Building Fences: An Interview with Mary Alice and James Earl Jones." *Theater*, Summer/Fall 1985, 68.

Henderson, Stephen. "Saturation: Progress Report on a Theory of Black Poetry." *Black World* 24 (1975): 4–17.

Henry, William. "Exorcising the Demons of Memory." *Time*, 11 April 1988, 77–78.

Hughes, Langston. "The Negro Artist and the Racial Mountain." *Nation*, 23 June 1926, 692–94.

————. "The Negro Speaks of Rivers." In *Selected Poems of Langston Hughes.* New York: Vintage, 1959.

Johnson, Malcolm. "New Wilson Play Needs More Work." *Hartford Courant,* 2 April 1990, A9, A11.

Jones, LeRoi. *Madheart.* In *Four Black Revolutionary Plays.* Indianapolis: Bobbs-Merrill, 1969.

————. "The Revolutionary Theatre." In *Home: Social Essays.* New York: Morrow, 1966.

————. *See also* Baraka, Amiri.

Karenga, Maulana Ron. *Quotable Karenga.* Los Angeles: US Organization, 1967.

Kowinski, William S. "The Play Looks Good on Paper—But Will It Fly?" *Smithsonian,* March 1992, 78–87.

Kucherawy, Dennis. "Charles Fuller: Haunted by History." *Theater Week,* 12–18 December 1988, 17.

Lida, David. "*Fences*: A Review." *Women's Wear Daily,* 27 March 1987, 8.

Livingstone, Sandra. "August Wilson: Regards from Broadway." *MPLS/St. Paul* 13 (September 1985): 184.

Marshall, Michael. "Spiritual Odyssey: August Wilson's *Joe Turner's Come and Gone*." *The World and I,* December 1987, 240–41.

Martin, Bill. A Teachers Guide to the 1991–92 Negro Ensemble Company Tour of Charles Fuller's We: *Sally, Prince, Jonquil, Burner's Frolic,* 9.

Merrill, Hugh. *The Blues Route.* New York: William Morrow, 1990.

Metraux, Rhoda, ed. *Margaret Mead: Some Personal Views.* New York: Walker, 1979.

Migler, Raphael. "An Elegant Duet." *Gentleman's Quarterly,* April 1990, 114, 139–42.

Mitgang, Herbert. "Wilson, from Poetry to Broadway Success." *New York Times,* 12 October 1984, C15.

Moyers, Bill. *A World of Ideas.* New York: Doubleday, 1989.

Neal, Larry. "The Black Arts Movement." *Drama Review* 12 (Summer 1968): 29 39.

————. "The Black Contribution to American Letters: Part II: The Writer as Activist—1960 and After." In *Black American Reference Book.* Edited by Mabel Smythe. Englewood Cliffs, N. J.: Prentice-Hall, 1976.

Nelson, Don. *Playbill,* December 1984, 8.

New York Recording Laboratories. Port Washington, Wisconsin, 1927.

Palmer, Robert. *Deep Blues.* New York: Viking, 1981.

Patrick, Michelle. "An American Voice." *Philip Morris Magazine,* March-April 1989, 40–43.

Pawley, Thomas D. "The Black Theater Audience." In *Theater of Black Americans.* Edited by Errol Hill. New York: Applause, 1987.

Plum, Jay. "Blues, History, and the Dramaturgy of August Wilson." *African American Review* 27 (Winter 1993): 561–67.

Pointsett, Alex. "August Wilson: Hottest New Playwright." *Ebony,* November 1987, 68–74.

Powers, Kim. "An Interview with August Wilson." *Theater* 16 (Fall/Winter 1984): 50–55.

Reed, Ishmael. "In Search of August Wilson." *Connoisseur* 217 (March 1987): 92–97.

Rich, Frank. "Family Ties in *Fences*." *New York Times*, 27 March 1987, C3.

———. "August Wilson Reaches the '60s with Witnesses from a Distance." *New York Times*, 14 April 1990, C13, C17.

———. "Panoramic History of Blacks in America in Wilson's *Joe Turner*." *New York Times*, 28 March 1988, C15.

———. 2"Wilson's *Ma Rainey's* Opens." *New York Times*, 11 October 1984, C1, C3.0

Richards, David. "The Tortured Spirit of *Joe Turner*." *Washington Post*, 9 October 1987, B1, B12.

———. "The Trouble with *Sally*." *Washington Post*, 2 August 1988, E4.

Robinson, Jackie. *I Never Had It Made*. New York: G. P. Putnam, 1972.

Rocha, Mark. "A Conversation with August Wilson." *Diversity: A Journal of Multicultural Issues* 1 (Spring 1993): 24–42.

Rosenburg, David. "Parallel Tracks: Yale Rep Does August Wilson's *Two Trains Running*." *Fairpress*, 12 April 1990, D1, D7.

Rothstein, Mervyn. "Round Five for the Theatrical Heavyweight." *New York Times*, 15 April 1990, sec. 2, 1, 8.

———. "A Star of *The Piano Lesson* Who Found a New Life Onstage." *New York Times*, 19 April 1990, C17, C24.

Santino, Jack. *Miles of Smiles, Years of Struggle: Stories of Black Pullman Porters*. Chicago: University of Chicago Press, 1989.

Savran, David. *In Their Own Words: Contemporary American Playwrights*. New York: Theater Communications Group, 1988.

Scherer, Mark. "*Turner* Never Comes at All." *Evening Capital* [Annapolis, Md.], 13 October 1987, B10.

Schomburg, Arthur. "The Negro Digs Up His Past." In *The New Negro*. Edited by Alain Locke. New York: Atheneum, 1925.

Schwartzman, Myron. *Romare Bearden: His Life and Art*. New York: Abrams, 1990.

"*Seven Guitars*: Synopsis." In *On Stage* [The Goodman Theater Newsletter], p. 4. Edited by Tom Creamer. Chicago: Goodman Theater Series Productions, 1994–1995.

Shannon, Sandra. "From Lorraine Hansberry to August Wilson: An Interview with Lloyd Richards." *Callaloo* 14 (Winter 1991): 124–35.

———. "The Long Wait: August Wilson's *Ma Rainey's Black Bottom*. *Black American Literature Forum* 25 (Spring 1991): 151–62.

Shklovsky, Viktor. "Art as Technique." In *Russian Formalist Criticism: Four Essays*. Translated and with an introduction by Lee T. Lemon and Marion J. Reis. Lincoln: University of Nebraska Press, 1965.

Spillers, Hortense. "Interstices: A Small Drama of Words." In *Pleasure and Danger: Exploring Female Sexuality*. Edited by Carole S. Vance. Boston: Routledge, 1984.

Stayton, Richard. "August Wilson Lets His Characters Go." *Los Angeles Herald Examiner*, 31 May 1987, C2–C4.

Steele, Shelby. "Notes on Ritual in the New Black Theater." In *The Theater of Black Americans*. Edited by Errol Hill. New York: Applause, 1987.

Suavage, Leo. "On Stage: Spring Salad." *The New Leader*, 18 April 1988, 23.

Tallmer, Jerry. "*Fences*: Anguish of Wasted Talent." *New York Post*, 26 March 1987, C4.

Taylor, Clyde, ed. *Vietnam and Black America: An Anthology of Protest and Resistance*. New York: Anchor, 1973.

Tighe, Mary Ann. "A Rough, Raw, Jazz-Filled Drama Makes It to Broadway on Ecstatic Word of Mouth." *Vogue*, October 1984, 95.

Titon, Jeff T. *Down Home Blues*. Champaign: University of Illinois Press, 1977.

Walker, Joseph. *The River Niger*. New York: Hill and Wang, 1973.

Waters, Muddy (McKinley Morgan). *Still A Fool* [album title]. Chess Records, [catalogue no. 31268] 1951.

Watlington, Dennis. "Hurdling Fences." *Vanity Fair*, April 1989, 102–13.

"Wilson, August." *Contemporary Literary Criticism*: Yearbook 1985. Edited by Sharon K. Hall. Detroit: Gale Research Company, 1986.

———. Interview with Julian Bond. *America's Black Forum*. Washington, D. C. 23 Feb 1992.

———. Personal interview. Washington, D. C. 9 Nov 1991. See appendix.

Winer, Linda. "*Joe Turner* Enriches Wilson's Cycle." *New York Newsday*, 28 March 1988, 7.

INDEX